POLICE RIOTS

Collective Violence and Law Enforcement

Rodney Stark

Focus Books

published by
Wadsworth Publishing Company, Inc.
Belmont, California

Rodney Stark's initiation into police circles came during several years as a reporter for metropolitan newspapers. Later, as a research sociologist at Berkeley during the rise of student dissent, he found it "impossible not to observe police operations in confrontation situations." He began fulltime study of police practices in 1968 under the auspices of the Center for the Study of Law and Society of the University of California, Berkeley. During that period he also served as a consultant on the police to the National Commission on the Causes and Prevention of Violence and to the San Francisco Mayor's Commission on Crime. Prior to this Stark had become well known for his many books and articles in the areas of prejudice and religious behavior. With Charles Y. Glock he is co-author of *Religion and Society in Tension* (Rand-McNally, 1965), *Christian Beliefs and Anti-Semitism* (Harper & Row, 1966), *American Piety* (UC Press, 1968), *Wayward Shepherds: Prejudice and the Protestant Clergy* (Harper & Row, 1971), and (forthcoming) *The Poor in Spirit: Sources of Religious Commitment*, UC Press. Stark has written for *Harper's, Trans-action,* and *Psychology Today* and his articles have appeared in many scholarly journals. Since Fall 1971 he has been Associate Professor of Sociology at the University of Washington.

The quotation on pp. 194-195 is reprinted by permission of G. P. Putnam's Sons from The Police Establishment by William W. Turner. Copyright © 1968 by William W. Turner.

© 1972 by Wadsworth Publishing Company, Inc., Belmont, California 94002. All rights reserved. No part of this book may be reproduced, stored in a retrieval system or transcribed, in any form or by any means, electronic, mechanical, photocopying, recording or otherwise, without the prior written permission of the publisher.

ISBN-0-534-00145-9

L. C. Cat. Card No. 78–178816

Printed in the United States of America

1 2 3 4 5 6 7 8 9 10—
76 75 74 73 72

Contents

	Introduction: Studying Police Violence	1
1	Collective Police Violence	15
2	Police Violence as Routine Behavior	55
3	The Sources and Targets of Police Anger	85
4	Tactical Errors	125
5	Strategical Misconceptions: Police Ideology	139
6	Internal Control over the Police	178
7	External Control over the Police	208
8	Changing the Police	225
	Footnotes	240
	Index	247

Preface

When I started the work that led to this book I had no intention of writing a book about the police. I was going to do only a short investigation of a particular disturbance in Berkeley during the summer of 1968. Several months later I agreed to take responsibility for a chapter on police responses to protest and confrontation for the Skolnick Report* to the National Commission on the Causes and Prevention of Violence. When that was finished I realized that I had incurred an obligation, at least to myself, to assess what I and others had come to call police riots. Had I foreseen this at the start I might have decided to do something else.

Frankly, I value a quiet life. I would rather not provoke police anger or be considered controversial. The hate mail generated by the considerable publicity given my previous work on prejudice has dwindled lately and I don't miss it. Unfortunately, this book will probably cause even stronger reactions. Yet it needed to be written, and no one else was likely to do it.

Although some very capable scholars have written about the police in the last several years (and I have learned much from them), typically they have been quite circumspect in dealing with controversial features of policing. This is because of their understandable need to retain their access to the police if they are to continue their work. Even delicate treatment of such matters as brutality has caused some scholars to be denied further opportunity for study. The only way around this impasse is for some of us to study the police without caring whether we can do a second study.

---

* *The Politics of Protest* (New York: Ballantine, 1969).

Preface

This study was sponsored by the Center for the Study of Law and Society, University of California, Berkeley, from funds granted by the Ford Foundation for a program of research on questions of criminal law and social policy. Neither the Center nor the Ford Foundation is in any way responsible for the views expressed or the conclusions reached. The study was further facilitated by the National Commission on the Causes and Prevention of Violence, in particular its Task Force on Violent Aspects of Protest and Confrontation, directed by Jerome Skolnick.

The study is based on four general sources of information:

1. Interviews with policemen, officers of police guild and union organizations, and police commanders in a number of major cities across the country. Most of these were obtained for use in my Task Force report on the police, and were conducted by Sam McCormick, a former Los Angeles policeman who was then enrolled in the Ph.D. program of the Criminology Department of the University of California.
2. A large number of scholarly studies, reports written for government commissions such as the Kerner Commission and the President's Commission on Law Enforcement and the Administration of Criminal Justice, grand jury, and other judicial investigations, and various semiofficial or blue-ribbon hearings on police behavior. Examples of the latter, which have proved invaluable, are the Cox Commission's report on Columbia University, The Byrne Report on the Free Speech Movement at Berkeley, a report of a citizen's committee on the April 27, 1968, peace march incident in Chicago, and a report by the American Civil Liberties Union on the Century City peace march in Los Angeles, June 23, 1967. Reports by specially appointed study teams of the Violence Commission, particularly the Walker Report on Chicago during the Democratic convention, were also invaluable.
3. Intensive analysis of police magazines, newspapers, pamphlets, newsletters, campaign literature, textbooks, manuals, and speeches by prominent police leaders. While this is a vast literature, it is amazingly uniform in its themes, judgments, and proposals; thus it is easy to generalize about it.
4. Newspaper and magazine accounts of episodes involving the police. Availability of these accounts was greatly facilitated by a daily clipping service provided by the U. S. Air Force for circulation among personnel of the Violence Commission. It must be acknowledged that there are pitfalls which must be avoided in the use of press accounts. For example, there is no reason to suppose that a reporter who has not conducted a systematic opinion poll has accurate knowledge of the proportion of policemen who voted for George Wallace (a question considered in Chapter 5). But the press is gen-

erally reliable for hard facts about given occurrances—for example, that nine policemen were indicted for brutality and that the mayor, the chief of police, and other officials said certain things in their public comments upon this affair. Much of the present study depends simply on demonstrating that certain kinds of events frequently happen and that certain kinds of statements are frequently made. For these purposes accounts gathered from the nation's press are sufficiently reliable and are the only feasible source of information.

I must acknowledge that the data on which this study is based are not all that I would have liked. In fact, final completion of the manuscript was delayed for a year while I submitted research proposals seeking funds to conduct a systematic survey study of a national sample of policemen. In my experience I have found that ethnographic studies (which are the predominate kind of scholarly study available on the police) often err badly when they attempt to estimate distributions of various traits across a population. I am certain that a solid body of survey data would reveal that many things we believe about the police are not so. I would like to have built this book upon such a solid data base. However, funds were not forthcoming despite considerable encouragement to believe they would be. Thus, my option was to say nothing or do the best I could with what I could get. Obviously, I felt silence was more irresponsible than risking error.

In conclusion I must acknowledge my debts to a number of persons. Sam McCormick conducted superb interviews of police union officials, excerpts of which appear throughout the book. A number of colleagues gave me critical advice: Norman K. Denzin, Charles Y. Glock, John Lofland, Sheldon L. Messinger, Philippe Nonet, and Philip Selznick. I was also substantially aided by a number of police officers, each of whom I have thanked personally. Finally, I must thank Joshua A. L. Stark, who made many attempts to type the manuscript.

R. S.
August 1971
Berkeley, California

Introduction: Studying Police Violence

... not to criticize the police may well be the most serious anti-police action.

This is a book about police riots. As a result it often must portray the police at their worst, unjustifiably beating, gassing, and shooting helpless and nonprovocative persons (and even other policemen they mistake for civilians.) However, anyone who thinks that it is an anti-police book either hasn't read it or hasn't understood it.

It is vulgar nonsense to be anti-police. Our society could not exist without them. It is because they are absolutely essential that it is so necessary to evaluate their performance. We *must* ask: Are they fullfilling reasonable standards of competence? Are they conducting themselves in ways which worsen some of the problems they are supposed to relieve? These are not anti-police questions, they are pro-police. Implicit in each one is an effort to understand how to improve the position of the police—in a sense, how to make their jobs easier and safer. Unfortunately, it is hard to criticize the police and not seem to be their enemy. In our present anxiety over law and order many claim we must protect police morale at all costs and repress all criticism. This is foolish and dangerous; there is no prospect for law and order, let alone justice, so long as substantial police misbehavior and incompetency continue. Thus, not to criticize the police may well be the most serious possible anti-police action.

Many policemen will reject such statements. Indeed, a major part of the present police problem is rooted in the fact that so many policemen are locked into a narrow us-against-them mentality and regard all criticism as a betrayal. Yet it is demonstrable that month by month the position of the American police is deteriorating. Their jobs are becoming more difficult, more dangerous, and their efforts less and less effective. To remain silent is to condone these trends.

Ultimately, of course, this study was not written for policemen. It is addressed to Americans generally. We get the kind of policing we deserve. If we want a different kind we must change those to whom we entrust this task and how we permit them to perform it. That is mainly what this book is about. I don't think we ought to have policemen who riot when confronted with particular kinds of persons in particular circumstances. I don't think the shotgun or the nightstick are acceptable or even workable solutions to political and social controversies. I don't think excessive use of violence by the police ought to be routine. I don't think police commanders should be unable to impose discipline on their men. And I think I understand something about why things are as they are and what can be done about them.

I take it as axiomatic that most police officials and commanders are responsible and humane men trying their best to cope with the terrible burdens of maintaining order in our urban society. I am equally sure that the average policeman is decent and well-intentioned, trying to do his duty as he sees it. Yet these same men gravely misjudge the meaning of some of the major facts of our time and can be swept up in hostile, collective outbursts of violence. It is not merely to condemn, but to understand how this occurs and what can be done to prevent it, that has brought me here.

Since policemen were first invented in the nineteenth century they have been a periodic source of public indignation and concern. For decades governmental commissions have issued reports on widespread police corruption and violence. But progress in reforming the police has been slow. Over the past few years tensions between how the police actually behave and how we think they ought to behave have been increasing. As previously submerged minorities have spoken out, condemnation of the police has become a major theme. Indeed, as the civil rights movement developed in the South it became inescapable that Southern policemen were not yet professionalized. And as black protest turned North there has been evidence that professionalization is not yet ingrained in Northern policemen either. Such indications have continued in police responses to campus unrest and the peace movement. Clearly, the police don't always do the right thing.

Nevertheless, before the Democratic National Convention met in Chicago in 1968 many Americans—especially white upper-middle-class adults—were inclined to dismiss these signs of trouble as isolated instances and the work of a few unsuitable policemen. The general news media both reflected and supported such an outlook. Evidence of police misconduct was treated gingerly, and such phrases as "police riot" and "police revolt" were left unwritten and unspoken.

This is no longer so. Today, the most respected newsmen and the most influential and responsible public news media use such phrases almost routinely. On the cover of *Life:* "The Police Rioted."[1] In *Fortune:* "The Way To Cool the Police Rebellion."[2] Similar examples can be found in the *Wall Street Journal,* the *Christian Science Monitor,* the *New York Times,* and most other major papers. Suddenly, articles on police misbehavior, political militance, and the like fill the nation's press and have prompted television news specials. Possibly the majority of Americans still remain uninformed, unsympathetic, or unconvinced.[3] But, clearly, a consensus exists among the influential, informed, and responsible sectors of public opinion that something needs to be done about the violent behavior of the police.

It all began in Chicago. While the police rampaged through the streets, beating and gassing with abandon, the demonstrators chanted, "The whole world is watching." And so it was. Hundreds of demonstrators and innocent bystanders were wantonly beaten, as were scores of accredited newsmen. Hotel rooms were invaded. McCarthy-for-President campaign headquarters was sacked and the staff roughed up. On the floor of the convention, television newsmen were punched, and delegates were manhandled and even hauled off to jail.

In the words of the *Walker Report,* the police were guilty of unrestrained and indiscriminate violence on many occasions:

[The police] violence was made all the more shocking by the fact that it was often inflicted upon persons who had broken no law, disobeyed no order, made no threat. These included peaceful demonstrators, onlookers, and large numbers of residents who were simply passing through, or happened to live in, the areas where confrontations were occurring. . . .
Newsmen and photographers were singled out for assault, and their equipment deliberately damaged. Fundamental police training was ignored; and officers, when on the scene, were often unable to control their men. As one police officer put it: "What happened didn't have anything to do with police work."[4]

Despite Mayor Richard J. Daley's efforts to bar the press from the streets of Chicago and the frequent police efforts to break cameras and intimidate photographers,[5] the news media provided remarkable coverage. And so we all watched.

Since then, there has been a rude awakening to the facts of life about police behavior; events in Chicago were unique only in the quality and quantity of media coverage. In most other ways the behavior of the Chicago police on this occasion was indistinguishable from police behavior in a number of similar recent events both before and since the convention. Indeed, the events during convention week were not new even for Chicago.

In April 1968, an outbreak of police rioting and violence occurred during a peace march in downtown Chicago. According to the account by D. J. R. Bruckner of the *Los Angeles Times,* this "police outburst . . . should have been a clear warning to [Mayor] Daley of what could happen during the convention."[6]

According to Bruckner, city officials had done all they could to hamper plans for the march by refusing meeting and parade permits—a pattern continued during the Democratic convention. Thus, in order to hold the protest at all, "a peace march by 8,000 persons had to make its way through the Loop piecemeal, obeying all traffic lights and staying on the sidewalks, as it moved to the civic center over a three-mile route."[7]

Bruckner provided the following account of what happened then:

Once in the plaza of the Civic Center, these marchers were required by police to keep moving. . . .
As one line of police on the inside of the plaza pushed out against the marchers, a line of police in the streets kept insisting that the marchers stay on the walk and out of the street. After about 30 minutes

of this squeezing tactic, the march line began to break, and many of the marchers were pursued and knocked down by angry police who chased them, in open defiance of shouted orders by their officers, and in the presence of Police Superintendent James B. Conlisk.[8]

Bruckner's account was substantiated by an independent investigating committee chaired by Dr. Edward J. Sparling, president emeritus of Roosevelt University, and which included such persons as Professor Harry Kalven, Jr., of the Chicago Law School and Warren Bacon, vice-president of the Inland Steel Corporation. This blue-ribbon committee reported after careful investigation that:

On April 27, at the peace parade of the Chicago Peace Council, the police badly mishandled their task. Brutalizing demonstrators without provocation, they failed to live up to that difficult professionalism which we demand. . . .

Yet to place primary blame on the police would, in our view, be inappropriate. The April 27 stage had been prepared by the Mayor's designated officials weeks before. Administrative actions concerning the April 27 Parade were designed by City officials to communicate that "these people have no right to demonstrate or express their views." Many acts of brutal police treatment on April 27 were directly observed (if not commanded) by the Superintendent of Police or his deputies.[9]

Of course, Chicago is not New York or San Francisco, as residents of both cities are quick to point out. But similar outbursts of police rioting and collective violence occurred more than once in both New York and San Francisco during 1968, and occurred in many other cities as well. Consider the following examples, selected from among the many which have been reported.

San Francisco One evening in January 1968, police attacked antiwar demonstrators who had gathered near the Fairmont Hotel on Nob Hill to protest a speech by the then Secretary of State Dean Rusk. According to eyewitness accounts by newsmen, police broke from their lines and charged into the crowd on wild clubbing forays. This was the beginning of a year of repeated episodes during which San Francisco police were charged with violent misbehavior both on and off duty: several outbursts of collective violence by the Tac Squad (tactical or riot squad) during disturbances in the Haight-Ashbury hippie community—during one of these, a black policeman in civilian dress was beaten by fellow officers; an off-duty foray by members of the Tac

Squad through the streets of the Mission District during which they forced pedestrians off the sidewalks and a number of young people claim to have been beaten—two officers were later brought to trial; and the year culminated in a whole series of outbursts of collective violence by the Tac Squad and other policemen during the long strike at San Francisco State College. News film shows officers breaking from their riot formations and charging crowds of students. Pictures show completely subdued demonstrators held by officers while another officer squirts Mace in their faces from a few inches away, and similar acts of unwarranted assault.

New York During March 1968, police suddenly appeared during a yippie demonstration in Grand Central Station and, without giving the crowd a legitimate chance to disperse, indiscriminately attacked and clubbed demonstrators, according to eyewitness newspaper accounts.[10] A month later in Washington Square, a similar police attack occurred.[11] In the spring, police repeatedly went on rampages during the Columbia University student strike—police misbehavior at Columbia has been widely reported, verified by an impartial investigative committee, and condemned.[12] Shortly after the Chicago convention an estimated 150 off-duty policemen beat several members of the Black Panther Party in the halls of a Brooklyn courthouse.[13]

Los Angeles During June 1967, police violently dispersed a peaceful demonstration by 15,000 persons who had gathered before the Century Plaza Hotel where President Johnson was attending a $500-a-plate dinner. In August 1968 bitter charges of police rioting, brutality, and unwarranted killing convulsed the black community after police attacked persons gathered in a park for the Watts Festival. Three citizens were slain and 35 were wounded during the engagement.

Paterson, New Jersey Police violence during racial disorders in July 1968 led the county grand jury to use such terms as "terrorism" and "goon squad" tactics in a presentment issued in October. The jury charged that groups of policemen seized individual Puerto Ricans and Negroes and gave them a vicious beating as an example to others, and that police deliberately damaged black-owned stores and shops.[14]

Berkeley, California During June 1968, police attacked a peaceful crowd listening to speeches in support of the French student strike, thus touching off a long weekend of police rioting and violence. Subsequently, during February and March 1969, a number of episodes of collective police violence occurred on the campus of the University of California, Berkeley, where members of the Third World Liberation Front were striking in demand of a college of ethnic studies.[15] Finally came the crisis over People's Park in May and "Bloody Thursday," when police fired on demonstrators protesting the middle-of-the-night erection of a fence around the disputed property. Although Alameda County Sheriff Frank S. Madigan justified the shooting (at first saying only bird-shot had been used, but admitting that some officers had fired lethal double-ought buckshot after an autopsy of a young man killed by police fire revealed marble-sized buckshot slugs) as necessary to protect his officers from the mob, eyewitnesses and a great number of photographs revealed that some of the officers engaged in a virtual turkey shoot—some victims were shot in the back while trying to flee, in circumstances posing no threat whatsoever to the police. I witnessed an incident in which one of a pair of officers casually shot a middle-aged man, who was standing with his back to the officers about 40 yards away. There was no disorder going on in that immediate area at the time. The police called no commands, gave no warning; one simply aimed and shot the man in the back. Then both officers turned and strolled away, making no attempt either to arrest their victim, who lay bleeding profusely on the sidewalk, or to help get him medical aid. The incident was witnessed by at least several dozen other people who were standing on balconies or front steps of their homes. There seem to have been many similar episodes throughout the afternoon.

This brief recital of recent police outbursts makes it clear that the events during the convention in Chicago were not simply another manifestation of the unsavory Chicago police tradition. It is closer to the truth to regard their actions as the conventional response of the American policeman in such circumstances. This study was prompted by the regularity with which the police behave in this fashion, posing a severe threat to democratic institutions. I began this book several months before the Chicago convention. For some time it had been clear to me that the American police were becoming more and more prone to erupt into disorder and collective violence in response to mass demonstrations, protests, and racial crises. But no one could offer any compelling explanations of why this was occurring. Was it, as the young spokesmen of the New Left charged, simply that our society is based on coercion and that the police will always try to crush and repress dissent? Or was it rather a crisis of "law and order"? Was it simply a "commie smear" or a plot to take over America? Was it, as the young black militants claimed, that the police are a bunch of "fascist pigs"? Were we headed for a police state? What did it all mean?

Since the study began, some aspects of the problem have changed. Most importantly, it is no longer so difficult to pursuade readers that the police sometimes do riot. Events and the media have taken care of that. But credible explanations of *why* they riot have remained elusive. It was to try to sort out the complexities of this urgent question that this study was undertaken. Why do policemen defy their commanders and break ranks to attack certain kinds of gatherings? Why do they go on shooting sprees in black ghettos?

As research proceeded, the initial question of why the police riot remained central, but the scope of the investigation expanded far beyond anything I originally had anticipated. Partly this was because my resources for research were greatly increased by my unanticipated appointment to the Task Force on Violent Aspects of Protest and Confrontation of the National Commission on the Causes and Prevention of Violence. But primarily this great expansion of scope was a necessary response to pursuit of the original problem.

It became clear that the propensity of the police for rioting and collective violence is simply a very obvious symptom of much larger forces which are transforming the nature of the American police. *Given the present state of affairs among our police, the fact that they are prone to rioting and violence is to be expected.* Thus, by pursuing the question of why the police riot, it became necessary to ask why the police are as they are. Why are so many policemen angry, fearful, prejudiced, militant, and politically disaffected? Why is the state of police training and tactics as it is? What effect does this have on police attitudes and actions? Why have police commanders, civil authorities, and the courts so little control over police behavior? These questions and many others are critical to an understanding of why police riot. Thus, the study grew into a rather broad assessment of the contemporary American police.

But, obviously, the study is not in any sense an attempt at a comprehensive study of the American police. Its central issue is why the police riot. Therefore, I have focused on the relationships among factors which I think produce police riots. In so doing many important features of the contemporary police are treated as givens. For example, it is important to understand that police recruitment, job satisfaction, training, and qualifications have been rather rapidly deteriorating over the past decade. But I shall not try to explain fully why this has happened; that would be a major study in itself. For purposes of this investigation I shall simply demonstrate that these changes have occurred and concentrate on explaining how they influence the police tendency to riot. At this point several widely held, but spurious, theories about the police should be disposed of.

Rotten Apples and Fascist Pigs: Common Misconceptions

Two nearly identical theories are widely accepted as *the* explanations of police violence and misbehavior. Both rest on imputed defects in the character or personality of individual policemen. If either theory were true, this study could be completed in two pages, for each offers a simple and brief explanation, which unfortunately mainly serves to cloud our understanding of the real issues. Ironically, the first of these explanations is supported by police spokesmen, the second by radicals and black militants.

The rotten apple theory blames police misbehavior on a few unsuitable officers. Police commanders frequently use the rotten apple imagery to distinguish from the rest of the force officers caught in corruption or misconduct. This preserves the respectability of the majority from the misconduct of a few. Frequently, police commanders are justified in using this device to protect the good name of their force. But far too often they also use it to argue that several rotten apples are to blame for what was clearly the action of a great many officers. Indeed, Chicago Mayor Richard J. Daley would have us believe that the misconduct during the Democratic convention was the work of nine officers!* Similarly, the Passaic County Grand Jury in its condemnation of police behavior during racial trouble in Paterson, N. J., fell back on the rotten apple theory:

This grand jury states its abhorrence and dismay at the actions of a relative *handful of misguided police officers* who, while sworn to uphold the law and provide protection for life and property, chose instead on this occasion to break the law and destroy private property, including that of private citizens not involved in any way with the disturbances.[16]

---

* This could best be called the superman theory of police misbehavior.

The effect of the rotten apple theory is to offer scapegoats to public indignation and to evade basic questions about the organization and character of police institutions.

Further support is lent to this notion by suggestions that higher pay and more selective recruitment would solve our major law enforcement ills. Recent efforts to set up elaborate psychiatric screening of recruits are based on the assumption that the major problem is to keep out certain kinds of defective and unsuitable candidates: the problem is defined as sick cops, not a sick system. But the weight of available evidence suggests the opposite: It is not so much a question of what a man is like when he joins the force as the kind of man he becomes and the kinds of situations in which he finds himself after he is a policeman.[17]

The fascist pig explanation is based on the same psychological assumptions as the rotten apple theory. Disagreement between the two is simply one of proportion. While the rotten apple theory argues for a *few* defective or misguided officers, the fascist pig theory argues that *most* policemen are defectives. Stripped of its angry rhetoric the fascist pig theory reflects a belief that is widespread among both social scientists and laymen about the modal psychological make-up of the police. It is commonly assumed that police work tends to attract those with an excessive love of power, especially the sadistic or authoritarian, and that therefore most policemen have authoritarian personalities. The rotten apple theorists often concur in the assumption that police work tends to draw such persons, but argue that only a few slip through the screening process and thus that only a minority of policemen are like this. The fascist pig theory maintains that under present conditions this tendency is permitted relatively free reign.

Both analyses reflect a widespread and vulgar penchant for curbstone psychologizing; neither can survive a confrontation with the evidence.

For all the seeming plausibility of the authoritarianism and sadism assumptions of the fascist pig theory, all available evidence indicates that police recruits, as a group, are *not* especially sadistic or authoritarian.[18] Quite the opposite, the average police recruit is a gregarious young man, with an interest in sports, some sense of social ideals and a rather unremarkable psychology.* So much

---

* Indeed, McNamara's data (McNamara, "Uncertainties in Police Work") show that rookies entering the New York City Police Department

for the mythic image of psychic jackboots and a fascist mentality.

Similarly, the rotten apple theory is not supported by the evidence. A recent study by Sam McCormick has shown that officers who are frequently involved in altercations with citizens cannot be distinguished from other officers (who rarely or never get into altercations) on the basis of any of a great number of psychological measures including authoritarianism.[19] This is not to say that departments don't have their "two-guns," policemen who are violence-prone, but that generally they cannot be identified on the basis of psychological scales.

Even without these studies it ought to be obvious that labelling the police as "pigs," "fascists," "Birchers," "sadists," and the like cannot explain collective police violence. Although the political and social beliefs of the police may indeed be a critical part of any comprehensive explanation of their behavior, it is obviously nonsense to settle for explanations limited to such factors. Plainly, the police don't run amok every night, nor do they beat most offenders. In some apparently very dangerous and provocative situations they remain cool and disciplined. In others they riot. Purely psychological traits, much less epithets, cannot account for these variations. Furthermore, the fascist pig and rotten apple theories hide more than they explain about the individual conceptions and attitudes of policemen. Both prejudge police conceptions of themselves and what they think they are doing, and why, when they engage in violence. As we will see later, the phenomenology involved is important and not so obvious.

Aim and Organization of the Study

The focus of this book is the phenomenon of the police riot. By the term police riot I mean a "hostile outburst"[20] in which the major participants are police officers. While we all know more or less what a riot is, it may be useful to consider one definition which guided this study: a riot, or hostile outburst, is "mobilization for action under a hostile belief. . . . Participants . . . must be bent on

---

scored considerably lower on a measure of "punitiveness" than did a large sample of community leaders! Niederhoffer, *Behind the Shield*, supports this point.

attacking someone considered responsible for a disturbing state of affairs."[21] This definition excludes collective violence stemming purely from panic—such as persons fighting to leave a burning building—as well as all irrational mob or crowd behavior (for instance, that persons were seized with some kind of collective psychosis, or such ideas as the "herd instinct," and the like). Riots, under this definition, involve some semblance of a governing ideology—a set of beliefs that someone is to blame for something which upsets, threatens, or otherwise disturbs those who participate in the riot. Riots are a directed form of action, they are against something or someone, namely those who are "to blame."

In Chapter 1 this conception of a police riot will be considerably expanded. First, criteria will be established by which we can distinguish a police riot from other kinds of events. Then, drawing on my observations of a number of police riots, and on published accounts of others, a prototype of the police riot will be presented. This prototype takes the form of an escalation model—the typical stages through which relatively commonplace situations are transformed into police riots. Then, to give concreteness to the model, two specific examples of police riots, illustrating the two major variations of the phenomenon, will be described in detail.

Having gained some understanding of what it is we are trying to explain, the remainder of the book is concerned with features of the police—their training, routines, circumstances, and beliefs —which cause them to engage in riots.

The first step in this explanation is taken up in Chapter 2. There I try to establish that excessive use of violence is a routine police behavior. It is routine in two senses. First, the police privately regard their use of violence as routine—in fact as legitimate —and their training instills a routine reliance on violence. Second, excessive police violence is statistically routine. Examination of a great deal of systematic data establishes that excessive use of violence is a common, everyday occurance in urban police departments. Thus, it is not the use of violence that makes police riots unusual events, but simply the concentration of police violence in a limited time and space.

But the police don't riot in just any mass situation, and they don't beat up just any kind of citizen. Chapter 3 tries to identify the particular kinds of people who arouse police wrath and explain why they do. Whom do the police hate and why? The central feature of the analysis is showing that the police, themselves, constitute a minority subculture in American society and showing how this subculture is especially divergent from certain other subcultures: minority groups, political dissenters, and youth.

The tendency for the police to erupt into riots in particular situations is also greatly facilitated by their inherent tactical incapacities and tactical misconceptions when faced with confrontation situations. Chapter 4 examines how police tactics often cause the trouble they are meant to quell. Four major tactical problems are examined: the incapacity of the police to operate reliably in large formations; the role of massive police deployment as a cause of confrontations and disturbances; the undue concern with their own safety that governs police tactical choices; and finally the misguided search for technical and mechanical solutions to human and political problems.

Behind tactics lies strategy. What the police believe about man and society plays a critical role in what they do and would like to do. Chapter 5 first attempts to characterize the central elements in police ideology and assess the validity of each one. Then an effort is made to explain why the police see the world as they do.

The first five chapters provide an explanation of why the police riot in particular situations. But a major question remains: Why are they able to get away with it?

Chapter 6 examines internal control over the police and finds it is largely absent. A major truth about the contemporary police is that they are virtually immune from departmental disciplinary action for using excessive violence against civilians. Part of this is due to an almost reflexive joining of ranks against any outside criticism. But a large part is due to the militance of police rank-and-file which leaves their commanders with very little authority to act against them.

Chapter 7 tries to demonstrate that external controls over the police are nearly as ineffective as are internal controls. Over the last few years the police have discovered their considerable political muscle. In showdowns at the polls with political authorities the police typically have won. Recently this has led to police candidates in local elections, and there are now several police mayors in major cities. Along the way, political control over the police has become extremely weak. At the same time the police also have effectively opposed the courts. Furthermore, many features of the court system make it ill-equipped to curtail police violence. The press constitutes another possible external source of control over the police. Since the Chicago police riot, the press has attempted to arouse concern over the behavior of the police. Unfortunately, like the courts, the press operates within narrow confines which impede its leverage with the police. But more important, the press has failed to convince the general public that the police really do misbehave. The final section of Chapter 7 assesses data on public opinion to understand why the public fails to condemn police violence.

Chapter 8 is devoted to proposals for changing our police and our police institutions to make them more effective in maintaining law, order, justice, and democratic principles.

1

Collective Police Violence

...the police were seen throwing rocks at fleeing citizens from rooftops....

In the Introduction, a police riot was defined as a "hostile outburst" during which the police unlawfully attack persons they blame for a "disturbing state of affairs." This chapter refines that definition. In it I try to provide criteria by which we can tell a police riot from other kinds of events, such as when the police utilize a considerable, but legitimate, amount of force against a group of civilians. Next, a prototype of the police riot, the stages through which incidents typically escalate into a police riot, is presented. Finally, in order to give concreteness to these generalizations two specific police riots are reported and analyzed.

I. What Is a Police Riot?

Readers of the Kerner Commission Report[1] or the Skolnick Report[2] or any of dozens of other books, reports, and articles on recent events in black ghettos or during student and anti-war demonstrations will have recognized that sometimes police behavior is indistinguishable from that attributed to rioters. It is not merely that sometimes the character of the police response in certain situations provokes riots, which it does, but that on some occasions the police seem to be *the major or even the only* perpetrators of disorder, violence, and destruction. *Such occasions are police riots.*

Recently police riots have often followed a ghetto disturbance or a confrontation with demonstrators. For example, two consecutive riots occurred in Newark during July 1967. Although the first was perhaps provoked by police, the rioters were ghetto blacks. But in the second, police officers were seemingly the only important participants. During the first riot, blacks damaged and destroyed white-owned stores. During the second, policemen damaged black-owned stores. Indeed, the second riot was only distinguishable from the first by a much higher casualty rate and by the fact that the rioters wore uniforms, were better armed and equipped, were paid by the public, and were immune from prosecution. This same pattern has occurred fairly often: in police- and National Guard–controlled territory in the later stages of the Detroit riot, and—according to the findings of a grand jury—in Paterson, N. J. during July 1968, to cite only two examples.

It must be recognized that sometimes the police behave in a disorderly way through panic and confusion, as when they shoot wildly and at each other in response to imaginary snipers.[3] But a true police riot is not simply an incident of bumbling or confusion —although certainly these factors may be present; it must involve a certain degree of intent to employ excessive force.

Nor is a police riot simply a fight between the police and a crowd. No reasonable person questions the right of the police to use necessary force (although on some occasions when justified force has escalated a crisis, the wisdom of using force may be questioned). Thus, when the lives of police or the lives of others are actually endangered by crowd behavior or when the police are otherwise unable to effect arrests for significant offenses, their use of the amount of force required can in no sense be called a police riot. Such police violence is legitimate. An event may only be called a police riot when the police during the incident collectively violate reasonable standards governing the lawful use of force. (These standards are described in Chapter 2.)

Full-scale police riots are not a unique form of police violence. As they will be treated in this study, a police riot is simply the most elaborate and extreme form of *collective violence*[4] by the police, differing only in degree and scope from an event in which only several policemen launch an attack on several citizens.

It must be recognized, however, that this study will not attempt to account for all varieties of the excessive use of force by the police. I shall exclude instances that can be explained on purely individual grounds, such as when a policeman beats a citizen against whom he has a private grudge, or a beating administered by a psychopath in uniform. I shall also ignore such institutionalized forms of police brutality as the "third degree," which is motivated by a desire to obtain speedy confessions and convictions, or brutality that is used primarily to punish offenders whom it would be difficult or unpleasant to prosecute, as is sometimes done with sex offenders.[5] All of these are important abuses of police power and ought to be suppressed. However, they do not constitute instances of collective behavior, and the reasons they occur are better understood. Collective outbursts by the police are currently more inexplicable and more dangerous. In addition, evidence presented in Chapter 2 suggests that perhaps the majority of police violence these days is collective, not idiosyncratic.

An event is a police riot when roving bands of *policemen set upon nonprovocative persons and/or property in an excessively violent manner*. When only one small group of policemen sets upon citizens and/or property in a single location it may be useful to call this a *police attack*. A *police riot* is any such event involving *two or more attacks*.

Nonprovocative persons are those who represent no significant threat to life, physical safety, or property (at least before the police set upon them; that police attacks often provoke counter-violence will be considered in some detail in later chapters). A young man standing on the steps of his home who gives "the finger" to passing police may insult their pride and provoke their wrath, but his actions are not provocative in the sense of providing a legitimate justification for being dealt with violently. Such a young man may be subject to arrest for his behavior, but to beat him or shoot him is legally and morally indefensible and constitutes a police attack. Similarly, carrying a picket sign advocating a cause with which the police disagree, having long hair, or being black may provoke the police, but is not legally provocative. Furthermore, nonviolent acts of civil disobedience may be unlawful, but they do not justify force other than that needed, for example, to carry away limp arrestees to jail.

One clear indicator that a police attack or riot has occurred is when persons are assaulted by the police and abandoned without being arrested, in other than a situation where arrest is impossible (for example, when police are too busy defending themselves or protecting life to make arrests). Often, of course, police do make arrests during a riot or attack. Indeed, they ordinarily justify their use of force by charging those on whom they have used force with acts of provocation such as resisting or fleeing arrest. Admittedly, often the police are justified in bringing such charges. However, when a citizen is beaten or shot and simply abandoned (when an arrest could have been made) the matter is unambiguous. If their use of force was legitimate, then the police were guilty of extreme dereliction of duty in not making an arrest. If the victim was not guilty of an offense that justified the use of force against him, then the police behavior was clearly felonious.

A second indicator of a police riot or attack is when police destroy or damage property without filing a report attributing this action to the necessities of duty. Even when filed, such reports can be fraudulent, but when none is filed, the grounds for calling the destruction wanton and unlawful seem clear.

II. The Prototype Police Riot: An Escalation Model

Police riots don't simply occur out of nowhere. They develop from a relatively common set of circumstances and escalate through a typical series of stages. An explication of these stages provides a fuller understanding of what police riots are and how and why they occur.

Stage 1: Convergence

A police riot can occur only if a relatively large number of civilians and policemen are present at the same time in a fairly restricted area. There must be someone for the police to riot (or counter-riot) against, and there must be enough policemen present to engage in rioting. It is difficult to say with any precision how many civilians and how many policemen are necessary in order to produce a police riot. I have heard of incidents involving only 40 or 50 civilians and 10 policemen. But ordinarily police riots have involved more than 100 policemen and at least 400 civilians. The convergence of large numbers of civilians and policemen in a single location is hardly unusual, and only infrequently results in a police riot (or any kind of riot). Most such convergences are simple crowd control and traffic direction operations produced by such events as parades and sporting events. Such convergences nearly always remain routine.

Stage 2: Confrontation

The potential for escalation into violence greatly increases, however, when convergence is accompanied by a conflict of interest, mutual hostility, or divergent definitions of appropriate behavior between the police and the civilians.

Three typical sources of confrontations are:

1. An incident, involving one or a few civilians and several policemen, attracts a crowd sympathetic to the civilians which in turn draws a large number of policemen to the scene in support of their fellow officers. This is typical of the genesis of ghetto confrontations and is also fairly common on college campuses.
2. A crowd gathers for a demonstration or protest march which offends the ideals of the police or which is designated by the police as illegal or potentially disruptive. The importance of police views of such events for the creation of confrontation is demonstrated by the differences when similar events (or the same event) are treated as a traffic problem on the one hand and an illegal assembly on the other. On several occasions peace marches lacking parade permits have been treated as merely traffic problems in Berkeley, but as illegal assemblies once across the boundary into Oakland. Trouble occurred only in Oakland.
3. Police are drawn to public recreational gatherings (such as love-ins, street dances, rock festivals, outdoor beer busts, and the like) which are judged by the police to be illegal, immoral, or a public nuisance.

The majority of confrontations do not escalate further. In order for escalation to continue, one or both sides must take action.

Stage 3: Dispersal

The potential conflict inherent in confrontations is activated if the police attempt to end the incident by dispersing the civilians. This decision may be forced upon the police by hostile or dangerous actions of the crowd. For example, the crowd may endanger the police by throwing bottles and bricks or by attempting to disrupt police lines. Or the crowd may endanger property, perhaps by smashing store windows. But frequently the decision to disperse the crowd is not forced upon the police by the action of the civilians. That is, for all that an assembly may be illegal (lacking proper permits) or distasteful, it poses no immediate threat to public safety or property. In such situations sometimes the police choose to disperse the crowd.

Stage 4: The Utilization of Force

Sometimes crowds disperse upon command or in response to police deployment and threats of arrest or gas. Sometimes they do not—often enough because of faulty police deployment they *cannot*. When they do not, and if dispersal remains the tactical goal, force is used by the police; police lines may advance brandishing riot batons; they may use these batons, tear gas, or firearms. The amount of force is usually increased as dispersal proves difficult to achieve. The more it is increased, the greater the likelihood that an excessive amount will be used. As will be taken up in detail in Chapter 4 and elsewhere, police commanders tend to maximize rather than minimize the use of force in order to maximize officer safety and to maximize dispersal. This is also true of individual officers. Furthermore, as we will see in Chapter 4, police command control and tactical integrity tend to collapse in contact with crowds and as greater force is employed. Thus, once introduced, *the use of force by the police tends to escalate rapidly into excessive use*. This is especially likely if the crowd offers any significant resistance (either real or symbolic) and/or if the crowd is made up of kinds of persons who arouse police hostility (blacks, students, radicals, and so on).

Stage 5: The Limited Riot

When excessive use of force by the police becomes relatively widespread during a dispersal action, this constitutes a police riot.

It is typified by the break-up of police formations into autonomous groups chasing fleeing civilians and charging into clusters of a crowd, beating people up. Sometimes this also involves uncontrolled use of tear gas, primarily in punitive ways (e.g., throwing canisters into homes and stores), and occasionally has escalated into wild shooting sprees (mainly during ghetto riots, but also at Jackson State and during Berkeley's People's Park incident). Whatever the level of violence reached, if the police cease their attacks when crowd dispersal is complete or very shortly thereafter, this is a limited police riot—limited to the single scene and incident.

Stage 6: The Extended Police Riot

In the aftermath of crowd dispersal, sometimes police riots do not stop. They may continue for several more days. If the initial riot and dispersal occurs on the home "turf" of the crowd—if a confrontation develops into a police riot in an area where the citizens live or typically congregate—a ghetto neighborhood, a student living area, a campus—then police attacks tend to continue well beyond the conclusion of dispersal. In part this is because in a sense the dispersal can never be complete. The targets of police wrath remain close by in their homes and shops. Furthermore, it is only under such conditions that the police are able to continue their riot once dispersal is complete. When a police riot occurs on neutral grounds—for example, in a downtown area—typically the civilians disperse to widely scattered places. The police have nowhere to go to continue the fray. But when police hostility can be attached to a neighborhood the possibility of continuing the attacks remain available. Thus, in Newark, police attacks on persons and property continued in the neighborhood of the disturbance several days after the rioting by blacks had ceased. In Berkeley, in the event to be discussed below, the initial confrontation and dispersal occurred on a Friday night, but heavy police action against the student community continued through Monday. It is also sometimes the case that continuing police rioting against such a neighborhood results in generating new crowds and new confrontations, thus renewing the cycle for some days. This is often what happens in campus situations.

The phases through which events move from convergence to an extended police riot indicate that there are a number of contingencies or decision points along the way. Much of the remainder of this study will be devoted to understanding why events so often take the particular turn they do and lead to police riots. It is also clear in this prototype that police riots grow out of interaction between the police and a group of citizens. Obviously, if civilians never provided the police with a confrontation or were always easily dispersed without force, police riots would be unlikely to occur. This is an unreasonable expectation, and ultimately civilian behavior—while it may contribute greatly to the likelihood of police rioting—does not explain or justify it. The mere fact of violence between citizens and the police does not constitute a police riot. The police must employ unnecessary, unlawful, and willful violence if we are to call an event a police riot. That can never be blamed on the victims of police riots, only on the police.

This prototype is intended primarily as a sensitizing device to critical questions of why police riots occur and what the phenomenon of a police riot is like. I now describe two specific police riots in order to provide the reader with a more concrete sense of the sequence of escalation and the behavior of police and citizens.

The first of these riots occurred in Los Angeles in the summer of 1967 during an anti-war march. It was a limited police riot which ended when the remnants of the crowd managed to depart for their homes. The second occurred in Berkeley during the summer of 1968 in the heart of the student living area. It was an extended riot. I have chosen to recount these two cases in considerable detail primarily because they were among those which were the subject of lengthy investigations. In most other instances of police riots one can only make educated guesses from fragmentary evidence about what happened. This is particularly true of police riots in minority communities. But except for the fact that guns were not used and no one was killed, these two police riots typify what I have been able to observe or reconstruct about the patterns of mass police misbehavior in other incidents.

Los Angeles

As I tried to get Laurie [her 4-year-old] away, I found a cop towering over me. "I can't move back, my little girl's brace is caught," I said.

"What the hell do I care," he replied, and hit me over the head with his night stick, knocking Laurie and myself to the payment.

On the evening of June 23, 1967, President Johnson attended a $500-a-plate fund-raising dinner at the Century Plaza Hotel in Los Angeles. It was still some months before the nation would begin to realize that the war in Viet Nam had cost Johnson his renomination to a second term—the Tet offensive and the New Hampshire primary would not take place until after Christmas. Still, the anti-war movement was developing rapidly.

A few weeks before the dinner members of the Peace Action Council, which had operated for nearly a year as a loose confederation of local anti-war groups, began to plan what they hoped would be their first sizable peace march. The demonstrators would parade past the hotel while the President was speaking.

As they planned, so did the police. Unable to block a parade permit, the police laid on ultra-tight security measures. Flaws in these measures, compounded by faulty decisions at the scene, produced first a confrontation, then dispersal, and then one of the bloodiest police riots ever unleashed on the peace movement.

In the event the police literally ran amok. They beat, herded, and abused a helpless, nonviolent crowd, composed mainly of terrorized, white, middle-class adults, who police actions prevented from dispersing. Infants, cripples, pregnant women, the very elderly—none was immune as the crowd was beaten from one cul-de-sac to another while motorcycles and squad cars careened among them.

In the aftermath of the riot, a vigorous public protest was launched, and, when an official investigation was not forthcoming, the American Civil Liberties Union of Southern California initiated a painstaking inquiry into what happened. More than 500 persons submitted written statements to the ACLU—some of them passers-by who had never been part of the protest march. A month after the incident, the ACLU published its report: *Day of Protest, Night of Violence.*[6] In reconstructing this police riot I have made considerable use of this document. I also conducted interviews with some participants, particularly with members of the Los Angeles Police Department. These interviews with the police unfortunately were off the record, and I may not quote them directly.

In what follows I first sketch the sequence of what happened.

Then I try to assess the extent and the character of the police violence. Finally, I try to suggest why the police acted as they did.

What Happened?

The gathering place for the march was Cheviot Hills Park, about a mile from the Century Plaza Hotel. By the day of the march the plan was to walk to the hotel and back again to the park. This was not a very good plan, but it was the only one available. A variety of plans proposing dispersal areas beyond the hotel and a rally *to draw people on from the hotel to the dispersal area*, had been rejected by the police and the hotel. This ultimately proved disastrous, at least for the demonstrators.

The crowd began to gather during the afternoon. The march was to begin at 7:30 p.m. From 5:00 o'clock on the crowd swelled rapidly as people arrived from work. It was a very good-natured and relaxed crowd. It was made up of the kind of people who knew nothing of police violence, who were accustomed to proper, even cordial interaction with the police. They were white, middle-class Americans. Many were business or professional men. Many were housewives. There were a great number of children and babies—many of whom were pushed along the parade route in strollers and buggies. There were, of course, a good number of students and some in hippie dress. But overall it was, as one observer described it, "one of the Goddamnedest most respectable crowds you could imagine. I mean it was mainly Beverly Hills solid types, all those cute, earnest women and guys in the $40 shoes."[7]

The pre-march rally began at 6:00. Dr. Benjamin Spock spoke quietly and persuasively about the immorality of the war. Muhammed Ali, recently stripped of his heavyweight title because he refused induction—"I got no quarrel with them Viet Cong"—advised the rally to remain nonviolent.

At 6:30, while the speeches continued, white-helmeted policemen accompanied a civilian through the park. He handed out leaflets. These were copies of a restraining order obtained that morning in Santa Barbara which barred demonstrators from committing a whole series of acts—many of which it is unreasonable to suppose they would have done. They were barred from using stink bombs, smoke-making devices, "loosing any animal on the premises" of the hotel, and so on. They were also enjoined from congregating in front of the hotel or entering any private property within the hotel complex.

Upon receipt of a leaflet some members of the crowd left thinking the march itself had been banned. It hadn't. But it had been made considerably more dangerous. For the police also barred all sound trucks from the parade, thus destroying the ability of parade leaders to communicate with, direct, or, eventually, to warn off the marchers. Some hand bull horns were passed out among monitors. These proved inaudible. Worse yet, it was impossible to get the word to the monitors about what directions they ought to give over their bull horns. Still the crowd was jovial and confident. Most people felt they didn't really need monitors to walk in a short parade.

By 7:00 the now 15,000 persons in the park began to line up in preparation for the march. Immediately, the police cracked down, giving a major hint of what was to come—"This is an illegal assembly. Your parade permit does not go into effect until 7:30." Fearing a confrontation, the march leaders got people to fall out of ranks and mill about until the appointed time when standing abreast would be legal.

At 7:30 the march began forming up again and the first ranks moved out the gate of the parking lot of the park. Here a Toyota pickup truck with sound equipment tried to join the parade. The truck was manned by several radicals who wanted to urge the crowd to engage in a massive sit-in once they reached the hotel. Parade monitors formed a linked-arm circle around the truck while the marchers flowed by in order to keep the truck out of the demonstration. The monitors took this action both because sound trucks were illegal and they feared their permit might be cancelled and because they did not want such advocates of civil disobedience associated with the parade.

The police noted the incident and moved in. Told what was going on, a sergeant said, "All right, we'll handle it." And they did. The sergeant motioned the truck out of the parade line and the driver signaled compliance and began to slowly turn the truck out of the march. Then an officer broke from the police lines and began to bash out the windows of the truck with his baton. Other police bolted and followed him and also began to smash the truck —on the doors, the windows, the body. Others followed. The police pulled people from the cab of the truck and beat them in front of the crowd. Several persons in the rear of the truck were beaten severely. "A policeman broke his club over someone, and then "grabbed a picket sign and continued slashing at people with it."

... the police came after the boy and girl on the back of the truck. They hit them with their night sticks, knocked them down, and pulled them off the back of the truck. At this point I could no longer see the blows land but the night sticks kept coming up above the side of the truck and down again, up and down again.

The police then beat everyone within reach around the truck, dragged several people off, beating them as they went, grabbed and beat and kicked several monitors and finally retired.

The behavior of the police in this incident was a preview of what was to come. The police seemed very angry. They erupted into violence or abuse easily. Numerous other early incidents of club waving, dangerous driving, and the like were reported. At 6:30 that evening a column of patrol cars, loaded with five officers to a car, on their way to the hotel stopped at a traffic light. On that particular corner four young Cal Tech students were distributing leaflets about an upcoming love-in. They good-humoredly offered them to the officers. Those in the first two cars took them and laughed. Then as traffic began to move, an officer reached out of the third car as it slowly passed. One youth handed him a leaflet. Suddenly the officer lunged out with his nightstick which he had hidden below window level and slammed the boy on the wrist. Officers in the following car yelled curses and an officer in the next car, now moving perhaps at 20 miles an hour, leaned out and swung with his club as he passed. He missed. But he would have many better targets later. Some tension built in the crowd as a result of police behavior and demeanor. But still, most seemed to expect no real trouble.

Meanwhile at the hotel, 1,300 police officers with another 200 in reserve had been assembled to seal the hotel off from the marchers. The first sign that police planning—despite an inch-thick special manual (*Century City '67*) prepared for the occasion—was ill-conceived was the fact that several thousand spectators, both sympathetic and antagonistic to the march, were permitted to gather in front of the hotel. Later, police proclaimed it was illegal to stand in front of the hotel, but by that time the crowd had already greatly contributed to clogging the route of the march past the hotel. For several hours those in front of the hotel had merely been requested to remain on the sidewalks by the police. The injunction obtained earlier, prohibiting congregating in front of the hotel, was not announced or enforced at a time when it might have still been possible for the spectators to leave.

And so on came the marchers. They had no internal communications. They had been denied a suitable dispersal area beyond the hotel. They were not marching past the hotel *to* somewhere, for they had been denied permission to hold a post-march rally. As a march leader put it:

There was no focal point beyond the hotel to attract those in the march. . . . Therefore, the hotel itself became the focal point.

Furthermore, it turned out to be virtually impossible for the marchers to pass the hotel. Passage was partly blocked by the crowd in front of the hotel. As the march approached, the police who had been positioned to keep the spectators on the sidewalks were withdrawn and the crowd permitted to spill into the street. Worse yet, the police positioned themselves at a critical bottleneck and blocked the only remaining space through which the march could have continued. As the march piled up and people began to mill around in front of the hotel the police continued steadfastly to block the traffic lanes through which it could have moved on through. There was no way to proceed, and no way to contact the line of march to halt. So the march continued to arrive and the crowd got denser. In effect, the police had created the very thing they said they most feared. They had stopped the march in front of the hotel and created a huge crowd. It would have been hard enough to keep the crowd moving in the best of circumstances. After all it was the presence of the President that had brought out so large a gathering in the first place. And the President was in the hotel. The hotel was the magnet. Given a predisposition for the crowd to be drawn to the hotel, police actions which greatly impeded the march made the creation of a large crowd certain.

As the crowd continued to build up in density, approximately 25 more militant demonstrators conducted a brief sit-in. The press of the crowd broke it up within five minutes. There simply was too little room.

The police felt something had to be done. They had no intention of permitting 15,000 people to stage a protest rally in front of a hotel in which the President was speaking. The police were probably right in wanting to avoid this situation. The reasonable course, however, would have been to open adequate passage for the march to leave the front of the hotel and direct the marchers out of the area. But reason was lacking. Instead, at 8:25, Captain Louis Sporrer took the microphone of the police sound van and announced that the assembly was illegal since, by stopping, the demonstrators had violated the terms of their parade permit. Quite true. He then ordered the crowd to disperse, *but he gave no instructions on how the marchers were to comply with this order. In fact the police had no adequate plan by which the march could disperse.* They simply confronted the front of the march in an area where all routes, except to the rear, were blocked or so clogged as to allow only a trickle of traffic. They seem to have wanted the parade to turn around on itself. Those in front could not accomplish this. The rear echelons coming along the route were not blocked off and turned back, but continued unsuspectingly to pour in, thus successively telescoping the line of marchers into a dense congregation in front of the hotel. In desperation to somehow comply with police orders some monitors instructed those near them in the crowd to march in circles (and thus keep moving). Impasse. Ahead an unyielding line of police. To the west was another line. To the east was a very steep embankment down from an overpass additionally blocked by a guard railing. To the rear only a sea of on-coming marchers unaware of why the parade was congregating in front of the hotel. Indeed, at this time police reinforcements blocked the last trickle of marchers edging by their lines.

The police asked the impossible. Of course they failed to get compliance. But they were determined none the less. They used motorcycle wedges to force an open space between the crowd and police lines. But as soon as they were opened, the density of the crowd forced those in front back close to the police again.

Then the police struck. They turned dazzling spotlights into the crowd and waded in swinging. They beat everyone they could reach while the crowd reeled back into tighter compression. Women and children were being pushed down underfoot, screaming. Attorney Judith Atkinson offered this description:

As the press of the crowd grew thicker, there were times when my feet were not on the ground. I was being carried along by the crowd. . . . People in front of us began to fall down. . . . As I turned around at this point, I saw a cop strike a white-haired, about sixty-year-old lady behind me with his club because she could not move forward. Cops to my right were now freely hitting and striking all people in front of them, prodding them as you would cattle, and I heard one cop as he struck a woman say, "They want to come to the show, but they don't want to pay the price."

After the initial charge the whole affair became a nightmare for the demonstrators. Most were forced to flee down a steep embankment (45° slope) into an underpass. The police bullied them over the edge. Many fell. The crowd was beaten and shoved hither and yon.

But once down the slope into the underpass they were again boxed in. Eventually, baton-wielding lines of policemen beat them back up the steep slope which was covered with slippery ice plant. The crowd formed human life lines and passed infants, children, and the elderly up the slope. The police beat whomever they could reach.

Finally, the crowd was cleared from the hotel area. Women seeking lost children were turned away from the site. Police lines began to move into the surrounding neighborhood and on towards the park. Demonstrators were harassed wherever police found them. Some were chased into Beverly Hills. Others were diverted from parking areas where their vehicles were parked. All groups larger than five were considered an illegal gathering. This was interpreted to mean no more than five could ride in a single automobile and led to many car stops. Police violence was directed at anyone still seen to possess a picket sign. Innocent passers-by were sometimes pulled from their cars and beaten or harassed.

The Extent of Police Brutality

In the aftermath of the police riot no systematic effort was made to determine the number of people beaten by the police or the number who were injured. This would have been extremely difficult to accomplish, since many suffered cuts and bruises for which they did not seek medical attention and many went to private physicians and clinics throughout the Los Angeles area. Nevertheless, early press accounts reported that 30 persons were treated at UCLA's emergency room. Furthermore, statements submitted to the ACLU give some hint of the widespread injuries inflicted by the police. One-hundred and seventy-eight persons reported injuries to the ACLU. Forty said they were hit on the head by police, 16 reported blows on the back or kidneys, and 97 reported blows on the neck, arms, legs, or chest.

The eyewitness accounts make it clear that a very large number of persons were beaten. Under the circumstances it is difficult to believe that any appreciable amount of the police use of force was justified.

Reading the various eyewitness accounts one can only conclude that most of the policemen who came into contact with the civilians used their clubs willfully and needlessly and that they hit about as many people as they could. The stories of elderly ladies and pregnant women being beaten and trampled were numerous, indicating the police were on a rampage against the crowd and had lost their heads entirely. It would serve no purpose to recount a litany of horror stories here. But considering what took place it is extremely fortunate that a number of people weren't killed.

Why Did It Happen?

Two main issues arise about why this police riot occurred. First, why was police planning so grotesquely inadequate? Second, once the confrontation had developed why did the police behave so brutally?

The first of these questions has to do with a faulty assumption about the kinds of people who opposed the war at that time and thus a serious underestimation of the size of crowd to expect. This in turn bears greatly on the second issue. The kind of people the police expected to turn out were those the police particularly hated and those who the police believed would pose a substantial threat to their safety. In addition to all of this, the police were anxiety-ridden by the fact that they were protecting the President of the United States. All of these factors led to the violence of the police once the situation developed.

In summer 1967, the Los Angeles police, like many Americans, believed that people who actively opposed the war were kooks, radicals, hippies, and subversives. But, while polls showed that a majority of Americans had not yet turned against the war, they also showed that a substantial minority (at least a third) did oppose the war at that time. This did not enter into police planning, however. They relied on the fact that earlier demonstrations against the war in Los Angeles had never drawn more than several thousand people. They recognized that a chance to protest directly against President Johnson would increase the size of the crowd, but I have been told that they did not expect many more than 5,000 persons to turn out. Three times that many did.

In judging anti-war sentiments to be deviant, they also assumed that those protesting would be deviants—hippies, students, radicals. This influenced their judgment of the threat of the marchers. It also, I believe, made them more intransigent in their pre-demonstration negotiations with the protest committee. From the beginning they pushed the demonstrators around. They were uncooperative in helping find march plans which would minimize the chance for confrontation or the need for dispersal and violence. It is a simple axiom of parade management that there must be dispersal areas, adequate route supervision, and the like. The police vetoed available dispersal areas and when the time came denied the parade organizers the use of sound systems to direct the march. They seem to have felt that the march should not occur, and when they found they had no choice but to permit it, essentially refused to condone it. Possibly they believed that the kinds of people they would be dealing with ought to be harassed and even set upon for their affront to the President, to "the boys over there," and to the civic reputation of Los Angeles.

In any event, I have been told that the plans for crowd control did not envision so large a crowd and that the police got caught short and were unable to improvise adequate tactics on the spot. Later, the then Police Chief Reddin said he gave the order to disperse the crowd when he looked down from a ninth story hotel window and saw a bulge in the crowd. Presumably from such a vantage point he might have worked out a dispersal route as well.

Amateurish intelligence work prior to the march helped the police misread the size and character of the crowd they would be facing. A private detective, hired by attorneys for the hotel, attended planning sessions conducted by the parade organizers and returned with lurid tales of conspiracies and diabolical plans: to unleash mice, cockroaches, and stinkbombs in the hotel, and other such outlandish schemes. The meetings were in fact open to the public and many of the detective's stories were based on suggestions offered by members of the audience. None was ever taken seriously by the planning committee.

However, such tales seem to have reinforced police beliefs that they were dealing with kooks and subversives. Certainly these impressions were widespread among the rank-and-file officers assigned to control the crowd. The rash of early violence and anger, long before the parade got anywhere near the hotel, indicated police sentiments and intentions. Statements submitted to the ACLU are filled with quotations of the police indicating they regarded the crowd as made up of disreputable people: "Get that damn Jew," "A bunch of dirty, Goddamned communists," "Animals and commies, that's all they are."

Finally, it is clear that the police were especially anxious because they were charged with the protection of the President of the United States. The major concern in their planning was to provide an impassable defense of the hotel. Thus officers with high-powered rifles were stationed on tall buildings throughout the area. A military helicopter hovered above the hotel armed with 20mm. cannon. The deployment of 1,300 officers was designed to defend the hotel against assault, not to facilitate dispersal or order.

The police view of their responsibility is perhaps best summarized by the words of one young officer to a housewife as police were forcing the crowd down the slope to the underpass:

I asked [him] why they were so violent; he was shaking with fear when he answered, "I'd push you off that cliff if I had to. The President's here."

Berkeley

A young black addressing a street meeting in the aftermath of the conflict:

Now you whites been done like we been done for years!

On a Friday evening (June 28, 1968), 124 Berkeley policemen, augmented by 32 police reservists, 10 University of California campus policemen, and 110 Alameda County Deputy Sheriffs, forcibly dispersed—with tear gas, riot batons, kicks, stones, and curses—a peaceful crowd of several hundred persons gathered on Telegraph Avenue, some of whom were listening to speeches in support of the French student strike. Thus ended a long era of good feeling between the community and the police, based to a considerable extent on the neutral policies of the police, who had previously dealt with rallies purely in terms of crowd and traffic control, regardless of political content.

During the long weekend disturbance that ensued, the conflict escalated. The first stones were thrown at the police. Gas cannisters were caught and hurled back. More beatings and gassing by the police occurred and eventually turned into what can only be described as a police rampage against unarmed and mainly non-provocative citizens. For several nights many policemen were lawless, dangerous rioters against a terrorized community.

What follows is an attempt to recreate and analyze what happened during this police outburst. The account is based mainly on the work of a short-lived, experimental Crisis Research Team which I organized just as the trouble began. This team of seven observers (including myself) conducted a close-up study of the Berkeley crisis as it occurred.[8] Members were on the streets throughout the crisis trying to keep track of events, running from the police, being gassed, talking to people, and making notes as best they could. In addition, the team conducted interviews with police officials, all members of the city council, businessmen, witnesses, victims, newsmen, clergymen, radical organizers, physicians, and nurses at area emergency hospitals—more than 500 persons in all. To augment these materials, 177 affidavits filed with the Berkeley Citizen Complaint Center of the American Civil Liberties Union were made available (without names).* In all, accounts by 221 persons who claimed to be victims or witnesses of police violence were available for analysis. This account also draws upon statements issued by a number of citizens and organizations, testimony before the city council, reports written by the mayor and by the city manager, and press and television stories.

* An ACLU staffmember checked against our list of interviewees in order to avoid any duplication, omitting ACLU affidavits of anyone we had interviewed.

The report is divided into three parts. The first is a chronological story of what happened. The second draws upon the reports of victims and witnesses to provide some conception of the frequency and variety of police rioting. The third explores briefly why the police acted against the crowd in the first place.

What Happened?

On June 19, 1968, the Young Socialist Alliance (YSA) applied to the City of Berkeley for a sound amplification permit for Telegraph Avenue—the heart of the campus community—for the evening of Friday, June 28. The permit was granted. Then the YSA announced that the sound amplification would be used for speech making at a rally to demonstrate solidarity with French students who had just lost their strike after narrowly failing to bring down the de Gaulle government. City officials countered that a sound permit was not sufficient, but that YSA would also need a permit to hold a street rally.

The YSA refused to request such a permit. Their leader, Peter Camejo, told a meeting of the city council on June 23 that under recent Supreme Court decisions on the right of free assembly such a permit was not legally required and that YSA would hold the meeting without one to challenge the local ordinance. This did not automatically necessitate a confrontation; rallies without permits are not unknown in Berkeley and in the past had been dealt with amicably by the police. Later police claimed that Camejo and the YSA were trying to produce a confrontation with the police, hence their refusal to apply for a permit. But, whatever Camejo might have wished, from past experience it is hard to believe that he could have had much reason to suppose he would be able to produce a confrontation.

In any event, publicity for the rally proceeded via sound trucks, handbills, and the underground press. It promised to be a typical Berkeley rally, which up to that time had been nothing more than long successions of speakers, some articulate, some not. Indeed, in this case there was not even an important local issue to turn out a crowd.

Meanwhile there were some sounds from city hall and police headquarters which in retrospect could have been a warning that this rally would be different. Several statements were released to the press that the rally was illegal, or that it would be illegal if the crowd grew beyond the sidewalks and into the street, thus blocking traffic. But this did not seem too grave a prospect. There would be monitors to direct the crowd, as there always are at Berkeley rallies. And besides, some clogging of the street is common on Telegraph Avenue on weekend evenings. Indeed, it was widely recognized that the YSA was holding the rally on Telegraph Avenue because of a justified lack of confidence in their ability to *attract* a large crowd—thus they were going where a crowd would be whether or not there was a rally. This becomes important shortly in assessing just how many people actually attended the rally, and thus in evaluating the police reaction.

But in addition to issuing statements about the potential illegality of the rally, unique preparations were being made by the police. Several days before the event the Berkeley police had decided they would use their mutual assistance pact with neighboring law enforcement agencies to assemble a large enough force to handle a riot. In the past no such action had been taken. Later I shall try to explain, based on interviews with Berkeley police commanders, why they decided that this particular rally was intrinsically much more dangerous than dozens of previous rallies which had been treated as simple crowd and traffic management problems and which had not prompted them to gather more than several dozen officers.

On the evening of the rally, 276 officers had been gathered to deal with the rally. Policemen controlled all rooftops along that section of Telegraph Avenue where the rally was to be held.

The rally began at 8:00 p.m. with the usual impassioned and somewhat boring speeches. As usual for a Friday night, the streets were packed with people. It was difficult to estimate how many people were actually attending the rally. At any given moment there were perhaps a thousand people in the block where the rally was going on. But many of them stopped and listened for a few minutes and then moved on. Others clearly were not interested at all, but were headed for the bookshops, coffee houses, and movies which are the heart of the Avenue scene. The consensus among Crisis Team observers and persons later interviewed was that there were about 200 people present who were serious about attending the rally and another two or three hundred mildly interested passers-by.

Until 8:50 p.m. the rally proceeded uneventfully. The presence of large police formations in nearby side streets had not yet come to be regarded with alarm in Berkeley. The monitors kept the streets clear and directed traffic. All was normal. And after the first several speakers the crowd began to dwindle significantly. As one respondent put it later, "I mean everybody was sympathetic with the French students but after you've said that, so what? I mean it wasn't like we could do anything. And, well, everybody has heard Camejo dozens of times. He doesn't grow on you."

At that point an unidentified young man suddenly urged the crowd to "liberate" the street. Presumably he was trying to put a bit more life into the sagging rally. About 200 people followed him into the street, despite protests by the monitors.

Berkeley Police Chief William Beall promptly declared the rally an illegal assembly, which, by blocking the street, it had become. Camejo exhorted the people to move back onto the sidewalk and asked the chief whether the rally might continue if they did so promptly. Beall retired to consult with his commanders. The crowd returned to the sidewalk, having blocked the street for approximately five minutes.

Then Chief Beall returned—the street was empty—and said no, the meeting was now illegal and must disperse. Several minutes later, at 9:00 p.m., police formations moved onto Telegraph Avenue, split the crowd, and pushed it onto two groups. City Manager William Hanley stated in his report to the city council that "by 9:30 the police lines were holding 200 people on Telegraph Avenue between Dwight [Way] and Blake [Street] and another 150 on Haste [Street] west of Telegraph." The situation remained static for awhile with some verbal abuse shouted at the police by a few members of the crowd while others attempted negotiations to resolve the situation. One group who tried to negotiate was made up of about a dozen persons, most of them Berkeley clergymen who typically volunteer as monitors for rallies, but also included City Councilman Daniel Dewey. Finally, as the police moved forward, this group interposed itself between a police line and part of the crowd. Councilman Dewey (who said he was present because he felt it important that council members observe demonstrations and rallies in Berkeley) said he and the clergymen linked arms and backed down the Avenue ahead of the oncoming police line out of concern "that the crowd be pushed back as nonviolently as possible."

When police lieutenant Charles Plummer approached the line, several clergymen tried to discuss the situation with him. He responded, "That's enough talk," and clubbed at their clasped hands with his bull horn. Lieutenant Plummer is a huge man, and he had little difficulty breaking the line of clergymen.

Then came a barrage of gas. A retired police commander with considerable experience in managing crowds both here and abroad was an eyewitness to police tactics at this point. In his judgment the use of gas was either done with extraordinary incompetence or with the intention of punishing the crowd, because the gas was thrown *behind* the crowd making them approach the police, and no dispersal routes had been left open. "The crowd could not disperse because the police had them boxed in," he said. In fact for some time, while the police had been seemingly demanding the dispersal of the crowd prior to the use of gas, dispersal had not been permitted by the police.

Choking in the gas, the previously passive crowd made desperate attempts at flight. Many were beaten by the police as they did so. After this came the first police rampage. Bands of policemen on foot and five to a car roved the South Campus area. Private residences were gassed. The Free Church and YSA headquarters were gassed. Unsuspecting crowds leaving movie theaters were gassed, clubbed, and even made to run gauntlets of club-swinging policemen. People were beaten in a seemingly random way, without any attempt being made to arrest them. (The second section of this account provides details and statistics on police attacks. I am concerned here only to provide a general outline of events.)

As the police violence erupted there came the first signs of fighting back. Some rocks were thrown at policemen—although as will be discussed later some of the rocks were thrown from the rooftops *by* policemen! Some building materials were dragged into the street to suggest barricades, and a number of trash cans (perhaps nine in all) were dragged into the street and set afire.

Well before midnight the streets were empty except for the police.

Saturday was another day. Residents of the South Campus area awoke to a still heavy pall of tear gas. As Telegraph Avenue came to life there was considerable anger and tension. Over breakfast in the cafés along the Avenue people recounted their experiences of the night before, read press accounts, and wondered what it all meant. Technically illegal or not, a peaceful and rather ordinary Berkeley rally had been broken up. Such a thing had never happened before. Many were inclined to put the blame on Alameda County Deputy Sheriffs, who, while they had yet to earn their dangerous and brutal reputation in subsequent Berkeley crises, were thought to be hostile to the Berkeley scene. Still, Berkeley officers had led and made the decisions. It was hard for many to accept this—relations with the Berkeley police had historically been benign. The normal Saturday crowds developed on the Avenue, but were infused with outrage, fear, and uncertainty.

By 3:00 p.m. leaflets were being circulated calling for a mass meeting under Young Socialist Alliance auspices at the intersection of Bancroft Way and Telegraph Avenue—the intersection adjacent to the Sproul Plaza entrance to the University of California campus. A second group—The Resistance, a small organization of street radicals—announced that a street dance would be held at the location of Friday night's rally.

At 7:00 p.m. the YSA "mass meeting" began with perhaps 200 persons. Speakers demanded that the city condone this peaceful rally and also open Telegraph Avenue for a street party on July 4th. Several speakers displayed gas masks and told where they could be bought. At 8:00 p.m. the rally voted to march down Telegraph to The Block, scene of the previous night's action. By 8:30 about 600 persons had gathered on The Block. Meanwhile, at 7:15 the Berkeley police had recalled all off-duty officers, requested reinforcements from the Alameda County Sheriffs, the California Highway Patrol, and the Oakland Police Department, and alerted the National Guard and all local hospitals. Subsequently the fire department and the public works department were asked to stand by.

This night the crowd was significantly different from that of the night before. There were many fewer middle-class and "straight" people. There were more juveniles—some who had come from Oakland and Richmond to "see what was happening." Traffic was diverted off Telegraph by members of the crowd. Several small barricades were constructed to close off The Block. Several people painted peace symbols on the street and sidewalk with spray paint. A rock band played, and many danced. A few—perhaps 40—listened to the speeches. As is normal during such impromptu street dances, it was not uncommon to see people smoking marijuana.

While the rally of the night before failed to stop or gather a really sizable crowd, rock bands and a street dance are always successful in doing so on Telegraph Avenue, especially on a Saturday night. By 9:30 p.m. perhaps as many as 2,000 people were taking part. Periodically, rumors circulated that the police were about to attack. But none appeared. Some said this was proof that Friday night was due to the Alameda Sheriffs. Things seemed back to normal.

This was faulty judgment. The police were in fact busy. They set up check points a few blocks from the scene and closed all exits from the area, diverting traffic. At 10:45 they gassed the first aid station at the Free Church.

By 11:00 the crowd began to diminish. The illegal assembly had seemingly been condoned for three hours. The police maintain they warned the crowd that they were an illegal assembly at 11:08. Perhaps they did, but no Crisis Team observers, members of the crowd we contacted later, or members of the press said they had heard such an announcement. Be that as it may, at 11:30 the police struck suddenly, violently, and in great numbers. Lines of riot-equipped policemen moved on the crowd from three sides throwing great numbers of tear gas cannisters. The crowd withdrew north along the Avenue back towards the university. The side streets were blocked—it was the only direction in which movement away from the gas was possible. Along the way large numbers of the ordinary Saturday night crowds which clog Telegraph were forced with them. As they neared the University the crowd was boxed in by another line of policemen advancing from the campus. The melee began.

Gas was everywhere. Demonstrators, street dancers, and great numbers of ordinary citizens tried desperately to flee. All exits were blocked, and flight required passing through police lines. In doing so, many citizens were beaten. There were 273 policemen in action. Many broke ranks and went on beating sprees. Sometimes squad-sized groups of officers chased and beat citizens.

Little knots of the most militant demonstrators reacted by breaking store windows and setting fire to trash cans. Others threw stones. An empty house owned by the University and scheduled for demolition was set afire.

At midnight someone threw a Molotov cocktail at a highway patrolman near the campus. He suffered serious burns on his lower legs. In the confusion of the moment a rumor seems to have rapidly spread among the police—possibly transmitted erroneously over the police radio—that the patrolman had lost his genitals as a result of the firebomb and was near death. This produced the most furious outburst of police violence during the entire crisis. The Crisis Team investigation located 27 persons who reported having been beaten *unconscious and left* by roving bands of policemen on Saturday night following this incident, and clearly only a relatively small proportion of victims were interviewed. All familiar with the American police recognize that injury, danger, or other difficulties suffered by a fellow officer galvanize the police. In this instance they had already been sporadically attacking the crowds. They were angry already. Thus, the attack on the officer with its attendant horrid rumors drove some policemen nearly berserk. The furious attacks which will be discussed shortly continued well into the night as did some further window breaking and stone throwing by militants. Police attacks were not particularly aimed at the militants (who were hard to catch). Instead, the police vented their rage on the community as a whole. And consequently it was mainly nonmilitants, often people standing in front of their homes or walking from restaurants, theaters, or a late session in their University labs and offices who took the brunt of the police violence.

At 3:30 Sunday morning a curfew was proclaimed for the South Campus area to be in effect from 7:00 p.m. to 6:00 a.m.

Sunday was a day of meetings and community mobilization. The demand for a July 4th street celebration, raised the night before, was widely agreed upon by those attending.

Meanwhile, during the afternoon policemen were deployed in substantial numbers along Telegraph Avenue. The curfew was extended from the South Campus area to include the campus itself.

At 6:00 p.m., approximately 300 people gathered in a park across from the city hall. It was a disorganized meeting. Berkeley Mayor Wallace S. Johnson joined the crowd and was spat upon. Some members of the crowd urged that he be beaten, others protected him. He left. At 7:00 p.m. many drifted away from the park meeting. Half an hour later a small band of militants marched from the park up University Avenue. Their passage was marked by window breaking in business establishments and some rock throwing.

This foray was met by police—approximately 700 of whom were gathered through the mutual aid arrangements. At 9:00 p.m. the curfew was extended to the entire city, but only enforced in the South Campus area. There were many fewer beating incidents. Instead the police began making arrests: 123 were picked up, four times as many as had been arrested during the first two days of the crisis.

Despite the relative calm, the massive police presence, and the curfew, several remarkable beating incidents occurred Sunday night. A restaurant was entered, damaged, and a young man dragged out, beaten, and left in the gutter. Two black men, one of them a minister, were chased and beaten by perhaps 50 officers. (Both incidents are taken up in greater detail below.)

From Monday on, street action cooled while community action heated up. An 8:00 p.m. to 6:00 a.m. curfew was in effect until Tuesday. There were a few dispersals of small groups gathered on Telegraph. There were a few more beatings. But the episode had run its course. However, marathon city council meetings began. The council demanded a report on police action from the city manager. Hundreds of citizens recounted their experiences to the council during public sessions. The curfew was cancelled. Attention focused on the demand for a Fourth of July street party. After much discussion the council granted a permit when Avenue businessmen and a number of clergy supported the demand, requested a permit, and undertook to monitor the event.

On July 4th a huge day-long rally was held. Thousands danced, ambled the Avenue, and listened to the rock bands. The crowd constituted a huge solidarity gathering of the University community—young and old, straight and hippie, moderate and radical. The police were nowhere in sight. There was no disorder.

The Extent of Police Violence

The preceding section sketched a considerable amount of violent police misconduct during this episode in Berkeley. Admittedly, there was also citizen misconduct. I hardly challenge the right of the police to move against such misconduct using the force necessary to make arrests or to preserve life. What is at issue is police behavior far beyond the bounds of such justification. I shall now establish that, whatever else may have occurred in Berkeley during this period, the police rioted.

As will be shown, police violence took two main forms. One involved lines of policemen charging, chasing, and beating unresisting persons on the street. The other involved four or five policemen piling out of a squad car to chase and beat citizens without provocation. In both kinds of incidents the victim was usually beaten and left lying where he fell while the police ran on or got back in their cars to seek new targets. Very few of those beaten were arrested; thus not even trumped up charges were used by the police to disguise their attacks. The hit-and-run attacks made from automobiles usually began after crowds had been dispersed and were especially frequent after midnight Saturday night.

In all, 37 citizens were treated for injuries at local hospitals—six for fractures, two of the skull. A much larger number were treated at impromptu first-aid stations, several of which were subsequently gassed and attacked by the police. Others were treated by private physicians.

In what follows, data from interviews with witnesses and victims will be presented to establish three main points about the nature and extent of police violence:

1. Tear gas was not simply used as "the best available means for dispersing crowds and controlling mass violence in a quick, decisive manner with a minimum risk of physical injury" as claimed in a report on the episode by the city manager. It was extensively used as a weapon of reprisal and terror against nonprovocative individuals and against the community as a whole.
2. Policemen indiscriminately beat nonprovocative persons, often in hit-and-run gang attacks, and engaged in various other indefensible forms of physical brutality.
3. Policemen systematically issued contradictory and impossible commands, made repeated threats, used abusive and obscene language, and otherwise employed terror tactics.

From its initial use against the crowd on Friday night, tear gas was *mainly* utilized as punishment and to create, not to disperse, potentially dangerous confrontations. I have earlier reported the expert judgment of a former police commander on the initial use of gas: that the crowd was not hostile and constituted no threat to the police; that the crowd was boxed in and thus the gas could not disperse them, only set them in motion within police lines; and that the gas was thrown at the back of the crowd, thus making it advance on the officers using the gas. Later in the evening a number of other gas attacks were reported.

Persons attending a dance at the student union and a movie on campus were tear-gassed as they attempted to leave. A professor who was at the movie reported that those in attendance had received no warning of the altercation going on several blocks away. He said, "old people and children were gassed, and gas was fired into a crowd near the student union that had made no provocative gestures, but had stopped, realizing that Telegraph Avenue was impassable."

Interviewers were told of a number of private residences that had been gassed, as were several emergency first aid stations, one at the headquarters of the Young Socialist Alliance, the other in the Free Church. Clergymen present at the Free Church reported that a number of canisters of tear gas were thrown down the entryway to the church on several occasions Friday night. The Rev. Jock Brown was badly beaten by a policeman as he stood at the entrance of the church directing injured persons inside. On one occasion two police officers in gas masks broke in the back door of the church, shouted unintelligibly, and then left. Later police broke into the church sanctuary, and then also withdrew.

On Saturday night the Free Church was again a scene of gassing. Later, Police Chief William Beall, Mayor Johnson, and "ten to fifteen officers" all in gas masks came to the side door of the church and "pushed their way in." Drawers and desks were searched. The police showed no warrant; indeed, the chief reportedly refused to speak to church leaders. The mayor and the police then withdrew without action or comment.

A convalescent home was also reported gassed, as were a number of private residences. Several witnesses described the following use of gas: a number of people were at a party in an apartment house on Haste Street (a block from Telegraph Avenue). A black girl at the party noticed police officers beating two black men on the street below. She and two young men shouted from the balcony of the apartment that the police should stop. No one recalls now exactly what was said, or whether obscene language was used. But the police reaction was to launch a tear gas canister up onto the balcony. The girl sustained cuts and burns on her legs which required medical treatment and, of course, all suffered from tear gas fumes.

Three reporters for the *Daily Californian* reported that they were caught up in the flight of people after police began their most savage outburst of beatings following the injury of a highway patrolman by a gasoline bomb. To escape they ran into an alley which turned out to be dead end. Police then fired four tear gas grenades at these three people.

At approximately 1:45 a.m. a policeman broke a large plate-glass window at a bookstore. The building was then gassed.

Although the city manager said no gas was used Sunday night, interviewers received testimony that it had been used several times. One complainant charged that a private dwelling was gassed without cause. Another claimed he was gassed at 11:00 p.m. on Telegraph Avenue at a time when he was the only person on the street!

This pattern of gas use by the police makes it clear that they used gas to vent their rage, rather than using it according to accepted tactics. If these actions do not speak with sufficient force, we have testimony on the loud words used by the police about gas. In one incident an officer entered a private establishment which was serving as a first aid station. An employee told the officer that if he didn't have a warrant he would have to leave. According to several witnesses the policemen then brandished a tear gas canister and said, "I don't need a warrant; I've got a tear gas bomb. Would you like that?"

In a similar incident a policeman who was asked to leave a restaurant by its owner waved a gas canister and responded: "Shut up, you motherfucker, or we're going to blow up your restaurant."

Nevertheless, gas was not the main resource of the police. Half of the witnesses and victims interviewed reported beatings. For Saturday night alone the Crisis Team obtained 50 accounts of being beaten. Only one of these victims was arrested. The others were beaten and left.

In a great many incidents, persons were set upon by roving groups of policemen—either moving on foot or in squad cars. These were not forays into crowds or groups of demonstrators.

Some victims were pedestrians walking residential streets, some were standing outside their homes, others stood in small knots of bystanders watching the scene. Five persons reported being attacked by groups of officers on foot on Friday night, seven on Saturday night. We received accounts of six incidents Friday night in which police jumped from their vehicles to beat one or more persons. Thirty-one such separate incidents were reported to us for Saturday night and eight more on Sunday and Monday nights.

In a typical incident police would drive up in their car and suddenly slam on the brakes when one or more of the five officers in the vehicle spotted someone or something which aroused him. The officers would scramble out of the car and run up to (or after) a victim, beat him with their batons, then return to their car and drive off. Frequently the target of the police beating was left lying unconscious, sometimes bleeding profusely from scalp lacerations. No one saw police issue either warnings or commands in any of these situations. Indeed, in most incidents witnesses stated that the police said nothing at all, except for some yelling of obscenities.

The typical victim was male, although perhaps surprisingly a third of the victims on whom we have information were female. More than half of the victims we interviewed were over 25 years of age. And most were "straight" in appearance. These last two findings may have been produced by a reluctance of younger and "hipper" people to be interviewed. A good many persons refused to be interviewed—some because they felt it would be futile (and perhaps they were right), others because they were suspicious that we might be fronting for the police. Thus, it must be kept in mind that these data probably considerably underestimate the actual number of police beatings. Crisis Team observers saw a number of beating incidents which later did not turn up in complaints and thus are not included in the statistics.

All witnesses and observers agree there were very few black persons present on the streets in the South Campus area during the weekend. Nevertheless, Crisis Team observers believed that the police were particularly likely to pick out any black they saw in choosing whom to chase or beat. It was reported that alerts were given over the police radio to be on the lookout for Black Panthers and other black militants. Reportedly police were warned to watch for Eldridge Cleaver especially.

Despite the fact that few blacks were present two of them were victims in one of the most flagrant and widely publicized incidents. A young black man, Raymond "Gypsy" Williams, was chased by approximately 50 police officers for more than a block down Telegraph Avenue on Sunday evening. They caught him just beyond Channing Way and beat him bloody and senseless (he had allegedly made an obscene gesture to a policeman). A black minister—in clerical collar—who attempted to intercede was clubbed down and arrested. About a score of newsmen witnessed this event, many of them photographing and filming it. The police then turned on them and smashed several cameras.

Also on Sunday night the Forum affair occurred—films of which shocked Bay Area viewers. Approximately eight policemen charged into the Forum restaurant–coffee house after a young man had allegedly shouted an insult at them. The police knocked down the railing in front of the outdoor coffee area, rushed inside pushing over tables and shouting angry curses, caught the offending youth, dragged him out under a rain of blows, and then discarded him unconscious and bleeding in the gutter.

The ratios of attacker to victim—perhaps 50 to 1 in the case of Gypsy Williams, and 7 or 8 to 1 in the case of the Forum victim—were not atypical. Most respondents claimed that the attacking groups of police officers greatly outnumbered the size of the civilian group set upon. On Saturday night, when the largest number of beating incidents occurred, there were 31 reported incidents of police attacks on persons who were either alone or accompanied by fewer people than there were attacking officers. Of course, not all officers in such groups always struck blows. Some stood and shouted encouragement. Some held victims while others beat them. Some were too slow to reach the victim before fleeter colleagues had finished the job. And some officers appeared to find the whole affair disgusting and simply stood to the side.

Most of the victims claimed they had not engaged in any illegal acts and furthermore that their presence in the area where they were beaten was not connected with the demonstration. Seventy-two persons who claimed to have been victims of police assaults claimed they had taken no part in any of the action during the four-day period. Eighteen victims reported to have been threatened, struck, gassed, or arrested while standing in close proximity to, or inside, their home or that of a friend.

On Friday night police attacks were confined to the Telegraph

Avenue vicinity, but on Saturday beatings were reported as far as five blocks west of Telegraph and ten blocks south of Haste Street. On Sunday, beatings were dispersed throughout the South Campus area.

On Saturday night several locations were particularly frequent scenes of police action. One of the most dangerous places to have been was the intersection of Telegraph and Parker. Seven respondents, including one clergyman, reported a series of beatings at this location over a period of two hours, during which perhaps 30 individuals were attacked. Here is one victim's description of the action as he wrote it up in a publicly released statement:

> Saturday night, having been out of town all day and at home all evening, I went out a little after midnight when fire engines went up our street. I did not know the demonstrations were still going on in any form. A few blocks from my own home, standing with a group of my neighbors, most of them middle-aged family types like myself, we saw Berkeley police attack and brutally beat a boy and two girls on the far side of Telegraph at Parker; the boy was clubbed repeatedly as he lay on the ground, kicked and stomped; the girls were "merely" clubbed as they dragged themselves along the ground, screaming. Our group made no hostile or provocative gesture, though a few people shouted, "stop it." A moment later we were charged by three *carloads* of blue-uniformed police who roared across the sidewalk, cutting us off from any escape. No order to disperse had even been given, though a Berkeley police officer had been standing no more than 20 feet from us during all of this. The police piled out of the cars, clubbed us, and cursed us. I myself was clubbed as I ran.

Another bad scene on Saturday night was the dark parking lot behind a restaurant which is located on Telegraph Avenue. The restaurant was tear-gassed and patrons fled the gas through the rear door into the parking lot. Here club-swinging policemen set upon them. One male student claims he was beaten by six policemen who attacked without warning. He suffered a fractured arm and required stitches in his head. A 34-year-old male claimed that he and 14 others were directed by one group of policemen to leave by a particular route only to be beaten by other policemen when they did so. He also required medical treatment for cuts. These are only the most seriously injured of many complainants from this particular episode.

Police also forced a number of citizens to run the gauntlet—to run past a line of policemen who struck at them as they passed. We received eyewitness accounts of three such incidents on Friday night and four on Saturday. We suspect that this may have been the work of one group of policemen. I have no way of knowing how many times they engaged in such performances.

On Saturday night the police were seen throwing rocks at fleeing citizens from rooftops overlooking Telegraph Avenue. This activity was reported in the British press and a British reporter provided us with an affidavit signed by 17 persons who claimed to have seen this occur. The reporter collected these witnesses on the spot while he was himself watching the police throw down rocks and a few tear gas canisters.

And finally we received assorted complaints of police-perpetrated damage to property. A policeman was seen knocking in a window at a bookstore. Others broke down the Forum's wrought-iron railing. Several persons reported damage to their residences after the police had forced their way inside. A number of others claimed the police beat their automobiles with riot batons, causing dents and breaking headlights. Several photographers had their cameras smashed. Others were forced to ruin their film. Two persons claim the police intentionally stepped on and smashed their glasses. In all, 16 respondents charged police with property damage.

Had we had more resources and more rapport we could have documented many more cases of police misbehavior during this four-day crisis. But it hardly seems necessary. Even a small portion of what we did record would be sufficient to establish that the police in Berkeley rioted.

Many will object that this report is biased because it does not provide a detailed account of violence and dangerous acts by citizens against the police. But the hostile actions of the citizens, whatever they may have been, are beside the point. I have not discussed actions taken by policemen to protect themselves or others from physical harm. I have discussed police attacks on persons who, whatever else they might have done to enrage the police, posed no threat. No one yet has died of being called a pig (although some may have died for saying it). Thus the police behavior, exemplified by beating persons and leaving them without bothering to make an arrest—when it would have been simple to throw the victim into the back of the police car and haul him off to jail—or making middle-aged couples run a gauntlet, was criminal, brutal, and immoral regardless of what other citizens may have done elsewhere.

Regardless of how many people steal, it is the job of the police to catch them, not become thieves themselves.

Why Did the Police Act?

No one really expected the police to move against the rally on Friday night. By doing so the police turned some portion of a peaceful crowd into militant antagonists and severely damaged public confidence at least within the University community. The police also initiated an escalating pattern of violence and counterviolence that has continued ever since. It is important to try to understand why the police chose this course not only for what it tells us about this particular event, but for what it tells of police ideology and tactical conceptions more generally. The Berkeley Police Department has long been regarded as a model of police excellence. Chief Beall was fond of saying that no department in the country had had so much experience in crowd and rally management and none had so successfully averted trouble in such situations. Until Friday, June 28, 1968, this was unquestionably true. Thus, if it could happen in Berkeley it could happen anywhere. Why did it happen?

Looking back, it is clear that one factor in the police decision was a growing hostility towards the Telegraph Avenue youth scene. Hippie dress, marijuana, radical politics, uninhibited public behavior, interracial couples all offended police prejudices, values, and conceptions of proper order (as will be taken up in detail in Chapter 3). Furthermore, the Avenue is usually very crowded. More people are drawn to it than can fit the sidewalks and there is no open space to relieve the congestion (a major factor in the People's Park conflict a year later). With the collapse of the San Francisco Haight–Ashbury hippie community under the pressures of the police, tourists, drugs, and rough elements, there has been some relocation to Berkeley. And as arrest and crime statistics show, petty thieves and toughs from elsewhere in the Bay Area have been attracted to Berkeley by its openness and excitement and have exploited the scene to commit burglary, theft, robbery, and rape. Even though the police know that the South Campus area residents are the victims, not the perpetrators of crime, they have reacted to the rising incidence of crime by proposing the easiest solution: remove the youth culture instead of protecting it. This tactic manifested itself in considerable police harassment—papering the area with jay-walking tickets, for example, or backing urban renewal schemes to physically obliterate the student scene. Thus, prior to the decision to disperse the crowd there had been a growing "turf" dispute between the residents of the South Campus area and the police. Quite simply the police took on the role of outsiders trying to take control of an area in which the residents had an extremely strong sense of community as well as commitment to a relatively unique culture. Through the ensuing friction the police came to be more and more alarmed about the challenge to their authority and more and more convinced that the Avenue was a growing peril to order, safety, and just plain decency.

Reflecting this attitude among the police is the fact that words such as "creep" and "freak" have been used almost routinely over the police radio to refer to South Campus people. (Recently, the new chief of police has asked his men to stop using these terms.)

This helps to account for why the police were so brutal after the action began, but it does not adequately account for the decision of police commanders to act in the first place. After all, the action did not begin accidently or in the heat of the moment. Considerable preparations had been made—scores of outside officers had been gathered, riot equipment had been issued, rooftops had been secured, and so on. What led the police to believe that they would or should need such preparations?

Interviews with police commanders elicited a murky and mysterious notion of a grave threat which they believed was going to materialize during what everyone else expected to be another ordinary Berkeley demonstration. These tales were told by the police with much indirection, innuendo, and knowing looks. It took some time to catch on to what they were talking about. But once I did it became possible for me, and for other interviewers, to test the interpretation which follows and to have it confirmed by the answers given.

In my interview with the chief of police, the first policeman to whom I talked after the episode passed, I laid out the puzzle as I saw it. What had made him think there was likely to be a great deal of trouble at the Friday night rally? What led him to prepare so large a force this time when previously only a few Berkeley officers had sufficed?

The chief responded in terms of a very mysterious "Them." He had made such preparations because of "Them." "They" were planning to move into the situation and exploit it to produce a violent outburst. "They," obviously, were people who wanted to launch the revolution. But who were they? I began by working through the various groups taking part in the rally and in the Avenue scene more generally. "They" were not Peter Camejo and his small band of Young Socialist Alliance members, according to the chief. He just snorted when I asked. He indicated that the department had dealt with Camejo and various Berkeley politicos for years, and like everyone else in Berkeley knew perfectly well that Camejo is harmless. Well then, were "They" the street people —the floating hippie population? At this point I got the distinct impression the chief thought I was hopelessly uninformed. "I am not talking about Berkeley people," he said at that point. "They have never been a real problem for us."

As our conversation continued I kept sliding back to who "They" were. It began to dawn on me that the chief believed that some outside band of anarchists, who knows from where, were secreted in Berkeley waiting for the YSA rally to run up the black flag and overturn law and order. Subsequent interviews with other police commanders and city council members turned up additional clues. FBI agents had been briefing the Berkeley police on the impending appearance in Berkeley of radicals from out of state. One council member said the FBI had informed the Berkeley police that people were planning to fly in from Chicago, New York, and New Orleans for the Friday night rally. Others said the FBI had warned of spotting vehicles in Berkeley belonging to campus radicals and various politicos from the East (in fact, such people normally come to Berkeley during the summer and many people from Berkeley ordinarily turn up in the East during the summer). For these and undoubtedly other reasons the Berkeley police became convinced that the YSA rally was the time when radicals were going to rise up. Consequently, they prepared to meet the trouble.

From then on, police preparations and expectations followed a self-fulfilling course (which will be considered in detail in Chapter

4). Arriving prepared for a major confrontation, the police found simply an ordinary and not very well attended Berkeley rally. But instead of concluding they had misjudged the situation, they concluded that they were being outmaneuvered. They maintained their original assessment, believing that because they had taken precautions the radicals had decided to postpone their outburst until another time when the police were not prepared to deal with them. Like any good tactician the chief apparently decided that if a battle were inevitable it had best be fought at a time and place of his choosing. I am convinced that the chief, suffering under the strain of expecting considerable trouble sometime soon, decided to make a demonstration of his strength and resolve the trouble while he had the manpower available. I believe he felt that such a demonstration would be chastening to the majority of the crowd, who in his judgment did not intend to engage in or support violence, and thus in the future those bent on disorder would not be able to exploit large crowds. Subsequently, when violence begot violence, the police took that as confirmation of their original suspicions—those who fought back, who threw rocks and pop bottles, who set trash cans afire, who broke windows, were "Them." There is, of course, a much simpler explanation of the citizen violence. "He who sows the wind shall reap the whirlwind." But the police reject such a possibility, preferring implausibly complicated conspiracy theories instead. As Chief Beall told the city council, "If we had not escalated our level of force as the demonstrators escalated their violence, we would have lost the city."

After the initial move against the crowd, the police continued to make preparations and tactical decisions which greatly increased the likelihood of violence, especially violence on the part of police officers. While watching police preparations Saturday night—they were loading cars with rifles and shotguns, putting large amounts of ammunition and gas into their trunks, deploying some mortars, placing snipers on rooftops—a British correspondent said to a Crisis Team observer, "They must be planning to fight a war." Understandably, policemen tend to judge the potential danger of a situation on the basis of the preparations made to deal with it, and they subsequently respond on the basis of their initial judgments. Thus preparations made "to be on the safe side" often increase the danger. Certainly bringing in large numbers of officers from outside Berkeley increased the sense of crisis among both the police and the citizens. Furthermore, these extra officers greatly overloaded the communications system and caused a breakdown in the command structure. There simply were not enough commanders to go around. In addition these outside officers were less accustomed to, and thus much more provoked by, the costumes and customs of the South Campus community. All of these factors played a part in producing the police riot.

Nevertheless, for all that Chief Beall decided, perhaps unwisely, to utilize his large and partly borrowed force to disperse the crowd and to continue massive police action, it would be extremely unfair to a responsible man to suggest that he either expected or encouraged the violent behavior of the police which followed. He did not. Nor, despite his unwillingness to publicly condemn what occurred or to take action against officers who committed brutal acts (for reasons which apply to most police commanders and will be reviewed in Chapter 6), was he unaware of what had actually happened.

This is clear in the excerpts presented below from a memorandum prepared for Chief Beall by the police sergeant he appointed to conduct an investigation of police behavior during the crisis. The results of this official police investigation, which were not made public at the time, confirm my account of a police riot. Indeed, it is an adequate summary of what I have written:

Memorandum dated August 21, 1968 [The following are excerpts]:

General Observations

Most casualties and complaints arise out of the same tactical situation ... the dispersal technique employing a (1) one-handed riot baton method by an officer in a (2) squad formation (often without a squad leader of supervisory rank) resulting in a (3) blow to the head of a recalcitrant civilian.

Both civilians and officers have reported observing a sort of "one-upmanship" phenomenon in squads without leaders of a supervisory rank. Each officer seems not to want anyone to feel that he is less zealous than anyone else in the squad, and in tense encounters, a spiralling force-level was observed.

Over 50 percent of the civilian casualties were head injuries, and all but two of these were caused by a riot baton.

None of the complainants stated that they felt that they had been singled out on the basis of their appearance, nor did they feel that they were the objects of a campaign of vengeance. The most common observation was that the police appeared to have "gone berserk" or "lost their cool" or otherwise acted in a nonrational way.

It is the opinion of the undersigned that this impression is due to a number of factors, but principally to (1) the inherent nature of a "brush-fire" operation, and (2) a lack of squad discipline due in turn to either (2a) the absence of a supervisory squad leader or (2b) the lack of civil disturbance training *in squads*. . . .

D. The observation was frequently made by civilians and officers that persons were ordered to disperse, but were hindered in so doing by our deployment, forcing them in some cases to "run the gauntlet."

E. A paradox is created when persons are ordered to disperse and then their resistance is met with a level of force which incapacitates them.[9]

Conclusion

This chapter has tried to characterize the phenomenon of the police riot. In essence, it is a process during which relatively commonplace situations are transformed into an outbreak of unrestrained police violence. But not everything which contributes to this process arises in the specific situation. Many factors merely come into play, or are activated by, the situation. Thus, to understand why the riot process occurs, we must understand many enduring characteristics of the police which shape their behavior in such situations. To ask why they do as they do, we must know who and what they are; what they normally do, what they want to do, and what they think they are doing.

2

Police Violence as Routine Behavior

What we must recognize about much excessive police behavior is this: it is not a dark sin of which police are ashamed or about which they feel guilty.

This chapter begins the task of explaining why the police riot. The central feature of police rioting is the widespread use of excessive force against civilians. Police riots are unusual events. But police use of excessive force is not. In this chapter I try to show that police brutality is routine. It is routine in two senses: it is statistically commonplace; and the police regard such excessive use of force as routine *and legitimate.* If this is true, police riots must be considered in a somewhat different light: only the scale of such riots is unusual, not the police behavior as such. The police normally use excessive violence against persons who anger, offend, or frighten them. What is abnormal about police riots is the number of policemen and civilians involved in a single incident during a relatively condensed time-span.

This argument will be developed in three main sections. First, I present criteria for judging when actions by the police legitimately can be called "excessive" or "brutal." Then I examine police norms about the use of force: how their attitudes and training support illegal uses of violence. Third, available empirical data is synthesized to make statistical projections of the extent of police brutality.

I. Identifying Police Brutality

Just what constitutes an act of police brutality? First, it is important to distinguish between rudeness, verbal abuse, and harassment on the one hand and physical mistreatment on the other. Many Americans feel they have been treated brutally by the police if they are subjected to insults or degradation.[1] Although such behavior obviously is unacceptable, the heart of the brutality issue concerns police misuse of physical violence. That will be the focus of this chapter.

It is not a simple matter to distinguish between legitimate and excessive use of violence by the police. The police are entitled to use "necessary" force in the performance of their duties. What is necessary in given situations is sometimes a matter on which fair-minded men can disagree. Indeed, police regulations governing the use of force vary from one department to another.

Nevertheless, although it may be difficult to specify precisely what degree of danger justifies police use of violence, we can establish some relatively fair rules of thumb. The following set was developed by Donald J. Black and Albert J. Reiss, Jr.,[2] for use by their field observers of police behavior:

A physical assault on a citizen was judged to be "improper" or "unnecessary" only if force was used in one or more of the following ways:

1. If a policeman physically assaulted a citizen and then failed to make an arrest; proper use involves an arrest.
2. If the citizen being arrested did not, by word or deed, resist the policeman: force should be used only if it is necessary to make the arrest.
3. If the policeman, even though there was resistance to the arrest, could easily have restrained the citizen in other ways.
4. If a large number of policemen were present and could have assisted in subduing the citizen in the station, in lockup, and in the interrogation rooms.
5. If an offender was handcuffed and made no attempt to flee or offer violent resistance.

6. If the citizen resisted arrest, but the use of force continued even after the citizen was subdued.[3]

It is important to recognize that the above set of directions, by which their observers identified instances when the police used improper or unnecessary force, seem very fair to policemen. Certainly they are entirely congruent with the following set of standards for the use of force by policemen developed by Nelson A. Watson, Project Supervisor in the Research and Development Section of the International Association of Chiefs of Police as a model for departmental guidance:

No action taken by an officer in defending himself, up to and including the death of his assailant, is brutal provided:

He is acting officially as a policeman within the boundaries of his legal powers.

He has sufficient cause, as would appear real and reasonable to a prudent man, to fear for his personal safety.

The means and the force employed by him are not such as a prudent man would consider excessive, unreasonable, or unnecessary.

There is no acceptable alternative available to him considering his obligation not to retreat from his official mission and his inherent right to protect himself.

When it comes to bringing a specific police mission to a successful conclusion—getting the job done—and there is no immediate or apparent danger calling for self-defense by the officer, his actions should be tempered by good judgment, common sense, restraint, and understanding. His actions would not fall within the definition of brutality provided:

He is acting officially as a policeman within the restrictions imposed on him by law.

He conducts himself impartially and dispassionately.

He is firm without being angrily unreasonable.

He provides reasonable opportunity for compliance with the law.

He uses force only after other means have failed.

The force employed is not more than is required to produce compliance.

The force is not of an uncivilized or cruel nature.

This proposed framework rules out any application of force after a person has submitted to arrest or complied with legal police orders.[4]

Such rules would seem adequate to identify instances of police brutality and provide a basis for enforcement. But there is another matter which clouds the issue of what is reasonable to expect of policemen.

A major problem in public discussions of police misbehavior is the defense that the police are, after all, only human—they become tired, fearful, and angry just like anyone else—and thus we ought to expect that "unfortunate" incidents will occur. Although partly obscured by his inimitable syntax, Chicago's Mayor Richard J. Daley argued that police attacks during the Democratic National Convention were perfectly understandable given the abuse they faced:

... Would you be the calm collected man you think you are? I saw many of you express emotions with less abuse than that. And to have your wife called the names that they were calling them and I'm certain for police are supposed to be human but you forget entirely the confrontation was not created by the police but by the people who charged the police.[5]

Mayor Daley reflected the views of the nation's police. As a Los Angeles police sergeant put it:

Policemen know what kind of men were on the lines in Chicago—men just like themselves, not especially patient or tolerant or self-controlled. They have lost their tempers with the public sometime in the past; they saw some Chicago coppers do the same thing. They felt justified when they did it, and they thought the Chicago police were justified, too. What else could they think?[6]

Indeed, the nation's number one cop, J. Edgar Hoover, expressed similar views about the Chicago police behavior in testimony before the National Commission on the Causes and Prevention of Violence:

The police are human. They are supposed to be both lawyers and sociologists, as I said, but they are still human. I don't think any of us in this room would be restrained if we had been hit with some of the things they have been hit with.[7]

Recently, the U. S. District Court in Chicago gave legal sanction to the view that police need not be any more impervious to abuse than any layman. Judge Joseph Sam Perry, 72, congratulated a jury which acquitted three Chicago policemen who beat reporter John O. Linstead of the *Chicago Daily News* during the convention disturbances. Linstead admitted he had shouted "Cut that out, you motherfuckers," at the officers as they beat two young people. The police did stop, and turned their clubs on Linstead, leaving him with head wounds requiring six stitches. Judge Perry told the jury: "The language that Mr. Linstead used ... was vile and degrading to the officers. He charged some of the officers with committing incest with their mothers in the lowest gutter language, which I suggest would be provoking in such a manner that any red-blooded American would flare up."[8] The U. S. Attorney pointed out after the trial that "for 200 years the law has said that no words can be provocation for an assault."[9]

To deny that filthy words or even bags of feces and urine thrown at them are sufficient provocation to justify police beatings incurs the risk of seeming anti-police—of appearing willing to complain about the abuse the police hand out, but being unmoved by the abuse they have to take. Is it fair to ask more of the police than of citizens generally? Here is the false premise: the notion that cops are only human; *we do and we must expect more of the police in their role as policemen than we demand of ordinary persons.* We expect members of *all* professions to be "more than simply human" in their professional roles. We do not expect heart surgeons to risk the life of a patient by having to stop to relieve themselves. While we recognize that most ordinary persons tend to be shy and not very fluent in a courtroom situation, we do not recognize the right of attorneys to similar failings. Most people are frightened of gunfire, but we expect soldiers to face it. In short, the essence of a professional is his capacity to perform his critical functions at a level of competence not matchable by nonprofessionals. As professionals, the police are *not* free to lose their tempers like "any red-blooded American."

Unlike Mayor Daley, J. Edgar Hoover, or the police, the majority of Americans concur with this view. As we will see in Chapter 7, 77 percent of Americans in a national survey would not approve of a "policeman striking an adult male for saying vulgar things to the policeman." Thus, the public accepts the position expressed by O. W. Wilson in his book *Police Administration:* "The officer ... must remember that there is no law against making a policeman angry and that he cannot charge a man with making him angry."[10]

But if most Americans agree with Wilson, most policemen do not.

II. Police Views on the Use of Force

Publicly, most police commanders have been unrelenting in their denials of police brutality. Privately, many of these same commanders speak of the excessive use of force by their officers as one of their worst problems. Chapter 6 discusses why, if they are so concerned, police commanders have had so little success in dealing with this problem. But a major impediment, and the one of interest here, is that most policemen reject the legal, administrative, and moral limits imposed on their use of force. They condone and even advocate using violence well beyond that permitted by these limits.

In his study of police violence, William A. Westley[11] found that 69 percent of policemen interviewed justified the use of violence on illegal grounds in response to his question: "When do you think a policeman is justified in roughing a man up?" Furthermore, this proportion is undoubtedly a low estimate because police answers were classified on the basis of the most important reason they gave, the one offered most heatedly or at greatest length. Thus, some of the policemen who were classified as offering legal grounds to justify violence also sanctioned illegal grounds, but with less emphasis. In any event, at least 7 of 10 policemen in Westley's study chose illegal grounds as their primary justification for "roughing a man up." Furthermore, the most common reason given (by 55 percent of those who gave illegal reasons) was that it is justified to rough a man up when he has insufficient respect for the police.

We are not discussing here persons who manifest their disrespect for the police by shooting at them or assaulting them. What is at issue are attitudes and deferential demeanor. Considerable evidence besides Westley's indicates that respect is a militant issue among American police and that a perceived lack of proper respect is a major, if not the major, grounds for becoming a victim of police violence.

On the basis of a systematic observational study of the police, to which we shall refer at length later in the chapter, Albert J. Reiss, Jr. reported that in nearly half of the incidents of excessive use of force recorded by his observers (who accompanied police), the precipitating factor was defiance of police authority.[12] In all of these cases, however, the form of the defiance was not physically, but only psychically, threatening to the officers, for only such cases were classified as excessive in the use of violence. As Reiss put it:

... Open defiance of police authority, however, is what the policeman defines as *his* authority, not necessarily "official" authority. Indeed in 40 percent of the cases that the police considered open defiance, the policeman never executed an arrest—a somewhat surprising fact for those who assume that policemen generally "cover" improper use of force with a "bona-fide" arrest and a charge of resisting arrest.

But it is still of interest to know what a policeman *sees* as defiance. Often he seems threatened by a simple refusal to acquiesce to his own authority. A policeman beat a handcuffed offender because, when told to sit, the offender did not sit down. One Negro woman was soundly slapped for her refusal to approach the police car and identify herself.[13]

Virtually all studies of the Los Angeles Police Department report that the "attitudes test" is a common part of L. A. police argot, and that for a policeman to say that a suspect "failed the attitudes test" justifies to other officers his use of violence, harassment, or bringing "chicken shit" citations and charges.[14] The "attitudes test" in Los Angeles indicates that in police–citizen interactions the police impose certain standards of deference and respect, and failure to meet this test merits reprisals. A number of other studies report that the police most frequently resort to excessive violence in an effort to "beat some respect" into victims.

An unidentifiable Berkeley patrolman (he was not wearing a badge) told a Crisis Team observer during the recent disturbances there, "If the parents of these cocksuckers had beat 'em when they were young, we wouldn't have to do it now." Then he added, "There's a whole bunch of these assholes who've learned some respect for law and order tonight. You better believe that, buddy."

Simply stated, the police believe that the key to law and order is considerable citizen respect for the individual policeman and that the way to instill such respect in those who lack it is with a night-stick, a blackjack, or a squirt of MACE in the face.

On the basis of his observations, Westley concluded that police use excessive violence because they feel their private grounds for doing so are equal or superior to the legal basis for the use of violence.[15] Furthermore, Westley's data indicated that to a great extent the monopoly on violence delegated to the police had been "appropriated by the police as a personal resource" to be used for personal reasons.

> ... policemen use the resource of violence to persuade their audience (the public) to respect their occupational status. In terms of the policeman's definition of the situation, the individual who lacks respect for the police, the "wise guy" who talks back, or any individual who talks or acts in a disrespectful way, deserves brutality. This idea is epitomized in admonitions given to rookies such as, "You gotta make them respect you," and "You gotta act tough."[16]

This use of violence to impose respect is hardly a police secret. A major goal of various police lobbying and trade-union organizations such as the Fraternal Order of Police and the many police protective or benevolence associations is to make such use of violence both legally and socially legitimate. Spokesmen for these police associations militantly defend the right of the police to use violence and force to obtain respect.

In an interview conducted by a representative of the Violence Commission,[17] John Harrington, national president of the Fraternal Order of Police, denied the existence of police brutality, dismissing such controversies as a "communist ploy," and then concluded:

> "When I was a young officer, I received the following instructions: if someone spits in your face, wipe it off and turn your back; if someone curses with the vilest language, pretend you don't hear. This is idiotic. The first person who spits in my face will lose his teeth; they have it coming to them."

Harrington's position accurately reflects the opinions of the 137,000 policemen in 37 states who belong to his organization. Nor do his views on these matters differ from those of officials of similar police organizations across the nation. Rather, Harrington's views reflect the strongly felt sentiments of the American cop.

Thus, the anger and contempt police direct against those who challenge their use of violence as brutal is not because the police refuse to admit they commit the acts in question, but because they reject the moral and legal standards by which this behavior is judged brutal. What we must recognize about much excessive police behavior is this: it is not a dark sin of which police are ashamed or about which they feel guilty. The average policeman believes such behavior is usually justified and even admirable. As a result, the reaction of the rank-and-file cop to growing public criticism has not been to curtail his use of violence or find ways to avoid violence, but to concentrate on not getting caught and not being subject to punishment if he is caught.

Chapter 6 will report the largely successful campaigns to defeat police review boards and police community relations bureaus staged by militant rank-and-file police organizations. These activities would make no sense if police really believed there was no brutality problem. But they make sense as a means by which policemen prevent their own standards of when to use violence from being subject to the legal standards governing police violence.

A second response by police to the growing conflict between their private standards and the legal standards of how and when force ought to be used, has been to search for substitute and less obvious means for violence. The advocates of MACE have quite unselfconsciously pushed it as delivering severe discomfort and pain without subjecting the policeman to the "social stigma" of smacking someone on the head with a nightstick. Television film of officers running up to prostrate or completely restrained victims and squirting them in the face with MACE from a distance of a few inches indicates that patrolmen have been quick to accept it as such a substitute. In Chapter 4 this and other aspects of modern police techniques and armaments will be considered at length.

But perhaps the primary response of the police has been to concentrate on not getting caught. As one police administrator who was indignantly demanding the names of officers Reiss's field workers had observed using excessive violence, said: "Any officer who is stupid enough to behave that way in the presence of outsiders deserves to be fired."[18] The moral was hardly lost on his men. Indeed, a number of researchers who have studied the police say that the major reaction by police commanders to their reports has been a sense of betrayal. They do not thank the researcher for bringing important facts before them, but rather feel that he has violated their trust by letting outsiders know what is taken for granted among policemen. Perhaps George Bernard Shaw was correct when he said that "all professions are conspiracies against the laity." Certainly in the case of the professional police it is true. In my experience it has been far easier to study convents and religious cults, which are famous for secrecy, than to study the police, who presumably are public servants.

Police use a variety of means to avoid being detected in the excessive use of violence and force. Chapter 6 will consider how police solidarity and discretion contribute to their impunity in using violence. It has also been widely recognized that police sometimes egg a suspect into resisting so they can justify roughing him up. The use of false charges of resisting arrest has also been well documented as has the practice of committing brutal acts in the privacy of police vans and station houses.

But perhaps the most alarming and revealing police practice for evading retribution for acts of brutality is carrying and using throwaways or alibis. Throwaways are knives and guns, often obtained from searches of suspicious persons, which patrolmen carry to plant on a victim of their brutality should they need convincing evidence of self-defense. Thus, they are often called alibi guns or knives. Can such practices really occur? Considerable expert testimony says yes, and that these practices are not even uncommon.

The observational study conducted by Black and Reiss under the auspices of the U. S. Crime Commission referred to earlier sustains these charges even though the observers were known as investigators of police practices and did not accompany individual patrolmen long enough to become intimates. Similarly, ex-FBI agent William W. Turner reports that after leaving the police academy young patrolmen are quickly reeducated by veteran officers who give them tips on how police work is really done. These tips may include "the advisability of carrying a hidden tossaway knife or gun that can be planted on a suspect to corroborate an excuse of self-defense."[19]

It is difficult to say how many American policemen actually carry throwaways. The mere fact that Reiss's observers found out that some of the police they studied (for only an average of two days each) in Boston, Cleveland, and Washington, D. C., carried them indicates that it can't be too uncommon or too closely guarded a secret among police. A second source of confirmation is that from time to time policemen are caught planting a throwaway on a victim. As Robert Conot reported, two Los Angeles vice squad officers, Richard L. Price and Daniel M. Samaniego, tried this tactic after shooting a 31-year-old Negro musician recently.

The Superior Court which threw out the case brought against the musician held the officers guilty of "conspiracy to obstruct justice." But perhaps the most important feature of this incident is what it revealed about the official attitude of the Los Angeles police and the District Attorney towards the use of throwaways, to say nothing of the shooting of suspects. Price was permitted to resign from the force, while Samaniego received a six-month suspension. Neither was prosecuted.[20]

The need for such practices as the throwaway could be interpreted as a tacit admission by policemen that they are triggerhappy. A policeman who believes it is sufficiently likely that he may need a throwaway so that he carries one is clearly a policeman who thinks he is likely to shoot first and ask questions later. There is no systematic way of knowing how many of the approximately 250 persons officially reported* to have been killed by the police each year were needlessly and even criminally slain.† But the following stories concerning two "mistaken" intradepartmental shootouts in New York City during 1968 suggest that the proportion may be scandalously high. Had the men slain in these incidents not been policemen, would the story have been told quite differently?

---

* It is true to form that the *Uniform Crime Reports* issued annually by the FBI provide detailed information on the numbers, circumstances, time of day, and so on, of policemen killed in the line of duty, but report nothing on citizens slain by the police. Thus, the only source on the number killed is the Bureau of Vital Statistics. They, of course, do not have the resources of the FBI to gather such information.

† A recent "study" of 32 cases of citizens slain by policemen in Philadelphia by Gerald D. Robin *starts* with the assumption that all were justifiable homicides and devotes itself to studying such things as time of day. (Justifiable Homicide by Police Officers," *Journal of Criminal Law, Criminology and Police Science,* June 1963, 225–231.) However, data he presents raise some grave questions. The rates for citizens slain annually per 10,000 police officers varies from 1.05 for Boston, 5.50 for Milwaukee, and on up to 35.41 for Kansas City, 38.15 for Miami, and 48.50 for Akron, Ohio. Similarly, the average annual rate of officers responsible for killing citizens (per 10,000 officers) varies from 1.41 in Boston to 63.43 in Akron. Can criminals be 45 times more dangerous to the police in Akron than in Boston? Such enormous differences in rates suggest either that the police in some cities are supermen, or that those in other cities are killers. Another recent study suggests the latter may be closer to the truth. Based on 30 cases over a three-month period, the conclusion was that one-third of the cases were "at best questionable and at worst murder made legal by deliberate oversight." Arthur L. Kobler, "A Report of the Characteristics of the Sample of Police Homicides in the United States," quoted in Cray, *The Big Blue Line,* pp. 157–158.

A Deadly Mistake

New York Three off-duty policemen, none apparently aware that the others were fellow members of the force, shot it out on a city expressway Tuesday night in what began as an argument over a stalled car. One of them later died, and another was wounded seriously.

Police said the shootings occurred shortly before 10:30 p.m. when a car driven by patrolman John Dalton, 41, stalled on the heavily traveled cross Bronx expressway.

Rookie patrolman Nicolo Danisi, 21, of the Bronx, who is training at the police academy, was caught in the traffic jam and got out of his car to investigate.

Police said that during an argument with Dalton, Danisi reached into his pocket for his badge identifying himself as a policeman but Dalton, fearing Danisi meant to attack him, pulled out his service revolver and shot Danisi in the head.

Detective Frederick Gibson, 28, of the Police Bureau of Special Services, arrived on the scene at this point, ordered Dalton to drop his gun, and when Dalton refused, shot him in the abdomen, police said.

"None of the officers knew each other was a police officer," said acting chief of detectives Joseph McLaughlin.

Dalton and Danisi were rushed by police cruiser to Jacobi Hospital where they were admitted in serious condition. Danisi died yesterday.[21]

Off-Duty Cop Kills Another

New York Two off-duty policemen exchanged shots in Harlem early yesterday, apparently because of mistaken identity. One was killed, the other wounded.

It was the second such incident in New York in recent weeks.

Police said Patrolman David Turman, 23, in civilian clothes, had taken a prisoner into custody and was carrying his pistol in his hand.

Taylor Johnson, 35, a Housing Authority patrolman also in plain clothes, challenged Turman and identified himself as a policeman, but Turman fired a shot wounding Johnson in the chest, police said.

Johnson fired one shot back, fatally wounding Turman, the police account stated.[22]

As will be considered in some detail in Chapter 7, the press often functions to inhibit police freedom to use force and violence in accordance with their own rather than with legal standards. This has been especially true of press coverage of police behavior in mass disturbances such as ghetto riots and confrontations with protest demonstrations. As a result the police have sought ways to avoid or prevent press coverage. Efforts first to prevent the press from covering events in Chicago and then to drive them from the scene by physical assaults have been widely publicized. Since then charges of beatings and broken cameras and other harassment have become more and more frequent from newsmen covering the police. The police generally acknowledge such actions. Throughout Task Force interviews with metropolitan policemen, hostility towards the press and expressions of the need to keep the press away from police action were among the most common themes.[23] A great many American policemen blamed the press for "sticking their noses into police business." Others were disdainful of the naiveté of the Chicago police in dealing with the press. An Oakland policeman, an official of the Police Officers' Association, criticized the Chicago police for using white riot batons—the Oakland police learned long ago not to use white batons because they show up too well in photographs. "We have black batons," he said, "and we hit low and aim to knock the guy out with one blow. Those white batons look bad."[24] None of these policemen denied that newsmen had been assaulted by Chicago policemen. Many volunteered their belief that the press had gotten what they deserved.

In the last several years the black police have begun speaking out on the subject of police violence. New organizations—Officers for Justice in San Francisco, the Afro-American Patrolmen's League in Chicago, the Society for Afro-American Policemen in New York, are prominent examples—have sprung up to articulate the resentment and resistance of black policemen to racism within their department and brutality by their fellow officers. Through these militant new organizations, the black police have charged that frequent acts of brutality are committed by the police. In several cities the black police organizations aid citizens in bringing charges of brutality against the police. *Newsweek* reported that tensions created by blacks objecting to the treatment white officers were giving citizens has led to black and white cops pulling guns on each other in Detroit and Chicago. In New York and Washington, *Newsweek* reported, black policemen have physically prevented white officers from beating up black prisoners. In San Francisco, black officers protested so vigorously about police brutality at the San Francisco State College disturbances that they were relieved from campus assignments. "All this shouldn't surprise anyone," says Patrolman Leonard Weir, president of New

York's Society for Afro–American Policemen. "The white policeman is acting like he's always acted. It's the black policeman who's acting differently."[25]

It is also important to recognize the extent to which police norms about the use of violence are inculcated and sustained—perhaps unintentionally—by their training. The police rookie is given considerable training in the use of firearms, the nightstick, and in hand-to-hand combat. He is trained to use force and to see force as vital to his competence as an officer. Unfortunately, this training is rarely accompanied by training in restraint. Few departments conduct any serious training in violence reduction or give much more than lipservice to the notion that force is only to be used very reluctantly and carefully. To the contrary, much police training is designed to encourage reflexive reliance on force. Indeed, a widely adopted police science textbook gives only a few superficial lines to restraint (and then mainly for such reasons as avoiding civil suits) but devotes considerable attention to the problem of "buck fever"—the inability of officers to fire at a suspect. The author writes:

> The killing of another human being is a serious matter, and should not be taken lightly. However, the officer's life and safety is much more important, and steps should be taken to discover these tendencies and either correct them or direct the officer into another field of employment.[26]

He then proposes to have officers trained with wax bullets to react to movies of danger situations so that they draw and fire on the basis of "a conditioned response."

Perhaps this author's discussion of how and why to use the police club provides the clearest demonstration of how the police are trained to regard violence as their right.

The Use of the Police Club

Like the revolver, the police club presents many problems to the new officer because of his prior conditioning from the movies, TV, and the comic strips.

What is the police club for, and how is it used?

Most people will agree that the police club is both a defensive and offensive weapon, but there is much confusion on its use. If a word association test were given to the average citizen, and the words "police club" were mentioned, the corresponding word that would likely come to their minds would be "head." It seems natural for the club to be used on the opponent's head, yet if there were a cardinal rule for the use of the police club, it would be "not to hit a person on top of the head with the police club." So natural is this reaction, that veteran officers who know better have, on occasion, because of the excitement of the fight, hit their opponent on the head. Why then, if this tendency is so natural, shouldn't an officer hit his opponent on the head?

1. It can kill them. If you want to kill the person, use the gun, that's what it is for. It is possible that they might have a silver plate in their head, or have some deformity of the brain.

2. You seldom knock them out. In most cases, the purpose of using the club is to subdue the opponent or knock him out. With the police club, this seldom occurs. Many times the club will break and still not knock the person unconscious. (Neither of the broken clubs in the illustration knocked the person unconscious.)

3. If the club breaks, it is psychologically defeating. It is not only embarrassing but psychologically defeating to put everything you have into a club, and then end with just a stub in your hand. (It makes it worse because instead of knocking the person out, it just makes him more angry and violent.)

4. The victim usually bleeds profusely. Even though the break in the skin is small, the bleeding is quite profuse, and this will gain the sympathy of bystanders and promote charges of police brutality. When the blood runs down over his face, it looks as though he has received a severe beating even though he may have only been hit once.

5. It brings "police brutality" charges. Nothing will promote police brutality charges faster than hitting a person over the head with the police club. Some departments have forbidden the club to be raised above the head. Leftist agitators often have photographers mix with the crowd for the sole purpose of taking a picture of a police officer with his club raised over his head. This makes very good anti-police propaganda.

6.. The person can be left insane. Because the club comes down on top of the brain, it is quite possible to leave the person insane or "simple" for the rest of his life. There have been cases where the person not only went out of his head, but seemed to gain superhuman strength, and became a serious menace to both the police and bystanders.

7. The officer opens himself for attack. When the officer raises his club, as he must to hit a person on the head, he opens himself for any number of defensive actions. It puts him in a very bad position strategically.[27]

There is nothing here to suggest that the police club should only be used as a last resort and then used as humanely as possible. The police are subsequently advised to attack the collar bone, knees, nose, Adam's apple, and the like—not because it is more humane, but because it is more effective and more covert. Police brutality is dismissed as a matter of appearances (blood running over a victim's face and the sight of raised clubs) and of leftist plots and propaganda.

The whole tone of the material conveys the message that personal safety of the police comes first and that violence is subject only to tactical, not moral or legal, restrictions. This is the implicit message of most police training. And the message gets across.

In the next section, data will be presented to assess the extent to which the police actually engage in acts of brutality. But whatever they do it seems certain what they think: that violence is essential to the job of policing and that rules limiting the use of violence were made to be broken.

III. The Incidence of Police Brutality

For decades now commissions appointed by state and federal governments to investigate the police have almost routinely condemned the extent of brutality by policemen. Indeed, in 1930, the National Commission on Law Observance and Enforcement summarized its findings in a book entitled *Our Lawless Police*.[28] It charged that police practices in America were "so appalling and sadistic as to pose no intellectual issue for civilized men."[29] Again in 1935, following the Harlem riots, a commission appointed by the mayor reported widespread police brutality against blacks, including mutilation and murder.[30] The President's Commission on Civil Rights condemned widespread police brutality in its 1947 report.[31] The U. S. Civil Rights Commission in 1961 found that "police brutality is still a serious problem throughout the United States."[32] In 1967 the Crime Commission reported excessive brutality was still "a significant problem."[33] In 1968 the Kerner Commission devoted considerable effort to a series of proposals to curtail police brutality.[34] And so it has gone.

How widespread is police brutality? Various commissions have hedged on this problem by calling the extent serious, and adding that even a little would be serious. Nevertheless, it is obvious that "a little" would be a much less serious problem than "a lot." However, defining "a lot" or "a little" is a fairly subjective judgment. As a provisional standard, I would say that if there were one incident of police brutality in a metropolitan precinct or district every two months, this might be "a little." Several times a week would be "a lot." Several times a day, outrageous.

But how can we determine such frequencies? One important way is to ask representative samples of citizens about their personal experiences with the police. If a reasonable basis can be established to insure that people are giving mainly truthful answers, then we can project the findings of such surveys into the sampled population to arrive at an estimate of how widespread police violence is. Several such surveys have been done recently.

1. *Los Angeles*

Contrary to the flat denials of the late Los Angeles Chief of Police William H. Parker when asked about brutality—"There is no brutality!"[35]—a recent study of a representative sample of black residents of South Central Los Angeles indicates otherwise. Its major findings are shown in Table 1.

Respondents were asked about six major varieties of police misbehavior from the use of insulting language to the use of unnecessary force in arrest and beating up prisoners in custody. For each, respondents were asked whether they thought such things happened to people in their area, had it happened to someone they knew, had they seen it happen, and had it happened to them personally. Responses to the latter are enclosed in the box in Table 1. Twenty-three percent said they had suffered from lack of respect and the use of insulting language by the police. Twenty percent said they had been rousted and frisked and 19 percent had been stopped and their cars searched. The variation between answers to these questions and the others lends considerable credibility to the answers given. Reports on Los Angeles police practices indicate considerable field interrogation, which shows up in these data as roust and frisk and as car searches. The searching of homes is much less frequently done by the Los Angeles police, and these data vary in precisely the same way as what is known about actual

Table 1 Percent Distribution of Negro Responses to 24 Questions about Police Brutality (N = 586)

	Lack of respect, insulting language	Roust and frisk	Stop and search cars	Search homes	Unnecessary force in arrest	Beat up in custody
Do you think it happens to people in this area?						
Yes	71.3%	71.9%	68.5%	42.5%	65.5%	65.2%
No	11.8	12.2	14.1	24.4	14.0	11.1
Don't know	15.5	15.2	16.0	31.7	19.5	22.3
No answer	1.4	.7	1.4	1.4	1.0	1.4
Has it happened to you?						
Yes	23.0	20.9	19.3	5.1	7.8	3.9
No	58.2	58.8	58.8	65.4	68.5	69.8
Don't know	.2	0.0	0.0	.2	0.0	0.0
No answer	18.6	21.2	21.8	29.4	23.7	26.3
Have you seen it happen?						
Yes	38.6	41.1	39.9	15.2	36.9	20.8
No	40.2	38.9	38.6	54.8	41.6	54.4
Don't know	0.0	0.0	.2	.2	0.0	0.0
No answer	21.2	20.0	21.3	29.8	21.5	24.8
Has it happened to someone you know?						
Yes	41.5	37.9	37.4	20.8	32.1	34.4
No	38.4	41.6	39.6	49.2	42.5	40.0
Don't know	.2	.5	.2	.2	0.0	.2
No answer	20.9	20.0	22.8	29.8	25.4	25.4

Source: Walter J. Raine, "Los Angeles Riot Study: The Perception of Police Brutality in South Central Los Angeles" (Los Angeles: Institute of Government and Public Affairs, University of California, 1967), mimeographed.

police behavior. Most who claim to have been frisked or to have had their cars stopped and searched do not claim to have had their homes searched—thus the data do not indicate that persons were willing to accuse the police of just anything.

The most important figures, of course, are in the last two columns of the table. When asked about the use of unnecessary force in arrest, 36.9 percent said they had seen it happen, 32 percent said it had happened to someone they knew, and 7.8 percent said it had happened to them. Similarly, to the question, "Do police beat up people in custody" 20.8 percent claimed to have seen it, 34.4 percent said it had happened to someone they knew, and 3.9 percent said it had happened to them.

These percentages on personal experience of abuse by the police are very large. The population of the area from which the sample was drawn was about 300,000 at the time of the study. When the percentages reported in Table 1 are translated into numbers of people, they gain considerable impact. Thus, 3.9 percent—the number who report they have been beaten up by the police while in custody—means 11,700 black residents of only one section of Los Angeles claim to have been beaten. This total is not unreasonable, although it may appear so at first glance. As Raine pointed out in his report:

This would seem inordinately large if it happened to all 11,700 at one time. However, the question is asked without any time restriction; presumably it could have happened at any time in the past.

Since the median length of time in Los Angeles of this population, as estimated from our sample, is 16.8 years and there are 365 days in a year, we might estimate that on 6,100 days the possibility occurred for members of this population to be arrested, booked, and beaten or roughly handled. This gives an average of slightly less than two per day (assuming that different persons are beaten each time).[36]

Two beatings a day in the Watts area of Los Angeles! Projecting the 7.8 percent who claim to have been the victims of unnecessary force while being arrested into the population produces 23,400 victims. This yields an average of about four victims a day, or a combined *total of six cases of police brutality daily in the South Central part of Los Angeles.* Clearly there are sufficient numbers of policemen in the area to make these averages entirely plausible. If there were 700 officers assigned to the area, each would merely have to commit a brutal act about once every four months to produce the average of six victims a day, or 2,190 victims per year.

But are these citizen reports credible? I have already suggested that they are because of the systematic variations in what is reported. But there are other reasons to put some trust in them. For one thing, these projections closely agree with what several expert white informants, including an attorney and a police officer, estimated the incidence of police misbehavior in this area to be.[37] These estimates were made completely independently and without knowledge of the survey data. Another reason to put confidence in these statistics is that they are in close agreement with those obtained in a much larger study (reported below). Such consistency argues for accuracy.

This incidence of police misconduct is also reasonably congruent with the arguments made against charges of widespread brutality by the police themselves. In an earlier section I discussed the police argument that they are only human. In private conversations with policemen this line of reasoning has often been used to deny the obviously false image of the police as a bunch of bloodthirsty brutes. The following paraphrase characterizes many similar conversations: "Hell, I'm not a nut. Nobody I know of on the force likes to beat up people. But everybody loses his temper once in awhile, especially if you have to do the things cops have to do. Cops are only human too. But we're not hot-heads either. I rarely fly off the handle. Hell, it's been months since I got really mad."

This could well be true. In my experience most policemen don't usually go around looking for trouble. But what they fail to recognize is that if each policeman only loses his temper once or twice a year and roughs someone up, a very large number of citizens will get roughed up during the year. Thus their violence may seem occasional to individual policemen, when in fact for the force as a whole it is routine.

But we need not rely wholly on such tests of the plausibility of these data. For the sake of argument let us assume that half of these respondents were either lying or were in error—what they defined as unnecessary force would not be so judged by impartial and reasonable observers. Assuming this to be the case, we still have to confront an average of 1 beating up in custody and 2 unnecessarily rough arrests per day in this community. By the standards I adopted at the beginning of this section, this is still much more than what I would call "a lot"—it seems to me to be an outrageous incidence of police brutality. Whether or not others share my definitions, I think all reasonable persons would agree that this incidence of police misbehavior is unacceptable.

2. *Fifteen American Cities*

If the only survey study available on citizen experience with the police were based on black people in Watts, there would be some temptation to dismiss the findings we have just considered as peculiar to that particular community and its historic frictions. However, the main questions on police behavior contained in the Watts study were incorporated in a large and very carefully conducted study of persons 16-years-old and over in 15 major, non-Southern, American cities.[38] The study was directed by Angus Campbell and Howard Schuman and the sampling and data collection were conducted by the Survey Research Center of the University of Michigan.[39] The study was sponsored by the Kerner Commission.[40]

The relevant results, based on 5,759 interviews conducted during January 1968, are shown in Table 2. The findings for blacks are quite congruent with those from the Watts study. Thus, while 23 percent of the black respondents in Watts said they had been treated without respect and subjected to insulting language by the police, 15 percent of the black respondents in these 15 major cities reported similar experiences with the police. Similarly, 20 percent of the black people in Watts said they had been rousted or frisked and 13 percent of black people in the 15 cities study reported being frisked. Finally, while 7.8 percent in Watts reported being mistreated during arrest and 3.9 percent said they had been beaten up while in custody, 4 percent of the black people in these 15 cities said they had personally been unnecessarily roughed up by the police.

Table 2 also permits an examination of the experience of white citizens with the police. All comparisons show whites are less likely than blacks to think the police misbehave, to know people who have been mistreated, or to have been personally mistreated by the police. Nevertheless, white citizens *do* report police misbehavior. Seven percent say they have been subjected to insulting language by the police; 4 percent say they have been frisked without good reason; and 1 percent say they have been personally roughed up unnecessarily by the police. Among both blacks and whites there are substantial sex differences; women are much less likely than are men to report being mistreated by the police—a fact which lends credibility to the data, for obviously the police are much less likely to rough up women, and thus the data conform to reality on this point. Data presented by Campbell and Schuman in their report also show substantial age differences among both whites and

Table 2 Citizen Reports of Police Misbehavior in 15 Major American Cities

"Some people say the police don't show respect for people and use insulting language. Do you think this happens to people in this neighborhood? Has it ever happened to you?" (*In percent*)

	Negro			White		
	Men	Women	Total	Men	Women	Total
Yes	20	10	15	9	5	7
No	40	49	45	15	19	17
Don't know	2	0	1	1	1	1
Don't think it happens in their neighborhood	38	41	39	75	75	75
	100	100	100	100	100	100

"Some people say the police rough up people unnecessarily when they are arresting them or afterwards. Do you think this happens to people in this neighborhood? Has it ever happened to you?" (*In percent*)

	Negro			White		
	Men	Women	Total	Men	Women	Total
Yes	7	1	4	2	0	1
No	50	56	53	18	23	20
Don't know	1	2	2	0	1	1
Don't think it happens in their neighborhood	42	41	41	80	76	78
	100	100	100	100	100	100

"Some people say the police frisk or search people without good reason. Do you think this happens to people in this neighborhood? Has it ever happened to you?" (*In percent*)

	Negro			White		
	Men	Women	Total	Men	Women	Total
Yes	22	3	13	6	1	4
No	36	55	45	16	24	20
Don't know	1	2	1	0	0	0
Don't think it happens in their neighborhood	41	40	41	78	75	76
	100	100	100	100	100	100

Source for all of the above tables: Angus Campbell and Howard Schuman, "Racial Attitudes in Fifteen American Cities," in *Supplemental Studies for the National Advisory Commission on Civil Disorders* (Washington, D. C.: U. S. Government Printing Office, 1968), pp. 42–43.

blacks, with the young much more likely than the old to report police misconduct.[41] Again this closely conforms "with police records of the age characteristics of arrestees of both races."[42] The police have much more contact with the young. This is also confirmed by a recent study of the police which found that the police felt younger people to be a much more serious problem to them than older people.[43] These confirmations of the data by outside criteria increase confidence in their validity.

If we take these findings seriously, what do they indicate? First of all it seems clear that blacks, males, and younger people are much more likely to experience police misbehavior than are others. But more generally, it indicates police misconduct and brutality occur on a rather large scale. Four percent of the black residents of these 15 major cities translates into tens of thousands of citizens who have been physically mistreated by the police.

If these percentages apply to the country at large (and the percentages might be much higher elsewhere since these cities have highly professional police forces, and the percentages would almost surely be much higher in the South) then we must accept the estimate that several million Americans have been physically mistreated by the police—perhaps a million black people alone.

Furthermore, the survey did not ask *how many times* an individual had been roughed up by the police; only whether or not it had *ever* happened. But it is obvious that some people have much more contact with the police than do others and it is equally obvious that some proportion of those who claimed they had been roughed up had experienced this more than once. Thus, the number of persons who say they have been roughed up considerably *underestimates the number of incidents* in which the police have committed acts of brutality.

If we assume two million Americans have been roughed up by the police and if we assume that half have had two such experiences (surely an underestimate considering that many have had four or five such incidents and the fact that people in jail or prison or on the bum—those most likely to have had such experiences—were not included in the sample),* this would produce an estimate of three million instances of police roughing up a citizen unnecessarily. Since there were about 400,000 law enforcement officers in America at the time of the survey, this works out to $7\frac{1}{2}$ incidents of roughing up a citizen for each of them.

These projections are admittedly crude. But at the very least they make it quite clear that we are not discussing a rare event. If we can place even partial confidence in the results of these surveys, we must recognize that physical abuse of citizens by the police is endemic in American society.

In my judgment these studies were carefully and well executed and should be accepted as valid. Nevertheless, we need not rest the case that the police frequently do commit needless acts of violence on survey data. We may further consider the results of a systematic observation of the police in action. Here we need not worry about the possibility of false charges by irate or prejudiced citizens.

---

* The sample design did not include inmate populations, and there has long been a problem in locating certain "marginal" members of the population for survey studies or for census enumeration. Indeed, the U. S. Census Bureau now believes that failure to find male adult blacks for inclusion in the census may be so severe as to have led them to seriously underestimate the size of the black population in America. If the error is of the order of millions of persons, as some experts believe, then such matters as differential black/white crime rates may be seriously distorted—the rate for blacks being greatly inflated by being computed on much too small a base. Since this same problem applies to survey studies, and since those blacks most likely to have been beaten by the police—young males—are probably seriously underrepresented in the data, one must conclude that the proportions of persons estimated to have been beaten by the police is seriously underestimated in these data.

3. Observations of Police Violence

In the first section of this chapter the set of criteria by which a team of 36 observers classified physical assaults on citizens by police as "improper" or "unnecessary" were outlined. The study was conducted by Donald J. Black and Albert J. Reiss, Jr., for the President's Commission on Law Enforcement and Administration of Justice (The Crime Commission) during 1966.[44] With departmental permission, the observers rode with a number of policemen randomly chosen from selected precincts in three major cities: Boston, Chicago, and Washington, D. C. (all three of which were included in the 15 Cities Study, as well).

The observers spent an average of about two working-shifts riding with each officer selected for observation. They used an elaborately constructed "incident booklet" to record the details of all police–citizen encounters which occurred.

It might seem unlikely that the police would use unnecessary force while in the presence of an observer. In fact, 54 of them did so during the brief period when they were under observation. As Reiss put it, "people cannot change their behavior in the presence of others as easily as many think." Furthermore, when a policeman "becomes involved in a dispute with a citizen he easily forgets that an observer is present. Partly because he does not know what else to do in such situations, the policeman behaves 'normally.' "[45] Still, as Reiss pointed out, one ought to assume that some modification of behavior is likely in such a situation and thus that his data "represent a minimal picture of actual misbehavior."[46]

Before proceeding to an evaluation of the statistical rates provided by the Black and Reiss data, it seems important to give the reader some sense of the nature of the 37 incidents of police brutality—with 44 victims—witnessed and recorded by the observers. These were not incidents of minor misconduct or questionable judgment. Indeed, judging from the incidents they have reported as occasions when excessive force was used, it seems likely that Black and Reiss have leaned over backwards to restrict their findings to only blatant cases, which is a second reason to regard their findings as a low estimate. Consider the following:

White officers responded to a man with a gun . . . and heard three shots fired. Then the white man with the gun got a drop on the officer

—somehow they got the gun away and handcuffed him ... When they got him to the station garage, they kicked him all over, but the principal one was the officer who had been in danger when the man had the drop on him. He beat him as the others held him up. I got to the scene and the lockup man whistled for them to stop but they didn't. The Lieutenant arrived with everyone else and said there's going to be a beef on this one so cover it up and go find the empty shells. Someone call an ambulance (he needed it badly). Then the Lieutenant took complete control. They got the shells, got a complainant who said the three shots were an attempt to kill the officer, and he would sign a complaint, say he called an ambulance, etc. They wrote a cover for the incident. The officer who beat the man most was shaken by then but the others gave him support, telling him how brave he was and how wise he had been not to kill the guy at the scene, etc. They then set about to pull all the stories in order and I was carefully notified of it in detail so I would have it straight. I had enough rapport with these officers that they talked about it even after. The man was in pretty bad shape when he got to the hospital.[47]

... as the two [policemen] were moving across the precinct shortly after 10 p.m., a white man and a woman in their 50s flagged them down. Since they were obviously "substantial" middle-class citizens of the district, the policeman listened to their complaints that a Negro man was causing trouble inside the public transport station from which they had just emerged. The woman said that he had sworn at her. The older policeman remarked, "What's a nigger doing up here? He should be down on Franklin Road!"

With that, they ran into the station and grabbed the Negro man who was inside. Without questioning him, they shoved him into a phone booth and began beating him with their fists and a flashlight. They also hit him in the groin. Then they dragged him out and kept him on his knees. He pleaded that he had just been released from a mental hospital that day and, begging not to be hit again, asked them to let him return to the hospital. One policeman said: "Don't you like us, nigger? I like to beat niggers and rip out their eyes." They took him outside to their patrol car. Then they decided to put him on a bus, telling him that he was returning to the hospital; they deliberately put him on a bus going in the opposite direction. Just before the Negro boarded the bus, he said, "You police just like to shoot and beat people." The first policeman replied, "Get moving, nigger, or I'll shoot you." The man was crying and bleeding as he was put on the bus. Leaving the scene, the younger policeman commented, "He won't be back."[48]

The watch began rather routinely as the policemen cruised the district. Their first radio dispatch came at about 5:30 p.m. They were told to investigate two drunks in a cemetery. On arriving they found two white men "sleeping one off." Without questioning the men, the older policeman began to search one of them, ripping his shirt and hitting him in the groin with a nightstick. The younger policeman, as he searched the second, ripped away the seat of his trousers, exposing his buttocks. The policeman then prodded the men toward the cemetery fence and forced them to climb it, laughing at the plight of the drunk with the exposed buttocks. As the drunks went over the fence, one policeman shouted, "I ought to run you fuckers in!" The other remarked to the observer, "Those assholes won't be back; a bunch of shitty winos."[49]

Within a large city's high-crime rate precinct, occupied mostly by Negroes, the police responded to an "officer in trouble" call. It is difficult to imagine a call that brings a more immediate response, so a large number of police cars immediately converged at an intersection of a busy public street where a bus had been stopped. Near the bus, a white policeman was holding two young Negroes at gun point. The policeman reported that he had responded to a summons from the white bus driver complaining that the boys had refused to pay their fares and had used obscene language. The policeman also reported that the boys swore at him, and one swung at him while the other drew a screwdriver and started toward him. At that point, he said, he drew his pistol.

The policemen placed one of the offenders in handcuffs and began to transport both of them to the station. While driving to the station, the driver of one car noted that the other policeman, transporting the other boy, was struggling with him. The first policeman stopped and entered the other patrol car. The observer reported that he kept hitting the boy who was handcuffed until the boy appeared completely subdued. The boy kept saying, "You don't have any right to beat me. I don't care if you kill me."

After the policemen got the offenders to the station, although the boys no longer resisted them, the police began to beat them while they were handcuffed in an interrogation room. One of the boys hollered: "You can't beat me like this! I'm only a kid, and my hands are tied." Later one of the policeman commented to the observer: "On the street you can't beat them. But when you get to the station, you can instill some respect in them."[50]

There is no point in pursuing such stories further. The illegal and brutal behavior of the police in each incident is patent. And remember, all of this occurred in the presence of a trained observer whose true identity was known to the policemen in question and who was taking notes throughout!

Based on these careful and systematic observations of the police, Reiss has published statistical estimates of the extent of police brutality.[51] His gross figures were misused by the Kerner Commission as indicating that misbehavior occurred very rarely, in only "about three-tenths of 1 percent" of all officer–citizen encounters.[52]

But Reiss subsequently pointed out the fallacy in such gross rates:

> A rate depends, however, upon selecting a population that is logically the target of force. What we have just given is a rate for all citizens involved in encounters with the police. But many of these citizens are not logical targets of force. Many, for example, simply call the police to complain about crimes against themselves or their property. And others are merely witnesses to crimes.
>
> The more logical target population consists of citizens whom the police allege to be offenders—a population of suspects. In our study, there were 643 white suspects, 27 of whom experienced undue use of force. This yields an abuse rate of 41.9 per 1000 white suspects. The comparable rate for 751 Negro suspects, of whom 17 experienced undue use of force is 22.6 per 1000. If one accepts these rates as reasonably reliable estimates of the undue force against suspects, then there should be little doubt that in major metropolitan areas the sort of behavior commonly called "police brutality" is far from rare.[53]

The overall rate for the Black and Reiss data is 31.5 per 1000 suspects; 3.2 percent of the suspects who had contact with the police were unnecessarily beaten!

Of the 37 cases of brutality observed, with 44 victims, in 15 cases no one was arrested. In 13 cases "force was exercised in the station when at least four other policemen were present." Reiss reported that half of the victims suffered injuries no worse than being "physically bruised." Three of the 44 victims were hospitalized with their injuries.[54]

Finally, Reiss reported that in only one of the 37 incidents was a complaint filed with the police department about officer misbehavior.[55] If this is any reasonable indication of the proportion of incidents which will be reported through a citizen's complaint, the thousands of complaints filed each year with American police departments are indeed but the tiniest tip of the iceberg. During 1967, Los Angeles reported receiving 400 citizen complaints about unnecessary use of force by the police.[56] At 37 to 1 that would suggest 14,800 incidents, which is suspiciously close to the following projection based on the Watts data: If the population of the Watts area—300,000 people—yields 6 cases of police brutality a day, then one would project 45 cases a day in the whole city if the same rate held. This would add up to 16,420 cases a year. Such projections are of course entirely speculative; there is no way of really knowing whether the 37 to 1 complaint ratio is a sound estimate. But the fact that various procedures lead to rather similar estimates is highly suggestive.

The Black and Reiss data also established some rates based on their observation of police. In the 37 incidents over the seven-week observation period, 54 policemen were observed using too much force.[57] Thus, of all the officers observed, approximately 1 of every 10 was seen engaging in brutality. But this does not mean that only 1 of 10 officers ever commits such acts. Officers were observed only for an average of about two working shifts. Thus the data show that in a two-day period, one of ten policemen in this study used unnecessary force or violence. Obviously this rate does not hold for the nation; if it did there would be several million incidents of police brutality each year. Nevertheless, these data offer persuasive eye-witness evidence that police brutality is a relatively common occurrence.

Conclusion

This chapter has been devoted to demonstrating that unnecessary use of force by the police is a relatively routine occurrence. The case seems conclusive. The police advocate illegal use of force. Official commissions have frequently reported that the police do engage in brutality. Survey studies show that significant numbers of Americans claim they have been the victims of police brutality. And, finally, systematic observations of the police in action indicate that such behavior is relatively common.

The reason for examining police brutality in a book that is devoted to studying police riots is to show how the unnecessary use of physical force is a routine part of police behavior. This being the case, it is easy to understand why the police are likely to resort to unjustified force in situations when they are admittedly under extra stress: during confrontations with mass demonstrations and protests or during riots. Hitting people is the customary police tactic for dealing with trouble. A police riot, then, is unusual primarily as a situation. Ordinarily the police do not gather in large numbers nor do they normally deal with "suspects" *en masse*. This is what makes it a riot—*that the police are doing collectively in a short period of time and in a small area what they would ordinarily be doing in pairs or very small groups across a very large area over a longer time.*

3

The Sources and Targets of Police Anger

The police are not only different from most of the rest of us in terms of their conceptions about the world, but like nuns and hippies they have a distinctive garb which sets them apart.

Sometimes the police riot. But they don't riot against just any group of citizens who happen to be handy. Fraternal lodge or veterans' parades are unlikely targets. Peace marches are not. Furthermore, while we have seen that police brutality is relatively routine behavior, not everyone is equally likely to become a victim of it.

The purpose of this chapter is to identify and explain the most salient targets of police anger and thus of police violence. Who do the police want to get, and why?

A useful starting point is L. L. Bernard's summary of the kinds of conflict situations which often give rise to mob actions and riots:

Mobs develop with special ease under social conditions in which conflicting interests, ideals and controls are prevalent. The presence in close proximity of two or more races with fairly distinct customs, traditions and standards; of distinct social classes, such as capitalist and labor, rich and poor; of radically distinct religious alignments, each sect or religion holding firmly to its own tenets; of two rival gangs, each intent upon dominating the situation; or of two or more political parties, each with its patronage and graft to protect and candidates to elect, is especially conducive to the appearance of the mob spirit and mob action. Such conditions easily evoke race, class, religious, or partisan animosities and hatreds, which become chronic prejudices.[1]

What bearing do remarks on ethnic and religious conflicts, prejudice, class hatreds, and the like have on explaining why the police riot? It is not merely that police violence is often directed at minority groups, although that provides an important clue. Nor is it that the police simply represent the official, majority culture and thus come into conflict with such minority groups. Rather, it is fruitful to think of the police as themselves constituting a fairly distinct subculture, much akin to ethnic and religious minorities.

In this chapter I shall try to outline the ways in which the American police constitute a minority subculture and how this is both a cause and a consequence of the estrangement the police feel from the rest of society. This analysis will then be taken one step further to show that the police subculture especially conflicts with other subcultures which have interests, norms, and ideals different from those of the police and that this conflict is exacerbated by the prejudice and fear that typically accompany such conflict. Specifically, I shall show that the police subculture is especially in conflict with that of blacks and other racial minorities as well as with the subculture of political and social dissenters, both student and adult—conflicts fraught with reciprocal anger, hatred, violence, and fear.

A third source and focus of police anger inheres in the present predicament of the police. Increasingly they are being asked to perform tasks which are beyond their means. This further encourages the police to feel embattled, increases their isolation and their hatred and fear of minorities and dissenters—whom they blame for their predicament—and leads them to strike out at those "who are to blame."

I. The Police as a Minority Subculture

To say that a group constitutes a subculture is to be able to point to certain important and distinctive features that set it apart from other subcultures or from society at large. Typically, this term is applied to distinctive ethnic and religious groups. We can easily recognize that the Amish, Orthodox Jews, Mexican–Americans and other similar groups are subcultures—little islands of identity with unique customs, histories, outlooks, and ideals, afloat in the larger American culture. The concept often is applied also to various groups organized around the violation of laws or norms—for example, homosexuals, prostitutes, addicts, and the like. It is recognized how these special "worlds" are maintained through group solidarity, the sense of loyalty and belonging inspired in individual members, and through limited and circumscribed interaction with "outsiders."

Since the police exist to enforce the rules of the society at large, it may seem odd to conceive of them as making up a minority subculture. Thus, what follows will try to provide a basis for Westley's characterization of the police as:

> ... a social group which tends to be in conflict with and isolated from the community; and in which the norms are independent of the community.[2]

In terms of their values and view of the world, the police differ considerably from the majority of ordinary citizens. These differences are especially great vis-à-vis certain other minority subcultures. Furthermore, the social solidarity of policemen is pronounced and their insulation and isolation from "outsiders" is acute.

In his study of the police, Skolnick noted that "the police, as a result of combined features of their social situation, tend to develop ways of looking at the world distinctive to themselves."[3] One of the primary ways in which the police outlook is unusual is its conception of order.

It is impossible to state clearly what is meant by public order, which the police are asked to maintain. Partly this is because what might constitute disorder depends so much on circumstances. Wilson summarizes the inherent ambiguity of the concept of order as follows:

> ... public order is nowhere defined and can never be defined unambiguously because what constitutes order is a matter of opinion and convention, not a state of nature.... An additional difficulty, a corollary of the first, is the impossibility of specifying, except in the

extreme case, what degree of disorder is intolerable and who is to be held culpable for that degree.[4]

Given this uncertainty, reasonable men can and do disagree over how much disorder is safe or permissible. Furthermore, different constituencies and different social groups hold varying conceptions of what constitutes public order. In a military setting, for example, conceptions of order are extraordinarily restrictive. As Skolnick remarked, even tiny variations in detail of dress will be regarded as disorderly since the military conception of order "abhors individual differences."[5] In contrast, participants in other social settings (the university, for example) uphold permissive conceptions of order. Here even quite exaggerated differences in dress and deportment are felt to be irrelevant to stability. The point is that both individual and subcultural conceptions of disorder vary greatly in our society. At one extreme are what have been called low-risk conceptions. From this point of view the stability of public order is seen as fragile and thus that the maintenance of a free society requires unqualified respect for law and authority. The limits of variability and protest must be held to a narrow range, lest anarchy ensue. Threats to these standards of order must be put down quickly and firmly. High-risk conceptions of order, on the other hand, regard the social bases of order as considerably more durable, capable of sustaining considerable challenge and disarray. From the point of view of high-risk conceptions, it seems feasible and desirable to run greater chances of disorder in the interests of individual liberty, diversity, and keeping the legal system responsive to changing demands. The Army, the Old Order Amish, Trappist Monks, prisons and the like reflect extremely low-risk conceptions of order. Universities, bohemian districts, and fraternal order conventions reflect high-risk conceptions.

The conception of order held by police is extremely low-risk. They are trained to regard anything that is slightly out of the ordinary or irregular as suspicious—a potential threat to order. Skolnick suggests that predictability is the primary desideratum to the police in evaluating potential disorder.[6] Colin MacInnes stresses this characteristic of the English "copper":

The true copper's dominant characteristic, if the truth be known, is neither those daring nor vicious qualities that are sometimes attributed to him by friend or enemy, but an ingrained conservatism, and almost desperate love of the conventional. It is untidiness, disorder, the unusual, that a copper disapproves of most of all: far more, even than of crime which is merely a professional matter. Hence his profound dislike of people loitering in streets, dressing extravagantly, speaking with exotic accents, being strange, weak, eccentric, or simply any rare minority—of their doing, in fact, anything that cannot be safely predicted.[7]

The reasons the police are dedicated to a low-risk conception of order are many. One is obviously the fact that those charged with maintaining order will prefer to minimize the ambiguities of judging what is potentially disruptive by accepting the most restrictive definition. In addition, police feelings of danger will encourage them to take the fewest possible risks. The fact that some variety of behavior or state of affairs could *conceivably* lead to danger or disorder is typically regarded by police as sufficient basis for suppression. Furthermore, as Skolnick has pointed out, the paramilitary character of police organization influences their conception of order.

To the degree that police are organized on a military model, there is also likely to be generated a martial conception of order. Internal regulations based on martial principles suggest external cognitions based on similar principles. The presence of an explicit hierarchy, with an associated chain of command and a strong sense of obedience, is therefore likely to induce an attachment to social uniformity and routine and a somewhat rigid conception of order.[8]

The extremely low-risk conception of order held by the police is not shared by major sectors of the public and is especially discordant with the outlook of many American subcultures. This is not only an endemic source of conflict with the police, but is both a symptom and a source of a special police subculture. From the point of view of this special police world, society seems a disorderly, unpredictable and untidy place, fraught with dangers and potential breakdown. There are a number of other critical ways in which the police world-view is distinctive.

The police are not only different from most of the rest of us in terms of their conceptions about the world, but like nuns and hippies they have a distinctive garb which sets them apart. Furthermore, like nuns, the police are virtually cloistered from the world except when performing their occupational duties (during which time they admittedly mainly view an odd portion of life). There seem to be a number of reasons for this social isolation of the police. Skolnick provides an important insight:

Typically, the policeman is required to enforce laws representing puritanical morality, such as those prohibiting drunkenness, and also laws regulating the flow of public activity, such as traffic laws. In these situations the policeman directs the citizenry, whose typical response denies recognition of his authority and stresses his obligation to respond to danger. The kind of man who responds well to danger, however, does not normally subscribe to codes of puritanical morality. As a result, the policeman is unusually liable to the charge of hypocrisy. That the whole civilian world is an audience for the policeman further promotes police isolation and, in consequence, solidarity.[9]

Put another way, because they must enforce laws that impinge on common social and leisure activities of the community, the police—who also engage in many of these same activities[10]—attempt to protect themselves by segregating their social lives out of sight of ordinary citizens. Nearly every city of any size in America has its police club, maintained by the local police protective or fraternal organization. These are private clubs whose membership is restricted to policemen and certain chosen citizens, usually persons whose activities connect them with the police (bail bondsmen, assistant DAs, and assorted police buffs). These clubs hold a number of parties and banquets throughout the year and typically maintain a bar and game room which is open nightly. Here, out of sight of the public, policemen do their drinking, dancing, gambling, loud talking, philandering, and fighting, much like other highly masculinized occupational groups. Skolnick reported that "Much alcohol is usually consumed at police banquets with all the melancholy and boisterousness accompanying such occasions."[11] Or as Horace Cayton reports from his police days:

Deputy sheriffs and policemen don't know much about organized recreation; all they usually do when celebrating is get drunk and pound each other on the back, exchanging loud insults . . .[12]

The police clubs bear some resemblance to the rooms set aside for "teachers only" in the public schools, and for much the same reason. They provide a secure place where persons subject to strict norms in their public performances can "come off it"; where they can be "off-stage."[13]

In addition to clubs run by their protective or fraternal organizations, police tend to segregate their other organizational affiliations within a special police-dominated world. Thus, as Jacobs reports of the Los Angeles police, there are special police posts of veterans and military groups, "a police Masonic lodge, police religious groups, shooting clubs, and the FIPO, a right-wing political group of the Fire and Police Departments."[14]

Skolnick regards police segregation of their social activities as a defense against the discrepancy between the moral regulations the police enforce and their own norms and behavior in these same areas.[15] In any event an important consequence of this segregation is that it further sets the police apart into a world of their own, reduces their off-duty contact with nonpolicemen, and thus facilitates the extent to which the special features of their occupation produce a distinctive outlook and subculture.

But it is not only their party and club life that the police segregate from the nonpolice world (and from black policemen as well, for racial exclusion is widespread). The simple fact is that policemen spend an unusual proportion of their off-duty time with other policemen.[16] Indeed, the wives of policemen probably spend vastly more time with the wives of other policemen than is typical of the wives of most occupational groups. Among policemen, one commonly hears mention of "police families" indicating their propensity for social solidarity. In much the same way military people speak of "service families" or "navy families," and for much the same reason. Still, military social solidarity is reinforced by frequent transfers and by on-post housing. The police manage their solidarity in the midst of the nonpolice world.

"There's only so much you can have in common" with civilians was the way Mary Gannon put it recently. Her husband is a sergeant on the Washington, D. C., force. She said that when she has a "real problem," she talks it over with the wife of another policeman. "There's things I can discuss with a police wife that I can't discuss with anyone else," she said.[17]

Police social solidarity has many sources. One obvious source is the fact that the police experience a shared sense of danger and must rely on one another for protection. The norms of teamwork, cooperation, mutual responsibility—in short, to help your buddy

and look after him—are extraordinarily high among policemen.[18,] *
As Janowitz has put it about military men, "any profession which is continually preoccupied with the threat of danger requires a strong sense of solidarity if it is to operate effectively."[19] In fact, police work is not nearly so dangerous as policemen think it is (see Chapter 4), but what they think is all that matters for creating solidarity.

An additional source of police solidarity and of isolation from the ordinary citizenry is the fact that suspicion is an institutionalized feature of the police role. Policemen are continually looking for cues that identify others as a potential source of danger, disorder, or law violation. One manifestation of this suspiciousness is the way in which the police systematically violate norms of public behavior, especially those governing staring at strangers. For example, we ordinarily look away from one another as we meet on the street unless we know one another and are initiating an exchange of greetings. But policemen, freed from this norm by the authority of their uniform, stare at people they pass in the street or in bars or in passing cars, and so on.† Furthermore, the suspicious-

---

* Jacobs, *Prelude to Riot: A View of Urban America from the Bottom* (New York: Random House, 1967), p. 36, provides the following quotation from the *Board of Rights Manual* of the Los Angeles Police Department: "A strong protective feeling has always existed among policemen. Many policemen will jeopardize their own position to protect a fellow officer. One of the principal reasons for policemen believing that they must 'stick together at any cost' is the prevalent opinion that the public is generally opposed to them personally. This protective belief is shared by many supervisors as well as rank-and-file policemen."

† There is an interesting connection between this police habit of abnormal watchfulness—of violating rules about staring and the like—and the widespread belief among plainclothesmen that somehow criminals and deviants can "smell cops." From conversations with many detectives it is apparent that they realize they are continually spotted as officers by persons in public places, but they are at a loss to give a rational explanation of how this occurs. Consequently, they seem to accept a magical explanation that criminals somehow develop a sixth sense for detecting cops. From my observations it seems clear that, during their years spent as uniformed officers, detectives develop styles of public behavior—such as walking into bars and giving everyone the once-over—which violate norms of conventional behavior. These styles become so much a habit that they continue them when they don civilian dress and thus give powerful cues to their true identity. Cops have certain unusual ways of acting and continue to act in these ways as detectives. Of course they are also inclined to wear heavy shoes, to be of above-average height and weight, to travel in pairs, to wear their hair like soldiers, and keep their coats buttoned to cover their guns. In upper-class establishments they are sometimes mistaken for gangsters.

ness of policemen makes them less desirable as friends for ordinary citizens. The nature of the policeman's role tends to overflow the norms of friendship and to violate the integrity of trust on which friendships must rest, a fact which both the police and conventional persons find objectionable. It is hard to be intimate with a person who is supposed to arrest you for common and petty violations which intimates would ordinarily know about. And for the policeman, there lurks the threat of being compromised by finding out such things. As Skolnick put it: "The policeman may not get on well with anybody regardless (to use the hackneyed phrase) of race, creed, or national origin. Policemen whom one knows well often express their sense of isolation from the public as a whole . . ."[20]

An additional factor in the social isolation of policemen, which has received too little attention, is simply that they work odd hours. For example, an officer starting today on the San Francisco force can expect to spend his first 12 years working nights or evenings. As a result, policemen—especially in their early years on the force when they and their wives are probably establishing friendship ties with other couples—are at home when other people are working, and at work when others normally engage in leisure and social activities. Thus the police, like other occupational groups with unusual hours—such as cabbies, cocktail waitresses, and the like—can be expected to rely heavily on their workmates for their friends because they are collectively out of time with the rest of the world.

With the widespread change from beat patrolling on foot to radio dispatched patrol cars, another factor has been added to police isolation. Where once policemen became acquainted with people on their beat—even if within the constraints of on-duty contact—now they move through a community of strangers. In the words of the Kerner Commission Report:

> The patrolman comes to see the city through a windshield and hear about it over a police radio. To him the area increasingly comes to consist *only of lawbreakers*.[21]

For, as Paul Jacobs put it, the radio dispatcher

> . . . never tells them to stop by and congratulate Mrs. Johnson because her son has just won a scholarship to college—the police officers don't even know Mrs. Johnson exists, and the only time they see her

is when her next-door neighbor gets drunk and beats up his wife, and then Mrs. Johnson is just another black face to them, peering at them from the outskirts of the crowd.[22]

The Kerner Commission expressed considerable concern over this loss of contact between policemen and the people living on their beats.

If an officer has never met, does not know, and cannot understand the language and the habits of the people in the area he patrols, he cannot do an effective police job.[23]

The Commission went on to recommend new patrol practices that would include "getting the patrolman out of the car and into the neighborhood and keeping him on the beat long enough to get to know the people and understanding the conditions."[24] Whether or not such changes would improve policing and police–community relations (and the Commission acknowledged potential problems), the fact remains that patrolling by car adds on-the-job isolation of the police from the general public to their extensive off-duty isolation.

In their isolation, and supported by their intense solidarity, policemen feel that the society at large is unsympathetic, even hostile. Studies have shown that more than two-thirds of the police have an acute sense of citizen hostility or contempt.[25] On the other hand, ordinary citizens *do* tend to distrust the police, to reject their stringent conception of order, and to be apprehensive about police behavior. Out of this intergroup conflict arise the stereotypes and prejudices that ordinarily appear in such situations. The police tend to regard us all as potential threats to their safety and to their conception of order. We reciprocate by regarding them as potential oppressors. Such hostile images are especially prevalent between the police and certain other American subcultures: ghetto dwellers, blacks, radicals, hippies, teenagers, students, and the like. (Subcultures formed on the basis of law violation such as prostitutes or gamblers are omitted here because they represent a different case, and because police seem less prone to hostility towards what they see as conventional criminality). To the police these special subcultures seem to pose a grave potential threat, and worst of all, the nature of the threat is unpredictable.[26] Members of these subcultures regard the police as a continual source of repression, harassment, and hostility. (Evidence of this mutual hostility will be presented later in this chapter.)

It has long been recognized, by both scholars and the police, that the police use a variety of cues—most of which in themselves do not constitute violations of law—to identify persons as potential sources of trouble, danger, or criminality who should be stopped for questioning. Skolnick wrote of this as a "perceptual shorthand"[27] used by the police, which often is based on judgments about gestures, language, and attire which the police find unusual or suspicious. Piliavin and Briar report, for example, that the police are particularly suspicious of young men seen "strutting."[28] The importance of this use of cues is that *a large proportion of these cues are based on police-held stereotypes about subcultures with which the police subculture conflicts.* That is, these cues are not only or perhaps even mainly those that indicate something about the individual *per se,* such as skulking in a darkened doorway, or acting "nervous" after seeing a patrolman, although certainly the police do respond to such cues as well. Rather, the police commonly act on cues that simply identify a person as a member of a particular subcultural group. Thus, it is police suspicion and hostility towards the group that implicates the individual. When members of such groups complain that they are constantly singled out even though they haven't done anything, it is often true. To such groups this is patently police harassment. To the police it is simply routine, legitimate police surveillance. Several illustrations will make the point. One Berkeley patrolman told an interviewer that he always stops all black teenagers he sees after dark carrying any item of value, especially radios. His working premise is that black teenagers are thieves and by investigating in this fashion he is likely to catch some with property they have just stolen. Since a very high proportion of this group in Berkeley carries radios, he must be busy. The youths, on the other hand, begin to wonder if it's a crime to be young, black, and own a radio. Similarly, during the tense curfew period in Berkeley in the summer of 1968, the police radio gave instructions to use cues indicating political preference and other indicators of subcultural membership. According to the deposition of a Berkeley English professor who monitored the police radio during the curfew, orders were transmitted to "stop all cars with the usual bumper stickers" or those containing "unkempt types."

Thus, the police not only constitute a relatively distinct and unusual subculture within our society, but much of what they do stems from basic conflicts and cleavages between their own subculture and other subcultures. Thus, we have worked back to our initial starting point—Bernard's analysis of the strain that stems from conflict between religious, racial, and ethnic groups and the chronic prejudices that ensue. The next section examines these conflicts in detail.

II. Subcultural Conflict: Prejudice, Hostility, and Fear

This section will be devoted to the bitter fruits of conflict between the police and some other relevant groups, especially blacks, student and radical groups, and hippies. First of all I examine the prejudice and hostility that infect relations and contacts between the police and these groups. Then I examine the actual basis of real conflict from which these reciprocal prejudices stem.

Because of the potentially inflammatory and sensitive nature of what is to follow some general observations seem a necessary introduction. As I have repeatedly tried to make clear, this book was not written to indict the police or to muckrake. The matters involved are far too serious. I am sensitive to the plight of the policeman in our increasingly complex and agonized society. The policeman is daily the man on the spot. He must deal with the concrete manifestations of problems that the general society has shown neither the wit nor the will to solve. Continually the police are required to act, when no one has told them what is to be done. As the Kerner Commission has justly put it:

His [the policeman's] role is already one of the most difficult in our society. He must deal daily with a range of problems and people that test his patience, ingenuity, character, and courage in ways that few of us are ever tested. Without positive leadership, goals, operational guidance, and public support, the individual policeman can only feel victimized.[29]

It must be recognized from the start that in some of the subcultural conflicts between police and others, the police have both the law and the general public on their side. Some of the ways in which certain other subcultures tend to differ from the police subculture are illegal. Furthermore, the police are correct in their perception that members of some subcultural groups are more likely to pose a threat to police and public safety than are others. But, as I shall consider at some length, the main role played by cultural conflict is to generate prejudices and exaggerated perceptions of threat which in turn create unnecessary and unreasonable fears and hostilities on both sides. Thus, many cops are led to think there is no such thing as an unsuspicious young black ("all those young nigger studs are potential cop killers"), while ghetto dwellers are led to think all cops are "racist pigs."

It is in the hope that something can be done to remove the burden of prejudice, unwarranted fear, and hostility from these police–public relations that I approach this topic. Admittedly, even if all prejudice were to vanish overnight, substantial conflicts of interest and ideals would remain to produce tension and friction. Nevertheless, the eradication of myth, stereotype, hatred, and fear is necessary in order to find accommodations for the real conflicts and would undoubtedly make outbursts of violence by and against the police less likely.

The theoretical underpinnings for the analysis derive from the extensive work done by social scientists on racial and ethnic relations. It is well established that when two groups differing on highly valued traits such as religion, language, customs, and the like come into contact their conflicts tend to give rise to prejudice: they come to see one another in terms of invidious stereotypes and beliefs and to manifest suspicion, fear, and hostility. Indeed, in a classic research study, the generation of such phenomena of prejudice was observed among arbitrarily selected groups of boys at a summer camp.[30] When one or both groups feel that their own "ways" have a monopoly on virtue and legitimacy, these processes of prejudice are greatly encouraged.[31] Obviously, the forms in which intergroup hostilities will manifest themselves depend upon the relative power of the two groups involved. When one group is disproportionately powerful it tends to discriminate against, repress, persecute, and otherwise victimize the less powerful. The less powerful tend to respond by symbolic aggression and by acts of defiance, rebellion, and harassment.[32]

If the foregoing analysis is correct, and if the police are a subcultural group in conflict with other subcultures on important matters, several predictions ought to follow.

First of all we would expect the police and the other relevant subcultures to manifest considerable prejudice, hostility, and fear towards one another.

Furthermore, we would expect prejudice and hostility to increase directly according to the extent to which the two groups come into contact with one another, and, correlatively, that prejudice and hostility will be more common among individual members of the two groups the more often they come into contact.

In the subsections that follow the accuracy of these predictions will be assessed.

Niggers and Pigs: Reciprocal Images

In 1962 James Baldwin characterized the police in the ghetto as an army of occupation.[33] Since then there have been riots and sporadic gun battles and both blacks and policemen have been killed. Today the police in the ghetto are not so much an occupying force as they are counterinsurgency raiders: get in and out fast is the current tactic. Throughout this period black rage against white oppression has become increasingly focused on the police. The Watts' battle cry of "Get Whitey" has given way to the Black Panther call to "Off the pigs."

The police return these sentiments in kind. They both fear black people and openly express violent hostility and prejudice towards them. Los Angeles police greet each other with the old Lucky Strike slogan: LSMFT—which they translate as "Let's Shoot a Mother-Fucker Tonight."[34] Many policemen call their night sticks and riot batons "nigger knockers."[35] Nor has it been all talk. Reports from many cities, including Detroit, San Francisco, Chicago, New York, and Oakland indicate that police officers have attacked or shot members of the black community, often Black Panthers, at offices, social events, at home in bed, and even in the halls of a courthouse.

Police hatred and repression of black people is hardly new. Historically it has been mainly the police who enforced the cruel customs of racism. Nor was this a peculiarity of Southern lawmen. The Harlem Riot Commission Report of 1935 reserved its most severe criticism for the police:

The police of Harlem show too little regard for human rights and constantly violate [blacks'] fundamental rights as citizens.... The insecurity of the individual in Harlem against police aggression is one of the most potent causes for the existing hostility to authority.... It is clearly the responsibility of the police to act in such a way as to win the confidence of the citizens of Harlem and to prove themselves the guardians of the rights and safety of the community rather than its enemies and oppressors.[36]

Westley reported from his studies of midwestern police in the late 1940s:

No white policeman with whom the author has had contact failed to mock the Negro, to use some type of stereotyped categorization, and to refer to interaction with the Negro in an exaggerated dialect, when the subject arose.[37]

But if police racism is not new, it has undoubtedly become more urgent and intense during the past decade. For if the police have long hated and repressed black people, they have recently come to fear them; the black rage that once was dissembled behind a submissive, head-scratching façade has erupted into the open.

This section will examine evidence of the extent of reciprocal hatred, fear and violence between the police and black Americans.

The Police It may seem to many readers as naiveté, or mere scholarly ritual to bother to provide systematic evidence of police prejudice towards blacks. It may seem to be something that "everybody" knows. Still, police administrators continuously argue in public that their men are not bigots. Furthermore, even the most militant blacks would not claim that *every* policeman is prejudiced. But if not all, how many? Is it most, as blacks believe and as most impressionistic accounts of the police report, or is it few, as claimed by credible police administrators? The question hardly seems trivial. Fortunately, there is some hard evidence available.

In the Black and Reiss study, one of the things observers recorded were the racial attitudes and opinions of policemen. They did not solicit such opinions, but merely recorded what was incidentally expressed. Their field notes were classified along a continuum from "highly" or "extremely anti-Negro" to "pro-Negro."

Black and Reiss reported the following direct quotations to illustrate the meaning of their categories:

> The following exemplify the "highly prejudiced" officer: "These scums aren't people; they're animals in a jungle." "Hitler had the right idea. We oughta gas these niggers—they're ruining the country." "Bastard savages." "Maggots." "Filthy pigs." "They oughta ship 'em back where they came from." "Buffaloes."
> An officer was placed in the second category—"prejudiced or anti-Negro"—if he simply showed general dislike for Negroes as a group without making "extreme" statements as in the first category: "These people don't have enough respect for law and order." "Most of these niggers are too lazy to work for a living." "The trouble with shines is the way they run down a neighborhood—it's a real shame."
> The third category—"neutral"—was used for an officer who spoke of Negroes discriptively, without judging them. He neither condemned nor defended Negroes, their advocates, or their critics: "The colored are about like anybody else." "The main problem is education—Negroes just don't get enough schooling." "There are all kinds of coloreds, some good, some bad."
> The "pro-Negro" officer was outwardly sympathetic toward Negroes, or he defended Negroes against their critics: "These people deserve all the help they can get." "A.D.C. discriminates against Negroes." "They've been kept down too long. It's a disgrace for this country."[38]

It must be recognized that these criteria of prejudice are extremely severe by typical social science standards. No officer was classified as highly prejudiced for saying he would not want his daughter to marry a Negro, or for agreeing with such typical survey items as "Unfortunately, Negroes let their property run down." The violent hatred evident in the illustrations makes it clear that this is intense and freely expressed prejudice.

Consequently, the findings are a major cause for concern. As shown in Table 3, only one percent of those white officers studied could be classified as sympathetic to the problems of black Americans (in the authors' terms, "pro-Negro"), while 38 percent were extremely prejudiced and another 34 percent were prejudiced. Thus, 72 percent of the white policemen observed in this study expressed considerable hatred of blacks. Indeed, when those upon whom no information was available are excluded from the data, 84 percent are classified as prejudiced. Whether the correct proportion is 72 or 84 percent or something in between, the conclu-

Table 3 Attitudes of White Police Officers towards Negroes

Percent:	All white officers observed	White officers stationed in predominantly Negro precincts
Highly prejudiced	38	45
Prejudiced	34	34
Neutral	11	10
Pro-Negro	1	1
Difficult to obtain information	3	1
No relevant observation	13	9
	100%	100%
Number of officers	(510)	(181)

Source: Extracted from Donald J. Black and Albert J. Reiss, Jr., *Patterns of Behavior in Police and Citizen Transaction* (Washington, D. C.: U. S. Government Printing Office, 1967).

sion is inescapable that an overwhelming majority of these officers harbored extreme prejudice against black Americans. These are not the police of Nashoba County, Mississippi, or Selma, Alabama. They are the police of Boston, Chicago, and Washington, D. C. There is little reason to suppose that the police of San Francisco, Denver, or Philadelphia are any less bigoted, nor is there much statistical possibility for police in the rural South to be much worse.

A second finding shown in Table 3 is that white policemen in predominantly Negro neighborhoods are even more likely than are the police in general to be prejudiced. In this instance, it is clear, contact breeds contempt. Partly, of course, this is because frequently it is the lowest calibre of officers (as judged by police administrators) who are assigned to black neighborhoods. Both the U. S. Crime Commission and the Kerner Commission acknowledged this fact. Presumably, less capable, less intelligent, and otherwise lower-quality policemen will be more prone to prejudice. But, in addition, the fact of continuing contact with blacks makes manifest both the distinctive differences in values and customs between black and police subcultures and involves officers in apprehensive and hostility-laden interactions with blacks.

Robert Conot has provided a sensitive account of a young Los Angeles rookie patrolman and his shock at the open and militant racism of the older officers with whom he came in contact after his training period, and then his shock and repulsion when facing the "licentiousness," "violence," and "irresponsibleness" of the ghetto. He was not prepared by his background or his police training either to expect or understand what he saw. . . .

[He] recognized that the people—at least a majority of those with whom he came into contact—were so diametrically different from his concepts of decency and morality, so different in character from himself, that he would clash with them no matter what the color of their skin, no matter, even, that he was or was not a policeman. And as an officer sworn to uphold the law, the gulf was so wide—it seemed to him—that it could never be bridged. . . .[39]

And the only systematic interpretations he received of his perceptions of ghetto life were from fellow officers who called housing projects "nigger hatcheries" and told him that "the Negroes and their left-wing allies are the agitators and the underminers of the American system."[40]

This raises the question of why the police are so passionately prejudiced against black people. Conot implies that it is a product of the backgrounds from which policemen are recruited, their experiences with black people on the job, and the norms of racism which are institutionalized within the police culture.

We have seen in Table 3 a modest confirmation of one of these three sources. As earlier hypothesized, increased contact with blacks seems to make policemen more prone to prejudice.

It is also clear that policemen rarely come in contact with blacks except those suspected of crimes or who have been the victims of crimes. Little wonder that black soon becomes synonymous with trouble. The lack of contact with "law-abiding" or "respectable" black people in the line of duty is further exacerbated by the isolation of the police from civilians in their social lives. For within the police subculture policemen will not have their prejudices undermined by friendships with black policemen: discrimination is widespread in police recruitment[41] and promotion,[42] and flagrantly practiced by police social clubs and encouraged in friendship patterns.[43]

Conot reports that a black Los Angeles rookie was told by a white officer who had become his friend in the police academy: "I hope you'll understand. I'm intending to make a career out of the force. And there are people who keep telling me it doesn't do me any good to be seen buddying up with you. I just can't ignore it any longer."[44]

The black officer understood too well. When, during his training at the academy, invitations had been passed out to all the white rookies to join various police social clubs and to their wives to join the patrolmen's wives' association, none had been received by black rookies. It has also been long understood in Los Angeles that no black officer will pass his oral examination for promotion above lieutenant.[45]

Los Angeles does not have the most racist police department in the country. Chapters 5 and 6 will indicate the racist sentiments prevalent among the police in a number of cities, including Cleveland, New York, Detroit and San Francisco. Black officers in several California cities have recently publicly protested harassment by white colleagues and discriminatory patterns within their department (see Chapter 2). The Kerner Report indicates the extreme disparity between the proportion of blacks in the community and blacks on the police force in many American cities.[46] For example, in Detroit 39 percent of the population is black, while 5 percent of the policemen are black; in Oakland, California, the comparison is 31 percent and 4 percent; in New Orleans 41 and 4; in Baltimore 41 and 7; in Kansas City 20 and 6; in Newark 40 and 10, and in Washington, D. C., 63 and 31. The cities which come closest to parity (Chicago, 27 and 17, and Philadelphia, 29 and 20) still have blacks significantly underrepresented on their police forces. And major, non-Southern, metropolitan areas are probably the least discriminatory in police hiring patterns. As of 1968, there were fewer than 60 black state police officers in the entire nation![47]

Not only are there few blacks on police forces and usually no blacks in police social and fraternal circles, some of the few blacks who are policemen have taken on the prejudices of their white colleagues and thus provide further reinforcement for the racism of white cops. Black and Reiss report that 30 percent of the black officers in their study expressed prejudice against black people. Indeed, of those who expressed their feelings one way or the other 61 percent were classed as prejudiced![48]

Several experts on police science argue that racism among the police is mainly a product of training, not recruitment. Burton Levy, once a strong advocate of police–community relations programs to ameliorate prejudice and conflict, has recently argued that the problem is primarily located within the police system, not between the police and the community:

> ... to put it more bluntly, the police system can be seen as one that is a closed society with its own values, mores, and standards. In urban communities, anti-black is likely to be one of a half-dozen primary and important values. The department recruits a sizable number of people with racist attitudes, socializes them into a system with a strong racist element, and takes the officer who cannot advance and puts him in the ghetto where he has day-to-day contact with the black citizens. If this is an accurate description of the urban police system (and my personal observations over the past five years tell me this is so), then the reason is clear why every poll of black citizens shows the same high level of distrust and hostility against policemen.[49]

Levy's judgments are supported by Donal E. J. MacNamara, who teaches at the John Jay College of Criminal Justice, New York City's police academy, who argues that the prejudices recruits bring into the department are "tremendously reinforced because they are part of the community attitudes of this police group of which he becomes a member."[50]

This brings us full circle from the start of the analysis in this chapter. As an insulated and isolated subcultural group the police experience conflict with certain other distinct subcultures, in this case that of black Americans. Out of such conflict, prejudice arises. Furthermore, prejudice against blacks is an institutionalized part of the police subculture into which new recruits are socialized and which is self-sustaining.

If we accept that the American police are overwhelmingly prejudiced against Negroes, one may still wonder whether or not their prejudice carries over into overt, official behavior. Even if it doesn't, as Skolnick has shown, even-handed law enforcement often results in discriminatory consequences.[51] For example, a $100 fine can be a severe punishment for the poor. Nevertheless, if the police did administer justice without regard to color, we would be greatly encouraged, but no observer of the police believes that this is the case.

Still, it is difficult to demonstrate that the police do discriminate in their performance of duty. A simply listing of blatant episodes does not suffice, for the police can argue that these are rarities in terms of the absolute number of police–black contacts. One then turns to statistics in order to show that police are more likely to treat blacks in certain ways than they are whites. But this is difficult, because various factors are confounded. Thus, while it is true that the police are more likely to conduct "field interrogations"—the new technical euphemism for "roust"—with blacks than with whites, it is also true that they make arrests of a higher proportion of blacks than of whites they stop.[52] Similarly, while the police are more likely to search blacks than they are whites, it is also true that they more often find weapons on blacks than on whites whom they search.[53] Thus for all of these discrepancies along racial lines it can be argued that they merely reflect the greater crime rate among Negroes. The fact that the discrepancies may reflect both discrimination *and* greater cause cannot be demonstrated without more elaborate data than are available.

One set of findings by Black and Reiss are suggestive, however.[54] They report that white policemen are much more likely to adopt a friendly or even jovial manner with whites whose behavior they are investigating than they are towards blacks, *even though blacks are less likely than are whites to be antagonistic in such situations*. This difference in treatment cannot be attributed to black provocation.

Be that as it may, Black and Reiss concluded from an overall examination of their findings that in the *normal* run of events police don't seem especially discriminatory in their handling of blacks (of course, they tend to be rather brusque and suspicious with both whites and blacks). What struck their observers was "the great disparity between the verbalized attitudes of the officers, in the privacy of the patrol car, and the public conduct of the officers in encounters with Negroes and members of other minorities."[55] Indeed, judging by the comments reported to have been made by these policemen, and the kind of hostile feelings and talk reported by most other observers of the police, one might expect them to follow through on some "nigger knocking" or LSMFT proposals fairly often. In fact, policemen usually do nothing of the kind. For even though the police have considerable discretion in the use of violence, they too are greatly constrained in what they can actually do. Thus, Black and Reiss argue that police–citizen transactions tend to fall into a routine independent of police sentiments.[56]

This is probably true. However, the fact that police are constrained not to act on their true feelings in most routine encounters with blacks raises a very critical point for outbursts of collective police violence. *The fact that they suppress their strong feelings of hostility in day-to-day dealings may well result in the police behaving even more brutally in situations such as demonstrations or riots when the normal controls operating on them are temporarily weakened or suspended.* At such moments police may vent rage that has been building up for weeks or months while they had to suppress their day-to-day anger. This leads to questions of the controls that normally restrain the police and the occasions under which these controls break down, which will be the main topic of Chapter 6. Our interest here is in the way that the apparent disparity between what police feel about blacks and what they ordinarily do in their dealings with blacks operates as a source of strain, a basis for police remarks during outbreaks of violence that "we've had a belly-full of these bastards."

Black Views of the Police Thus far we have considered pursuasive evidence that a substantial majority of policemen simply hate blacks. We shall now see to what extent these feelings are reciprocated.

It is hardly news that the new generation of articulate and militant black leaders hate and fear the police. From the Oakland ghetto comes the cry "Keep the Pigs out of the Black Community," pushed into the public consciousness by the sophisticated and outraged young leaders of the Black Panther Party. In Watts, teenagers scream at police, "Hey, fuzz! The way you look your mother was a monkey's whore!"[57]

Recently, some militants have given the ultimate demonstration of their hatred and anger towards the police: they have become cop-killers. If it is true, as the many careful studies report, that there were virtually no black snipers at work during the riots of 1966 and 1967,[58] when scores of Negroes were shot by police and the military who suffered virtually no casualties themselves, by the summer of 1968 a few blacks were sniping. Since then random shootings of policemen, ambushes, and bombings have become more frequent.

Nevertheless, anger towards the police is not limited to nationalists, militants, or teenagers. There is hardly a black public official in America who has not spoken out against police practices and called for reforms. They have been joined in this by large numbers of the most substantial private citizens in the black communities. Nor can there be much doubt that hatred and fear of cops percolates through the streets of the ghettos, among the middle-aged and elderly, among physicians, lawyers, and the clergy, as well as the young and the dispossessed.

In its careful assessment of the grievances felt by blacks in riot-torn cities, the Kerner Commission found that "police practices" were the most intense and widespread grievance. As weighted by commission investigators, "police practices" were *seven times* more important than "white attitudes" as a source of black grievance, and more than twice as important as inadequate education.[59]

This coincides with Huey P. Newton's explanation of Black Panther policy in suppressing the "Get Whitey" cry that was spreading among young blacks during and after the Watts' riot and turning their attention to their "real oppressors, the pigs—black or white." The Panther attitude is that reactions against "Whitey" were racist, while opposition to the police is justifiable.

But, if stripped of hostile rhetoric, there is some justification for Black Panther statements about the police, the anger of some blacks towards the police has a quality of apparent unreason. *All police actions vis-à-vis members of the black community are interpreted by many as racist regardless of the circumstances.* And there is a militant resistance to confronting any of the many real problems of ghetto crime with which the police and black residents alike must cope—unwillingness to testify, for example. For all that the police exaggerate reality, it is nevertheless true that the norms of personal violence in the black community are substantially in conflict with those of white society, with the legal system, and with security of individual life.[60] Thus, while blacks are undoubtedly much less dangerous than the police think they are, they are demonstrably more dangerous to the police, society in general, and particularly to other black people than are whites.[61]

Black Americans do have a higher crime rate than do white Americans—even when social class is controlled.[62] One of the most frequent complaints against the police by black spokesmen is that they do not adequately enforce the law in the black community.[63] The police reply that adequate law enforcement is impossible without citizen cooperation and that black people will not cooperate, for example by testifying against other blacks.

But while all this may be true, in extremely critical ways it is beside the point. Present relations between the police and the black community are not merely based on the past and present police racism and brutality, reinforced by black hostility and the social disorganization of the ghetto. Rather they are rooted in the condition of black communities as colonized enclaves—communities not only exploited and deprived, but whose economy, politics, and other critical institutions are externally controlled. In this situation, as is widely recognized, especially by black leaders, the police are the primary, direct means of repression. As Robert Blauner has put it:

Police are key agents in the power equation [maintaining blacks in a colonized condition] as well as the drama of dehumanization. In the final analysis they do the dirty work for the larger system by restricting the striking back of black rebels to skirmishes inside the ghetto, thus deflecting energies and attacks from the communities and institutions of the larger power structure.[64]

So long as black Americans must continue the fight to free themselves from their colonized status, to gain economic and political autonomy, the conflict with the police will continue and probably worsen as police escalate their response to black rage. Indeed, even if, by some miracle of human relations training, white police were cleansed of their racist beliefs and feelings, the conflict would remain so long as the police were interposed between black aspirations and resistance of white society. As will be discussed in detail in Chapter 8, a necessary first step to restore the situation is community control of the police—so the police truly represent the internal needs for order of the communities (black or white) they police, rather than imposing their own conceptions of order or those of some external constituency. A continuation of the present course would seem inevitably to lead to guerrilla war.

A Note on Other Racial Minorities This chapter focuses on relations between blacks and the police because of the extreme prominence of conflicts between the two in recent times. But it must be recognized that the general contours of the whole discussion apply to nonwhites generally: the police are as prejudiced against most other nonwhites as they are against blacks and treat them as badly or worse when they have sustained contact with them. In the East, especially New York City, conflict between the police and Puerto Ricans is intense. Throughout the Western states in the vicinity of reservations it is often risky for Indians to be found by the police after dark, especially in small towns. Often Mexican–Americans are treated the same way. Indeed, in California and the Southwest, tensions between the police and the Mexican–American communities are nearly as great as those between the police and black communities. The recent shoot-out between New Mexico lawmen and Reies Tijerina and his followers drew attention to the escalating conflict. Since then there have been bloody conflicts in California between the chicano community and the police. Probably because Mexican–Americans predominately have lived in rural areas, these conflicts have escaped much notice until recently. But it is hardly a new phenomenon—Los Angeles was rocked by the zoot-suit and Pachuco riots in 1943, more than two decades before Watts exploded.

Recently students from minority racial backgrounds have been leading the way to a merger of nonwhite discontent. Under the collective name of Third World, the students have been fashioning a coalition of black, brown, red, and yellow power. Resentment towards the police provides a major unifying grievance in these student efforts.

Commies and Fascists: Reciprocal Images

This section will examine police attitudes towards social and political dissent, and the attitudes of such dissenters towards the police. Contemporary dissent includes very diverse persons and groups. Yet they are united by a shared concern about such issues as peace, poverty, racial justice, and increased individual participation in decisions which affect one's life—whether it be increased student participation in university affairs, increased participation of the poor in poverty, self-help, and welfare programs, or greater citizen control over the military and the police. Rather than spell out all the varieties and styles of contemporary protest, they will be lumped together for purposes of analysis. Indeed, the police do not view them separately, but regard them as a unitary group of "troublemakers and subversives." Similarly, protest groups in America have reached a common conclusion that the police are hostile and dangerous opponents.

The protestors are correct. The police do hate them. On this point there is unanimity in recent reports on the police.

In the judgment of psychiatrist John P. Spiegel, director of the Lemberg Center for the Study of Violence:

To the Irish or Italian police officer of working class background, black-skinned activists and youthful protesters are the embodiment of everything that is alien, evil, and destructive of the American social system. Militant youths and black militants are perceived not only as un-American, but also nonhuman. Ruled out of the human race, they become nonpersons and therefore deserving of intense attack, as one would attack a rattlesnake.[65]

Spiegel's judgments are supported by many qualified observers and much evidence. Here is a vivid account of his feelings, given to a *New York Post* reporter by a policeman who had participated in a violent dispersal of yippies from New York's Grand Central Station during the summer of 1968:

Here's a bunch of animals who call themselves the next leaders of the country.... I almost had to vomit.... It's like dealing with any queer pervert, mother raper, or any of those other bedbugs we've got crawling around the Village. As a normal human being, you feel like knocking every one of their teeth out. It's a normal reaction.[66]

Further insight into the intensity of police hostility towards demonstrators and protestors is provided by the following excerpt from a tape recording of the Chicago Police Department radio. At 1:29 A.M. Tuesday, during the 1968 Democratic National Convention the following dialogue took place:

Police Operator: 1814, get a wagon over at 1436. We've got an injured hippie.
Voice: 1436 North Wells?
Operator: North Wells.
[In quick sequence, there are the following remarks from five other police cars:]

> That's no emergency.
> Let him take a bus.
> Kick the fucker.
> Knock his teeth out.
> Throw him in a wastepaper basket.[67]

Similarly, columnist Charles McCabe tells of returning to the lower East Side of New York, his childhood home, and meeting a childhood friend who was now a policeman:

> We went to a corner saloon, together with a couple of buddies and we talked—mostly about cops. It was really terrifying. These guys, all about my age, had been to Manhattan and Fordham and St. John's. They had brought up decent families. But they had become really quite mad in their work. On the subject of hippies and black militants, they were not really human.
> Their language was violent. "If I had my way," said one, "I'd like to take a few days off, and go off somewhere in the country where those bastards might be hanging out, and I'd like to hunt a couple of them down with a rifle." The other cops nodded concurrence. I could only listen.[68]

A recent study of the police by *Fortune* concluded that "most policemen view young radicals from middle-class backgrounds with especially intense moral repugnance."[69] The editors of *Time* reported: ". . . police tend to be appalled by abnormal behavior and rebellions against authority. Most scorn long hair. . . ."[70] Consider the following unself-conscious, indeed self-righteous, report of a recent incident recounted by Los Angeles Patrolman George Suber at the semiannual meetings of the International Conference of Police Associations held in Dallas in 1968:

> You know, the way it is today, women will be women—and so will men! I got in trouble with one of them. I stopped him on a freeway after a chase—95, 100 miles an hour . . . He had that hair down to the shoulders.
> I said to him, "I have a son about your age, and if you were my son, I'd do two things." "Oh," he said, "What?" "I'd knock him on his ass, and I'd tell him to get a haircut."
> "Oh, you don't like my hair?" "No," I said, "you look like a fruit." At that he got very angry. I had to fight him to get him under control.[71]

Thus, as is clear from Suber's story, the police act on the basis of their anger against youthful protestors. As Berkeley economist and city council member Margaret Gordon put it, after a long episode of police violence in that city during the summer of 1968 (see Chapter 1): the "rage and frustration" of the police against nonconformist youth "can break out uncontrollably even in the historically well-disciplined and polite Berkeley police department."[72] And of course many apologists for the Chicago police have justified police attacks on newsmen during the Democratic National Convention because the police confused "hippie type" press personnel with demonstrators. Had they really been hippies, apparently, it would have been proper to beat them and thus the press had only themselves to blame for looking like hippies.[73]

The fusion of student protest with black power not only merges into a single target the two main hatreds of the police but adds an extremely horrifying (to the police) new element: interracial sex. Recently, the police have demonstrated often that they believe white female protestors are given to sexual activities with black militants. A number of young girls picked up in the mass arrest of more than 400 students during the student strike at San Francisco State College reported being sexually insulted and taunted by the police. Several reported that one policeman walked back and forth along the line of girls waiting to be booked holding his dark, wooden riot baton between his legs and asking the girls if it was "the right color" for them.[74] Given the prejudice of police against black people and that the average cop finds girl student protestors to be very desirable, and probably unobtainable sexual objects, the belief that such girls are available to black militants is extremely provocative. Indeed, according to John Hersey's reconstruction, the tragic events in the Algiers Motel during the Detroit riot were touched off by the anger of white policemen at finding white girls with black men.[75]

But it is not simply interracial sex or suspicion of political subversion that provokes moral repugnance among the police towards protestors: matters of conventional morality and sexuality in general also upset them. Indeed, the whole "New Morality," prevalent among older dissenters as well as youth provokes the police. As *Fortune* has pointed out, the police are heavily recruited from relatively puritanical moral backgrounds—often the puritanism of strict Catholic, blue-collar families—and especially from backgrounds in which the sexual double standard prevails.[76] They are easily shocked by sexual freedom, casual nudity, "filthy" speech by, or in the presence of, females,* "strange" clothing, long hair, rock music, drugs, and rejection of status ambitions. The response of the police to the moral climate of youthful dissenters is similar to their abhorrence of the "immorality" of blacks. In fact, to many policemen youthful dissenters are simply "white niggers."

Furthermore, the police have little or no sympathy for, or comprehension of, the issues which have been mobilizing mass protest both on and off campus. To them it is symptomatic of a "communist master-plan to destroy society." Recent interviews with policemen from a number of major cities reveal almost universal belief that protests and demonstrations are the work of subversives.[77] I shall take up this police point of view in detail in Chapter 5. But the following remarks by a San Francisco officer are representative:

I believe that most of these young kids that are involved in these demonstrations are just dupes. I think there is an organized conspiracy, supported by communists, to disrupt this nation. I read a book by an ex-FBI agent, I can't remember the name of the book, but in it he said there were six different methods by which the communists are attempting to disrupt this country, and I think he was right. I can't see anything to refute his claims. I think that we need the right to assembly and to demonstrate for people who have legitimate grievances, but I do not think that most of these demonstrators we have now do have legitimate complaints.[78]

Today's protestors, especially students, hate the police as passionately and even as blindly as the cops hate them. Anyone who has stood in a student demonstration when police arrive has experienced the immediate tide of almost palpable wrath that sweeps through the crowd: the pretty middle-class coeds beside you begin muttering obscenities about the "pigs," their faces flush and

---

* In this the black community as well as youth, dissenters, and the intellectual and artistic classes violate white working-class double standards under which it is properly masculine to talk "dirty," but only out of the hearing of the womenfolk. This mentality was exemplified by Chicago Mayor Richard J. Daley when he condemned convention demonstrators for their foul language. As Ralph J. Gleason so aptly put it: "[Mayor Daley accused the demonstrators of using] words that would not be used 'in a brothel'... and it has not yet entered his mind, I suspect, that the new generation knows only academically what a brothel is, in contrast to Mayor Daley's generation." "This World" section of the *San Francisco Sunday Examiner and Chronicle*, June 1, 1969, p. 43.

contort, and you know they believe they are gazing upon the face of unmitigated evil.[79]

Several days after the televised coverage of the rampages of the Chicago police, the Gallup Poll asked a national sample of Americans whether they approved or disapproved of "the way the Chicago police dealt with the young people." Fifty-six percent of Americans approved, while only 31 percent disapproved. However, among two major groups in the population the Chicago police did not get such overwhelming backing: only a minority of persons (47 percent) under 30 approved of the police and only a tiny proportion (18 percent) of black Americans approved.[80] Furthermore, a poll of young people conducted by *Fortune* several months later found that college students overwhelmingly disapproved of the behavior of the Chicago police.[81] Thus, anger at the police is not confined to a few radical students and black militants. *It is the predominant feeling on the contemporary campus.*

These feelings are a major factor in campus protests. The appearance of the police activates violent emotions which escalate both the volatility and the size of student protests. In combination with the intense anger of the police towards the students the situation immediately becomes volcanic.

Why do students and other dissenters refer to the cops as pigs? How did this implacable hatred develop?

Student hatred of the police has been building for a long time. In the beginning it was kindled by the abominations of Southern law enforcement against the civil rights movement. Indeed, these atrocities, many of them televised, outraged the nation and produced the major civil rights legislation of the 1960s. The effect on youth was especially deep because their commitment to the movement was profound. Furthermore, youth retained its commitment when the civil rights drive turned northward. Again the typical response to sit-ins and demonstrations was police repression, and student experience (at least vicariously) with police violence grew to include Northern as well as Southern police. This experience was further expanded with the growth of the peace movement. While middle-class America could and did doubt that police had really misbehaved in their dispersal of peace marches, students knew better. They (or their friends) were the ones who had been dispersed. Furthermore, while President Johnson could ignore the Kerner Commission Report, and thus minimize its impact on many adults, students read it in classes and student publications took it most seriously. Thus, the students knew that the report—produced by prominent members of the establishment—laid serious charges against the police. Thus, in the eyes of students it had become increasingly obvious that the policeman is not your friend unless you are white, short-haired, and apathetic about the primary moral and political questions of our time.

Furthermore, dissenters—both students and adults—have been in much closer contact with the black community than has the rest of white society. They have long heard the anguished cries of brutality coming from the ghettos.

And then there was Chicago. The main consequence of the Chicago police riot during the Democratic Convention, and the subsequent hard-line policy of Mayor Daley, has been to corrupt relations between students and the police for years to come. Now they expect the police to be used against dissent. Now they expect the police to be brutal. For many students the possibility of working within the traditional political system was permanently destroyed by nightsticks and tear gas on the streets of Chicago.

Recently I stood amid thousands of Berkeley students gathered on a grassy slope across the street from University Hall where Governor Ronald Reagan and the Regents were meeting. It was the morning after the governor had activated the National Guard to assist police in the campus crisis during the Third World Liberation Front student strike. Across the street hundreds of uniformed police stood in solid ranks facing the students. Hundreds more stood in reserve.

A girl next to me said loudly: "Do you know where we are?"

"We're in front of the West Gate," someone answered.

"You're wrong," she said. "We're standing in Grant Park and that building across the street is the Conrad Hilton."

This brief sketch barely outlines the process through which students and other protest groups have come to see the police as the enemy. But the important fact to be recognized is that however it came about, many Americans, especially students, do believe that the police are violent, brutal, and repressive. It hardly matters if the police in a particular confrontation behave impeccably—students are not prepared to dismiss the past very quickly. Even more unfortunate is the fact, as the revolutionaries among the students well know, that the police can almost certainly be counted on to mishandle their assignment and turn all the suspicion and hostility of students into blinding anger. Inevitably it would seem that at the very least a few officers will break formation and beat up a student before the eyes of the crowd. When this happened recently at Berkeley, a young sorority girl standing beside me, who was only a spectator and had earlier been indignant about the use of the word "pig" on a picket sign, began screaming: "Oh, God, they *are* pigs, they *are* pigs!" The next day I saw her in the picket line.

The growth of student anger against the police has recently escalated conflict to a more dangerous level. Nonviolence, as a doctrine rather than a tactic, has lost its force. Increasingly often a few students *do* throw stones and firecrackers at police formations. But more dramatic and dangerous: now when the police attack student crowds there is a good deal of fighting back. At Berkeley recently when a patrolman ran from his formation into the street and began to beat a student, another student ran out of the crowd and knocked him down, then both students fled into the crowd. Later, when the police threw tear-gas canisters, instead of fleeing the students grabbed them and flung them back. Other groups flanked the police and tipped over their unguarded vans.

In a subsequent Berkeley crisis, in May 1969, police raised the stakes of confrontation by shot-gunning students and gassing them from the air by helicopter. Next came a violent response by students: the Weathermen actions and the rash of bombings.

Student demonstrations were long wrongfully called riots—events during the Free Speech Movement at Berkeley in 1964–1965 were often called the student riots at Berkeley, despite the fact that the students never departed from nonviolence and passive resistance. But today student demonstrations often do become riots. They may soon be wars.

The students, protestors, and blacks are filled with hatred of the police. The police are filled with hatred of students, protestors, and blacks. We mix them at our peril.

III. The Predicament of the Police

This section explores some of the reasons why the police have become increasingly angry and hostile towards blacks and protestors, why their sense of social isolation has been growing, and consequently why they are so prone to react violently when confronted with mass protest situations. The necessary starting point is a careful examination of what it is like to be a policeman today.

It is impossible to exaggerate the gravity of the current predicament of the American police. They are caught between two contradictory developments: their job is rapidly becoming more difficult (some say impossible), while at the same time their resources —morale, material, and training—are deteriorating.

No recent observer doubts that the police are under increasingly unbearable strain because they are increasingly being given tasks well beyond their resources. The police themselves agree. Changes in the demands upon the police will be briefly sketched next. Then changes in the resources of the police will be reported.

Demands upon the Police

The general outlines of the growing demands being made upon the police are well known and do not require much review here. Increasingly, the police are asked to cope with the problems which arise because conditions in the black community remain intolerable and as black anger and frustration explode. Yet all intelligent police observers realize that the root causes of black rage, violence, and rebellion are beyond the means or authority of the police. As former Superintendent of the Chicago Police Department, O. W. Wilson, commented on riots in a recent interview:

I think there is a long-range answer—the correction of the inequities we're all aware of: higher educational standards, improved economic opportunities, a catching up on the cultural lag, a strengthening of spiritual values. All of these things in the long run must be brought to bear on the problem if it is to be solved permanently, and obviously it must be solved. It will be solved, but not overnight.[82]

While many would disagree with the specifics of Wilson's diagnosis, few would disagree with his general point. And since the publication of the Kerner Commission Report there is no longer much excuse for anyone not to understand the nature of the social ills underlying the symptomatic violence of the black ghettos. But while we all know what needs to be done, it has not been done. And it is the American policeman as well as the black American who must daily pay the exorbitant installments required by these unpaid bills. White America makes its police pay for its inaction and indifference.

James Baldwin's well-known characterization of the police as an army of occupation in the black community requires more, and more urgent, consideration. The police are set against the hatred and violence of the ghetto and are delegated to suppress it and keep it from seeping into white areas. Significantly, no one knows this better than the police who must try to perform a dangerous and increasingly unmanageable and thankless task. Throughout interviews with members of major urban police forces, a prominent theme was their resultant despair and anger in the face of worsening violence and impending disaster. All recent accounts about the police by scholars and journalists report similar feelings. As the *Saturday Evening Post* recently wrote of the police in St. Louis: "To many policemen, the very existence of [an emergency riot mobilization] plan implies that it will be used, and it is this sense of inevitability, this feeling that events have somehow slipped out of their control, that unnerves and frustrates them...."[83] And, of course, the police are correct. Events *have* slipped out of their control and they can do nothing much to regain control. Moreover, until society rights itself, they must live on the brink of danger and disaster. As one patrolman told a *Post* reporter, "the first guys there [responding to the riot plan]—they've had it. I've thought of getting myself a little sign saying 'expendable' and hanging it around my neck."[84] When the temperatures rise above 100 degrees in ghetto tenements overrun with people, rats, hopelessness, and anger, it is the police who are on the line, knowing full well that nothing they do can really help, while any mistake can bring fire and death. A New York policeman put the widespread apprehensions of the police simply: "Yeah, I'm scared. All the cops are. You never know what's going to happen out there. This place is a powder keg. You don't know if just putting your hand on a colored kid will cause a riot."[85]

Similarly, the police can do little to ameliorate the reasons for student and political protest. Many demands of the protesters—moral political leadership, peace, and reform of the universities—lie outside the jurisdiction of the police. But by meeting these demands and protests with lines of riot police, we transform them into problems for the police.

In short, we have forced the police into the uninhabitable role of acting as stand-ins for necessary political and social reform. If they cope with their nearly impossible situation by venting their rage on the most apparent and available source of their predicament—blacks, students, and demonstrators—it should occasion no surprise. Yet, in the process, the police themselves become a serious social problem. And efforts to restrain their activities seem further proof to the police that they have been deserted to stand alone against chaos.

Meanwhile, as the job of the policeman has become more important and more sensitive, society has also gravely neglected the police in quite direct ways. Law enforcement as an occupation has declined badly.

The Resources of the Police

Any way one looks at it, law enforcement is deteriorating. Relative to other comparable occupations, pay has declined considerably in the postwar era.[86] Correspondingly, the prestige of being a policeman in the estimation of the general public has fallen sharply, and there has been a serious decline in the quantity as well as quality of new recruits*—most departments have many unfilled vacancies and have lowered minimum hiring standards.

In New York, for example, according to a study conducted by Arthur Niederhoffer,[87] more than half of the recruits to the New York City Police in June 1940 were college graduates. But during the last decade the proportion of recruits with a degree has rarely reached five percent. Niederhoffer attributes this change to a decline in the relative financial rewards for being a policeman. He notes that: "in the 1930s . . . top-grade patrolmen in New York earned $3,000 a year. They owned houses and automobiles; they could afford the luxuries that were the envy of the middle-class; and they were never laid off. In the panic of the Depression, the middle class began to regard a police career pragmatically."[88] However, as the affluence of the country has risen in general, the relative rewards of police work have lagged badly. In late 1968, *Fortune* reported, "Patrolmen's pay in major cities now averages about $7,500 per year—33 percent less than is needed to sustain

---

* This was a standard theme in Task Force interviews with police administrators across the country.

a family of four in moderate circumstances in a large city, according to the U. S. Bureau of Labor Statistics."[89] In 1971, average police pay was 75 percent of the minimum standard of living wage.[90] This is less than skilled tradesmen, such as plumbers, earn. Meanwhile, we have encouraged police to aspire to a middle-class life style. To achieve this, many police "moonlight" on a second job—in 1968 a total of 6,486 New York City policemen were known to hold second jobs—[91] and have wives who work. Others—there is no way to know what percentage—engage in graft and corruption, which, in some cities has been described as "a way of life."[92]

Thus a decline in the relative salary of the police profession is at least partly to blame for the fact that, while we have increasingly become committed to professionalism among the police, in many of our great cities the quality of recruits has actually been declining. In fact, matters are worse than they might appear, for while the average level of education among police recruits has been declining, the average level of educational achievement in the population has been increasing rapidly. Thus, new police recruits are being taken from an ever-shrinking pool of uneducated persons; it is only such poorly qualified people who today find being a policeman a "good job."

Indeed, in many urban departments today the older policemen are better educated and qualified than are the young policemen—a reversal of the trend operating in almost every other occupation in America.* As an Oakland police captain with twenty-seven years on the force described changes in his department:

We are not getting the type of college people in the department that we were before. The guys that we're getting now have had a high school education, have gone into the army for a couple of years and have come out and are looking to get in the police department because of the good pay. Oakland is a relatively high-paying department, but still does not get educated recruits. We're not getting one twentieth of the people out of the junior colleges that we should get. What we're going to have to do is subsidize the education of these people.[93]

* *Fortune* estimates that fewer than 10 percent of American policemen have been to college (Dec. 1968). *Time* reported that Detroit police recruits come from the *bottom* 25 percent of high school graduating classes. (Oct. 4, 1968, p. 26).

Even more bleak is the picture painted by Dr. Maurice Mensh, a physician who cares for the Washington, D. C. police:

> This is an undereducated group. You should read what they write. They can hardly write.... And you put them on the street and ask them to make decisions that are way beyond their capacity.[94]

Moreover, such situations exist even in what are considered to be the more elite, competent, and educated police forces in the country. For example, in Berkeley, California, there has recently been a sharp decline in the educational level of recruits.[95]

The difficulty of attracting qualified recruits has prompted many departments to mount massive recruitment programs. In several cities billboard campaigns extoll the benefits of being on the force. After managing to fill only 33 of 1,000 new vacancies for police officers, the Washington, D. C., department recently launched a nationwide campaign with seven three-men traveling teams. They will concentrate on military posts and are authorized by Congress to obtain a soldier's release from service 60 days early if he agrees to apply to join the force. In the first weeks of the program as many as 15 percent failed even to appear for training after having obtained their early release.[96]

One consequence of all this has been a shortage of manpower on police forces. An examination of the Uniform Crime Reports of the Federal Bureau of Investigation shows that the number of full-time police employees per 1,000 population in America's cities has gone virtually unchanged since 1950, while the number of complaints handled by the police has increased enormously.* A corollary is, of course, the tendency to overwork and overextend our police.

Perhaps an even more significant effect of pressing manpower

---

* In 1960 there were 1.9 police employees per 1,000 population; in 1966, this ratio had increased to 2.0 employees per thousand. At the same time the number of serious criminal offenses increased 48.4 percent in just the six-year period from 1960–1966. Thus, while the number of indexed crimes jumped almost 50 percent, the number of employees was augmented by no more than 5 percent. J. Edgar Hoover, Director, Federal Bureau of Investigation, *Uniform Crime Reports for the United States, 1960, 1966* (Washington, D. C.: U. S. Department of Justice, U. S. Govt. Printing Office).

needs is the tendency to allow existing training programs to deteriorate because of the pressure for immediate manpower. There is considerable evidence that the new recruits are receiving less adequate training from within departments than in the recent past.* However, this deterioration has probably gone unnoticed outside the police. For while police academies have undoubtedly been upgraded in many cities and while their curricula have been immeasurably improved, frequently new recruits are not given much benefit of these improvements. Because of the overwhelming need for manpower, recruits often are hustled out of their training period and onto the streets before they have been adequately instructed. To appreciate the severity of this problem, one need only consider the following excerpts from Task Force interviews with New York policemen about officer training.[97] New York is an especially relevant example because it is generally regarded as a police department with outstanding training practices.

A Patrolman on a Brooklyn Beat There is no professionalization of this department. We're getting a bunch of dummies on this job now. We've got guys out on the street who haven't had any training outside of three or four days in the academy. We had one class that graduated in December and it had three weeks of training and we had another class that was in June for only I think it was two days, and they were put out on the street. The Mayor says we've got to have more policemen; so we put these guys out, and they shouldn't be there. And they keep saying, we'll send them back to the academy for their training later, and they've said this half a dozen times now and the guys are still out on the street. You know, they aren't even training these guys to shoot. . . . The way it stands now, we're putting uniforms on guys and calling them cops, but they're not cops; they don't know anything.

A Sergeant I was an instructor at the police academy last year and I know I had one of my classes turned out on the street after about three weeks. They're supposed to come back to work one day a week at the academy for what they missed, but it never happened. They're out there working now with just three weeks training. Last night I had a couple of young officers who had just a very short time on the job and only a few weeks in the academy and something hap-

---

* Charles Saunders, Jr., of the Brookings Institution, reports that some departments won't allow new officers to issue tickets—presumably because they haven't had enough training to cite the proper code violation—yet not only permit but require them to carry guns. *Fortune* (Dec. 1968), p. 150.

pened and one of the detectives fired his revolver and one of these young guys couldn't resist, he fired too. I'm really afraid of what's going to happen with these young guys. They're all eager to get in and do what they think is real police work, but they just don't have the training.

A Patrolman We had a young officer killed about two days ago, and I went and checked on his record myself, so I know this to be a fact. He had been out of the academy for a few months now and he had never had any training on how to handle a gun.

Indeed, according to a story in the *New York Times* more than 2,000 new policemen had been assigned to duty during the first eight months of 1968 without being cleared by the background investigation which "normally precedes appointment to the force."[98] The reason given by city officials was the urgent need to obtain new policemen.

Finally, there is widespread discontent among the police with the standard of their equipment and facilities. Lack of space forces them to pack holding cells and drunk tanks "like sardine cans." Task Force interviewers heard stories* from policemen who no longer tried to pursue speeders because their delapidated squad cars wouldn't go over 50 miles an hour. Most policemen have a huge backlog of overtime hours, piled up because of manpower shortages (most departments do not pay for overtime, but give compensating time off if and when the man can be spared). A policeman who heroically entered a blazing building and rescued several children sleeping inside told reporters, who asked what he had thought about while inside, that he was hoping fervently that he wouldn't ruin his uniform, because the family budget couldn't stand buying a new one. (Few departments provide uniform allowances.) Officers confronting a Berkeley student demonstration expressed envy of the toy-store walkie-talkies being used by student monitors. "They may be goddam toys," one said to me, "but they work. We ain't got shit." To which another cop said, "We just *get* shit, we ain't got it."

---

* Police complaints on lack of material must not be taken at face value. Some are simply a standard part of the strategy of getting larger appropriations. Some are simply grotesque: The Sheriff of Alameda County (Calif.) "explained" in May, 1969 that his men had fired lethal buckshot at student demonstrators—killing one and wounding others—because they ran out of less dangerous birdshot.

In sum, the police have less and less to work with, and more and more to do. They are less qualified and less trained, while being asked to perform tasks that the most idealized fictional policemen could not possibly handle.

Conclusion

Thus we arrive at some understanding of the sources and targets of police hostility. To a considerable extent the police regard all civilians as "outsiders"—as unsympathetic and a threat to order—because the police are a distinctive and relatively socially isolated subculture. But some civilians are more "outside" than others. Blacks, students, radicals, hippies, and other social dissenters are especially salient targets of police opposition, and the conflicts—both real and symbolic—between the police and these groups have created mutual distrust, unreason, and hatred. Police anger is further heightened by their changing circumstances. Their jobs are becoming more difficult while their resources for dealing with their responsibilities are deteriorating. Given these facts it is little wonder that the police lash out against their "enemies"—those who are considered to be responsible for what the police experience as a disturbing state of affairs. It should be clear that the police outlook is distorted by prejudice, ignorance, and their peculiar social location. But so long as their outlook stays as it is, they will hate and fear these particular categories of persons. And, given their monopoly on the legitimate use of force and violence, it is to be expected that the police will abuse their power to punish those they hate and fear.

4

Tactical Errors

It is not true that policing is an especially dangerous job....

The methods and means used by the police to perform their duties constitute the tactical level of policing (long-term goals and general beliefs about man and society constitute the strategic level, which is taken up in Chapter 5). This chapter concentrates on those aspects of police tactics which make them prone to riot when faced with confrontations. First I assess the incapacity of large police formations to execute basic riot control tactics. Then I examine the tactical operations of the police as a *cause* of disturbances and confrontations. Next I take up the unreasonable degree to which concern for their own safety controls police tactics. Finally, I sketch the tactical error of relying on mechanical panaceas which presently dominates police thinking.

I. The Tactical Incapacities of Police Formations

The basic doctrines and tactics of riot and crowd control derive from the military, especially from the experience of the British colonial army. Quite aside from whether such tactics are effective or whether in themselves they produce many unfortunate consequences (as discussed below) is the fact that *the assumptions on which most of these tactics are predicated cannot be met by modern American police departments.* To put it bluntly: the American police cannot perform at the minimum levels of teamwork, impersonality, and discipline which these military doctrines take for granted. Relatively green regular troops may be up to these standards, but even veteran police officers are not.

The important fact to recognize is that a policeman is not a soldier. The tasks for which each is trained and organized, and in which each normally engages, are entirely different. Often they require exactly opposite orientations and procedures. That the police are sometimes called upon to perform military tactics for which their organization, training, and outlook are unsuited is one of the dilemmas of contemporary policing.

Whether the tactics in question involve dispersing crowds, sweeping the streets clear of rioters or demonstrators, maintaining security in a cleared area, or using swift counterinsurgency strikes to put down potential outbursts, the basic tactical assumptions about rank-and-file personnel are those evoked by the picture of unwavering, lock-stepping lines of troops, advancing inexorably behind bayonets: a huge, many-bodied organism, utterly responsive to command and utterly impervious and impersonal. For some portion of such a line of troops to break ranks and charge the crowd is as unlikely as the punishment that would follow such behavior is harsh. A soldier is expected to do his duty, and his duty is to do exactly as he is told. The whole point of military training, organization, and discipline is to suppress individuality and personal sentiments, to subsume the person into the squad, the platoon, the company. Every effort is made to reduce individual discretion. For example, guard training instills total reliance on orders. No one is passed without proper credentials, even the commanding general. Standard guard instructions include calling the sergeant of guard in *all* cases not covered by orders.

Police training has opposite goals. Individuality, not teamwork is the basis of training and the basis of the day-to-day police operation. Policemen are trained and expected to initiate actions (stop suspicious persons and vehicles, for example) and to utilize considerable individual discretion in performing their duties (whether to issue a citation or just a warning; whether or not to arrest).

Indeed, even police conceptions of teamwork are primarily based on only a two-man unit. Furthermore, considerable rivalry is built into the police system. Promotion comes from distinguishing oneself from others primarily in terms of individual performance—making a good "pinch"—and not through team play. The police ordinarily are scattered in time and place—they patrol separate beats and are spread across three shifts. Thus, they have no opportunity to come to see themselves as a team, and no experience in team operations. In short, the police have atomistic operational experiences and an atomistic conception of operations. This was perhaps nowhere more clearly demonstrated than by police utilization of arriving National Guard units during the Detroit riot in 1967. As one National Guard commander complained: "They sliced us like baloney. The police wanted bodies. They grabed Guardsmen as soon as they reached the armories, before their units were made up, and sent them out—two on a firetruck, this one in a police car, that one to guard some installation. . . . The Guard simply became lost boys in the big town carrying guns."[1]

A second primary feature of police work which is antithetical to military conceptions is a *personal* versus an *impersonal* conception of patrol. Police are trained to see citizens as individuals—to pick out persons who seem suspicious or dangerous, to look for the faces of known felons or wanted men. Military training not only submerges a soldier into a group, but subsumes others into collectivities. The enemy is collective, not individual. Guarding applies universalistic rules to all persons who might be encountered. Crowds are crowds, not a number of individuals to be scanned for suspicious types.

When police march in a sweep line they do not view crowds confronting them entirely collectively. They tend to continue to be on the look-out for individuals among the crowd. When they see individuals who ring their private alarm bells they are inclined to go after them. In repeated instances, when some police have broken ranks and charged into a crowd it was not simply to unloose individual attacks on a collectivity but to attack specific members of the crowd who had aroused police anger or suspicion. This lack of impersonality is a thorough-going feature of the whole police system, not simply an attribute of patrolmen.

Recall from Chapter 1 that during the confrontation in Berkeley the police radio alerted all officers who were shortly to form skirmish lines to be on the look-out for Eldridge Cleaver and other Black Panther leaders. Similar instructions were issued concerning other activists. This was not unusual, but reflects a nearly universal police tactical policy. Most that has been written for the police about riot and confrontation tactics stresses looking for and *removing* real or potential leaders. An Institute of Defense Analysis paper on nonlethal weapons for the police points out in a discussion of the use of bright lights at night to "harass" crowds that they may also be "useful in destroying the anonymity of an individual in a crowd, especially as particular people can be singled out" and photographed, identified, or subsequently apprehended.[2] Getting the leaders is a basic tactical goal. But in practice it amounts to virtual instructions to the police to break ranks and go into the crowd. And it is precisely such a move that so frequently has sparked the breakdown of police restraint and command authority. The breaking of tactical formations—for whatever reason—violates the tactical assumptions on which riot control doctrines are based, virtually ensures a fragmentation of command, and severely weakens the police control of the crowd, thus increasing both the danger to policemen and their anger. Indeed, during the height of close-order military tactics in the eighteenth century, many commanders accepted galling fire on their flanks rather than risk readjusting the facing or formation of their troops under fire. They feared, with good reason, that moving troops might break and run.

Perhaps no more dramatic illustration of the inability of the police to fulfill military tactical requirements can be offered than the Detroit riot of 1967. Responsibility for riot control was divided between U.S. Army paratroopers on one side of town and a combination of Detroit police and the National Guard on the other. The Guard proved as untrained and unreliable as the police and between the two forces thousands of rounds of ammunition were expended and perhaps 30 persons were killed, while disorder continued. In paratrooper territory only 201 rounds of ammunition were fired, mostly in the first several hours before stricter fire discipline was imposed, and only one person was killed. Within a few hours, according to the Kerner Commission testimony,[3] quiet and order were restored in the section of the city under paratroop jurisdiction. These dramatic and critical differences seem mainly to have stemmed from discipline. The paratroopers had it, the police and guardsmen did not. The Army ordered the lights back on and troopers to show themselves as conspicuously as possible; the police and the guardsmen continued shooting out all lights and crouched fearfully in the darkness. The troopers were ordered to hold their fire, and did so. The police and guardsmen shot wildly and often at one another. The troopers were ordered to unload their weapons, and did so. The guardsmen were so ordered, but did not comply. The police logged hundreds of reports of sniper fire—the Army logged only ten such reports. In the evaluation of Lt. General John L. Throckmorton, commander of the paratroopers, the key to quelling a riot area is to saturate it with "calm, determined, and hardened professional soldiers."[4] I believe his evaluation was fully confirmed by events. Only soldiers (real ones, not civilians in National Guard uniforms) are capable of maintaining the discipline necessary for proper riot control tactics. The problem is, of course, that the police are on the scene when trouble breaks out, while the Army usually cannot arrive until events already have escalated considerably. Thus, to say "let the Army do it," is impractical, and probably undesirable on other grounds as well.

In response to their past failures with large formation tactics, many police departments have organized special "tactical squads" and have attempted to train them up to military standards of reliability. Thus far these efforts have not resulted in substantial improvements. Some of the most riotous police behavior I have witnessed (during Berkeley's bloody People's Park crisis and San Francisco State College's long strike) was the work of specially trained tactical squads. Some special sessions in close-order drill and in forming skirmish lines seem greatly outweighed by the deep hostility of the police towards particular groups, and most importantly by the lack of any substantial authority by police commanders. As will be considered at length in Chapter 6, internal control in most departments today is so lax that officers know they will not be punished if they disobey commands and charge into a crowd. Basically, it is discipline that sets soldiers off from policemen. But to achieve discipline among our police will require massive reforms in our police institutions.

Until such reforms occur, the decision to assemble the police into large units and to deploy them in confrontations is to run a substantial risk of a police riot. But this does not necessarily pose a Hobson's choice between anarchy or police violence. Often enough a decision *not* to deploy the police massively would *remove the need to do so*—massive deployment of the police often produces the very crises that deployment was meant to avert.

II. Police Deployment as a Cause of Disturbances

In both of the case studies of police riots examined in Chapter 1, at least one thing is clear: the police made a decision between treating people in terms of crowd and traffic control or in terms of an illegal assembly. In both instances they chose the latter. In both instances it is clear that the potential for confrontation and anger which led to police assaults on the crowds arose from this decision —the police could have treated both demonstrations in the same manner as they treat crowds leaving football games or groups with parade permits. Both crowds were substantially composed of middle-class whites who were not especially prone either towards violence or hostility toward the police. The police decisions to treat these crowds as "rioters" seems to have produced whatever rioting ensued.

Similarly, the Kerner Commission criticized police responses to potentially inflammatory situations as the major precipitating cause of ghetto riots. They quoted with approval from the FBI riot control manual which states:

The basic rule, when applying force, is to use only the minimum force necessary to effectively control the situation. Unwarranted application of force will incite the mob to further violence, as well as kindle seeds of resentment against the police that, in turn, could cause a riot to recur. Ill-advised or excessive application of force will not only result in charges of police brutality, but also may prolong the disturbance.[5]

The problem is, of course, how much force is the "minimum" necessary and what constitutes "excessive application." It seems clear in this passage as well as in the Kerner Commission discussion that the focus is on the toughness of police behavior—do they try to clear a street, do they use clubs, do they resort to gas, do they shoot? What is missing is an understanding that the sheer number of police present, and the nature and amount of weaponry they display, may as critically stimulate what comes to pass as anything the police actually do in terms of using their numbers or their weapons. Police preparations and deployment have two major potentially harmful consequences. First, as they create a confrontation and stimulate hostility towards the police. Secondly, as they shape police officer's expectations of danger and define intended levels of force to be used.

In a previous article I analyzed the sequence of events in several recent campus protests to demonstrate that:

The arrival of the police in strength on campuses, and their subsequent deployment and behavior, has transformed innumerable small student protests into mass demonstrations and then violence and rioting.[6]

A careful look at demonstrations at schools such as Berkeley, the University of Wisconsin, Sir George Williams University, and Duke University revealed a pattern in complete variance with common sense beliefs about the relation of police to protest. Typically, any potential for violence among student demonstrations remained latent until *after* massive confrontation by the police. Even more important, student protests remained quite small until *after* the arrival of police in large numbers. It was the presence of the police that brought out massive student participation. In fact, it was protest against the police presence, rather than new support for the issues being protested, that brought out the mass of students. A day-by-day study of Berkeley during a Third World Liberation Front strike (which began in late January 1969) revealed a recurrent cycle: a very small number of protestors (less than 300 shortly after the strike began), a display of police power, followed by a massive number of protestors which slowly dwindled, reintroduction of a massive police presence, a rekindling of mass student support until finally thousands of students confronted hundreds of policemen and a riot occurred.

Had there been no massive police presence, it seems extremely unlikely that any major difficulties would have ensued. Some colleges (Reed, Brandeis, and Chicago, for example) faced similar initial protest situations, but did not call in large police units; the crises did not worsen, but dissipated instead. On the contemporary campus a massive show of police escalates the confrontation.

Massive police preparations and deployment not only incite students and minority communities, they also unnecessarily alarm the police. During study of the Berkeley riot reported in Chapter 1, many observers were not only struck by the apparent unreality of police preparations, *but also by how anxious these preparations were making the police themselves.* As previously recounted, the police had arranged for scores of outside reinforcements several days before the initial event occurred—an unprecedented move. Then they issued riot equipment, took control of rooftops, and by the second day loaded large amounts of ammunition and firearms into their cars, deployed mortars and roof-top marksmen. As will be considered below, most of these preparations were undoubtedly done in the interests of preparedness—better to be safe than sorry. But it seems reasonable to suppose that such activities convey, perhaps inadvertently, a great deal of information to rank-and-file officers. Such preparations tell them that their commanders are thinking that they may be going out to face a bloody riot, that they may be fired on, that they may be facing urban guerrillas. These preparations also tell officers that their commanders mean to make an all-out fight for the streets, if necessary. They are "briefed" in this way about a situation in which they are in fact supposed to be cool, civil, disciplined, and restrained. Little wonder that they erupt into violence. Conversations with officers after a number of confrontations reveal claims that they were very frightened during the event. I am not skeptical of such claims. I think they are at the root of many tragedies. I am convinced that many guardsmen at Kent State were frightened. So were many policemen and guardsmen in a number of ghetto riots. But much of their sense of danger simply cannot have been produced by the events around them—bottles, stones, and catcalls simply aren't that frightening to a bunch of seasoned cops. Their fear was aroused well before anything happened by the level of preparations made. Troops moving through an area thought to contain the enemy are notoriously trigger-happy. Often precautions taken by police commanders convince the rank-and-file that they are indeed going into enemy territory.

III. The Obsession with Safety

I have pointed out above that the police often seem to over-prepare in terms of men and equipment for potential confrontation situations and, as a result, increase the fearfulness of their own men and the hostility of the civilian crowds. The cause of these over-preparations is, in my judgment, an obsession among the police with their own safety.

A constant theme in police periodicals, in public statements by policemen (especially when demanding greater discretion to use force) and in discussions about the police is: *danger*. Police wives speak of fearing the "knock on the door." This was also a common theme in Violence Task Force interviews with policemen. Several police union officials suggested that policemen were not performing their duties as fully as before because of fear of danger. And of course television police dramas show us that the policeman is in constant danger of losing his life.

It is true that police officers are killed in the line of duty. It is not true that policing is an especially dangerous job, however. As is shown in Table 4, compared to a number of other common occupations policing is notable for its relative safety. Yet we do not hear of the burden of fear sustained by farmer's wives, or the wives of construction workers—yet construction work is more than twice as dangerous as policing and agriculture is about one-and-one-half times as dangerous.

Furthermore, until the last year or so, the rate of policemen killed in the line of duty had been falling for the past 50 years.* Policing was getting safer, despite all the talk of our cities turning into jungles. In the aftermath of considerable police violence against radicals and minorities, policing recently has been becoming more dangerous. Policemen are being ambushed and bombed. This is most unfortunate, but it is exactly what I predicted (in the Skolnick

---

* Data reported by A. D. Biderman, "It's Getting Safer To Be a Cop," *Washington Post,* September 5, 1965, show that for the Washington, D. C. metropolitan area the line-of-duty death rate among police had dropped greatly since World War I. In the period of 1915 through 1934 about 1.5 officers per thousand were killed. Over the next decade the rate was .92; for the next, .40; and for the decade ending in 1964 it had dropped to .27.

Table 4 The Relative Danger of Policing

On-the-job deaths per 100,000 employees	Occupation
32.8	Law enforcement
44.1	Transport
55.0	Agriculture
75.8	Contract construction
93.6	Mining

Source: U. S. Dept. of Labor, "Monthly Labor Review," cited in *The Journal of Criminal Law, Crimonology, and Police Science*, Vol. 54 (1963), pp. 225-231.

Report) would happen if the police continued to use unrestrained force: their efforts to ensure their own safety have made policing more, not less, dangerous and have increased, not repressed, social turmoil. Even so, policing remains relatively safe.

Why then do the police think it is so dangerous (and I do not discount their statements as a subterfuge to justify repression and violence)? In my opinion it is the element of human intention in police fatalities as opposed to the accidental nature of deaths in most other occupations that leads to an obsession with safety. The truck driver must be on the lookout for dangerous or incompetent drivers and for natural road hazards, but he need not worry that someone will intentionally crash into him or mine the road. Similarly, the farmer, the miner, and the construction worker must be wary of hazardous situations and unforeseen accidents, but no one is trying to harm them. With the police, however, the major threat is from another human who is trying to kill or injure them. It is not the accidentally or carelessly dropped beam they must avoid, but the shots and blows aimed at them personally. In dealing with accidental and unintentional events a certain fatalism is encouraged. There is only so much you can do and after that it is a matter of being lucky or unlucky. But in dealing with the intentions of other humans there is a strong tendency to think safety is manageable. One is inclined to believe that if only proper precautions had been taken and if one were sufficiently alert and acute, danger could have been forestalled—use enough men and equipment, get them before they get you, watch out for suspicious types, and so on.

To some extent this is true. Many policemen have died because they failed to use proper restraining techniques, have inadequately searched suspects, or have otherwise violated their training. But probably in most instances only clairvoyance could have prevented the death. Every effort should be made to train and equip policemen to reduce the chances of death and injury. But the police also ought to understand clearly that they are being paid to take a certain degree of risk and that their safety does not come before public safety or the common good. Unfortunately, the police typically place their safety first and in recent years we have come to accept this priority. Thus, policemen in Berkeley fired shotguns into crowds of students because they felt imperiled by scattered rock and bottle throwing despite the fact that the police were wearing bullet-proof "flak" jackets, hard helmets, and face masks. Thus, Guardsmen at Kent State shot down students with rifle fire in the face of puny and petty threats to their safety. Thus, highway patrolmen at Jackson State riddled a dormitory because of the threat to their safety inherent in taunts and curses. Thus, police commando squads burst into Black Panther headquarters in the dark of night to serve insignificant warrants. And so it goes.

But consider the behavior of 200 U. S. marshals at the University of Mississippi in September 1962, facing a violent student and Klan mob of 2,000 who were trying to prevent the admission of James Meredith to the University. The marshals stood firm under barrages of bricks and sporadic sniper fire for seven hours, and 29 of them suffered injuries. They never broke. They never fired. They preserved life, property, and civil rights. Recalling this episode, consider how little we have now come to expect of the police and how greatly we have come to share their obsession with their own safety.

IV. The Search for Technical Panaceas

Understandably, police commanders would prefer to never expose their men to danger or to use night sticks and firearms on crowds. In consequence there has been a boom market for mechanical gadgets from wax bullets to tanks which might offer alternate tactical solutions to the problems of crowd control. No idea seems too silly for serious consideration. A recent compedium of gadgets either available or in the planning stage prepared by the Institute for Defense Analysis[7] describes the following:

    Barbed tape that springs from a box to form eight helices 12 feet long and 15 inches high.
    Nylon rope barriers modeled on portable horse race starting gates to channel crowds.
    Teflon confetti to make streets so slippery that crowds would be subject to slipping, sliding, and falling down.
    Semiliquid polymers which would have the same slippery-making capacity, but could be sprayed or pumped onto the streets.
    High-volume foam generators capable of laying down foam 5 feet high, 50 feet wide across a 200-foot-long street in 10 minutes, thus creating barriers for shutting off or boxing in crowds. The foam would also be extremely slippery.
    Water cannons firing dyed water to push back, knock down, and identify demonstrators. An electrically charged stream of water is reported in the experimental stage in West Berlin. The use of hot water was dismissed because of limitations in delivery equipment and the difficulty of "achieving useful effects safely."
    Hot air blowers to sweat out sit-ins.
    Cold brine projectors to freeze people into submission.
    Flood lights and flicker lights to dazzle the eyes.

    Many departments have bought tanks and armoured cars. Most have bought hard hats with face masks, flak jackets, shotguns, submachine guns, special-length riot batons, and gallons of Mace. Such items as lead-weighted gloves, deringers, and gas pens are hawked to individual policemen through magazine ads and direct mail. Recently some cities have purchased helicopters. Others have installed closed-circuit television monitors to watch the streets. Many departments have obtained police dogs.
    This frantic search for mechanical saviors reflects a naive sci/fi faith in technology. Consider the following excerpts from a Task Force interview with a police union leader:

I think that they might have to end up getting these people [criminals] and giving them a pill or some sort of psychiatric treatment. We can just obliterate everything that's been programmed into their value system and give them new values that are acceptable to a Christian society such as ours. In the future I can see the police flying around in space suits being called social service agents and our job would be to go around and arrest these people who do not have proper values and maybe after two or three arrests take them to a Center, a medical center, not a jail, where they would get the treatment necessary to change their values.[8]

The fallacy of technical solutions is four-fold. First, the extent of public disorder clearly is not sufficient to justify turning the police into a heavy weapons counterinsurgency corps. There is no need for such excessive firepower and equipment. Second, to the extent the police are so armed there is considerable danger that they will misuse these armaments. Weaponry tends to be self-justifying. Most gunfire by the police in riots and disturbances is directly attributable to the fact that the police were armed. Shotguns were fired because they were carried, not because the situation called for shotgun fire. Indeed, recently new riot regulations covering the National Guard specifically ban utilization of heavy weapons such as machine guns and tanks. In fact most guard units will not now issue rifle ammunition to the rank-and-file prior to an on-the-scene decision to commence firing. These decisions at the federal level run counter to the trends toward heavy weaponry among the police. Third, it is not simply that such weaponry is out of proportion to need, or that it is too likely to be misused, but such weaponry, as noted above, serves as a provocation to civilians and creates a false sense of danger and a too deadly definition of plans among the rank-and-file police. Finally, the major point against the search for technical solutions is that they are a failure. There was a strong negative correlation between the amount of force applied and the cessation of rioting in Detroit. Similar patterns were found by investigators of other civil disturbances.[9] Shotguns did not resolve the problems of Berkeley, but intensified them. A careful analysis of crime data after the introduction of helicopter patrols in several Southern California cities found that the relevant crime rates continued to rise.[10] This should hardly be a surprise. For the fact is that the social problems and political conflicts which generate disturbances are hardly amenable to mechanical suppression. Short of shooting demonstrators on sight (which would most likely lead to civil warfare, not peace) there are no mechanical panaceas which can solve these problems for the police. In the final analysis these are problems to be solved by the society, not by the police. And that includes the problem of how to provide disciplined, tactically restrained, competent policemen suitable for the policing of a democratic society.

Conclusions

The tactical incapacities and misconceptions of the police contribute to the occurrence of police riots in a number of ways. First, simply massing the police together, given their lack of discipline and tactical competence, provides an opportunity for them to attack crowds. Second, massive displays of police power provoke demonstrators and tend to produce confrontations and deeper conflicts. Third, police tactics mislead policemen about what is expected of them and increases their anxiety and hostility. The obsession with officer safety leads to overpreparedness, overreaction, and a disregard for the general safety. As the textbook on patrol procedures quoted in Chapter 2 put it, "killing another human being is a serious matter.... However, the officer's life and safety is much more important."[11] But to risk their life and safety is what they are hired to do.

We have seen in Chapter 2 that brutality is a routine police response to danger or anger. In Chapter 3 we saw who it was that the police were likely to be angry towards and fearful of—who they would like to be violent towards. In this chapter we have seen that their lack of tactical competence maximizes the opportunity for policemen to break ranks and do what they would like to such people. In fact, violence is about the only tactical competence the police bring to confrontation situations. Thus in a police riot the police are doing what they routinely do, to those they would most like to do it to, and they are doing the only thing they are adequately trained to do.

5

Strategical Misconceptions: Police Ideology

... when the police have violently treated moderate citizens as if they were bomb-throwing revolutionaries, how many bomb-throwing revolutionaries have they created?

Central to police conflicts with other subcultures and to their tactical mistakes in dealing with organized dissent is their general conception of how society is and how it ought to be—their strategic grasp of the "big picture."

What the police do is affected greatly by what they believe and value. Their responses to certain crises, problems, and persons are governed by their comprehension of what is going on and why. Their view of the "big picture" defines what is wrong, who is to blame, why, and what ought to be done about it.

The fact that the police view of such things is at considerable variance with the views of informed and influential civilians is an additional source of police alienation and their sense of embattlement. But more importantly, in my judgment what the police believe about many vital questions is simply incorrect and leads them to sentiments and actions which are inappropriate and often harmful.

This chapter first assesses what the police believe about a number of major issues and the accuracy of their beliefs. The second section attempts to understand why the police believe as they do.

I. The Nature and Quality of Police Ideology

This attempt to portray and assess predominant themes in current police thinking falls into three general sections.

The first deals with police beliefs about criminality and the causes of crime. In it I try to show that the police commonly subscribe to a number of dubious theories of criminality and crime causation which greatly influence their conclusions on how to deal with crime and criminals. Because much of what the police believe about crime is at best dubious and sometimes patently false, they find their efforts to act on their beliefs opposed by civil authorities, the courts, penal and probation authorities, social scientists, and others. In this sense police perceptions of these groups as "enemies" or "part of the problem" are realistic. Furthermore, the inadequacies of police theories of criminality often lead them to act in ways which do not help and often make matters worse.

The second section is devoted to the propensity of the police to explain events—especially protests, demonstrations, and civil disturbances—as conspiracies. I try to outline some of the general criteria by which the police identify conspiracies and to show how these judgments often are faulty. Important here is the fact that conspiracies understandably often cause considerably more alarm than do events which are "natural." And this often leads the police into a vicious, self-fulfilling cycle. The fact that the police see conspiracies where many other careful investigators do not causes them to be more alarmed by these events than is warranted. Consequently, they act in ways quite out of proportion to the inherent threat of the situation. Such police actions, in turn, often produce the danger and disorder they were meant to prevent and thus confirm the apparent validity of the initial police misperception.

The third section will sketch a portrait of the political, religious, and social views of the American police. In general, their views on these matters could be described as old-fashioned, and as a result the police regard current trends of social change as a decline into moral decay and as a harbinger of social collapse. The police see themselves as one of the last untainted bastions against the destruction of Christian morality and the American way of life. But I am getting ahead of the story.

Dubious Theories of Criminality

Lately, policemen across the country have begun to express considerable resentment towards social science. A police commander in Berkeley recently put it to me this way during a student demonstration: "It's the bleeding hearts bullshit you guys pump into them in class that gets them out here raising hell. And it's the bullshit you've pumped into the courts and the press that keeps us from taking care of them."

At issue is the contempt the police hold for social science explanations of crime causation and of protest and civil disturbance. The police generally reject social-structural and cultural theories of criminality. Instead, they see criminality mainly in volitional and individual terms. John Harrington, national president of the Fraternal Order of Police, said in an interview that society doesn't make ghettos, "the people who choose to live in them do." A well known police official often says "poverty doesn't cause crime, people do." And, of course, the National Rifle Association has long claimed that "guns don't kill people, people do."

The conflict between these and social science explanations rests on differing conceptions of human nature. Most American policemen are firmly committed to the traditional conception—stemming from conservative Christian doctrines and long reinforced by unsophisticated notions of rugged individualism and unregulated capitalism—that men are possessed of virtually unlimited free will. The basic assumption of this doctrine is that human behavior almost invariably transcends past experience and cultural, societal, and other external forces and can be understood almost wholly in terms of personal choices freely made. Thus, men get what they deserve because they are free to do what they want to do.

The following excerpts are from the opening chapter of a leading textbook used in police training. Here, free will assumptions in rather unsophisticated form are made clear.

... The authors do not share the modern "assumption of determinism" whereby behavior is deemed almost totally determined by instinct, heredity, and environment.

Certainly, freedom of choice can be overcome by violence or force, by fear, by sense desire, or through ignorance.... But just as certainly, our social existence is based on the assumption of personal moral responsibility which is concomitant with individual freedom....

The physical brain is a necessary condition for thought ... but the physical brain cannot have universal ideas, cannot form judgments, cannot reason, cannot will—only the spiritual soul.

... It is the immortal nature of the human soul that is the source of dignity of each individual person.

... One will regard man as a mere animal, subject to animal dependence on the material, subject only to an animal sense of motivation, and subject to the utter annihilation of animal death, *or,* one will regard man as a rational creature, free in action and thus responsible, and destined for eternal life.

It is well worth the time of any serious student of law enforcement to cogitate on the nature of man, for how a law enforcement practitioner regards himself and his fellow man often determines his course of action.[1]

One can hardly doubt the authors' concluding remark. It is precisely because the police so typically do hold these fundamentalistic theological views of man as the "captain of his soul, the master of his fate" that they reject social science explanations of criminality. And because they reject these explanations, they reject the proposals for controlling crime that follow from them. If one holds that poverty, poor home life and training, lack of education, hopelessness, and the like are important causes of criminality, then attempts to halt crime are directed towards alleviating these social problems and the handling of offenders turns to reform, therapy, retraining, parole, and the like. But if one rejects these factors as important sources of law violation and sees such acts as the freely chosen acts of intentionally "bad" people, then punishment, repression, and even revenge become reasonable lines of action.

So long as conflicting images of man remain merely the substance for philosophical and theological dispute, the matter cannot be resolved, nor does it matter very much. But, the issue is not merely academic. When these images are related to human behavior, in this instance criminal behavior, they generate contrary empirical expectations. In short, social scientists commit themselves to showing that the social and cultural factors which they believe contribute to criminality are empirically related to, or will predict, criminality. Those who hold a radically free-will image of man must assume that nothing in a person's past or environment will be related to subsequent criminality—that criminal behavior is not predictable by reference to social and cultural forces.

While it is obvious that social science has not produced theoretical models that will explain all individual criminality, it is also obvious that many of its assertions have received strong empirical confirmation. Of course, until such time as *all* such behavior can be predicted (an unlikely occurrence, if only because to do so would be both too expensive and too uninteresting), a residual of unexplained behavior will still allow some scope for arguing that human behavior is free in the theological sense to some degree. But present social science evidence simply does not permit a thorough-going free-will conception of man. Too much can already be predicted.

Why then do the police, and many other Americans as well, continue to deny the validity of social science in the face of firm evidence? In part this may reflect the fact that moral and theological convictions are notoriously resistant to refutation. Be that as it may, a widespread misunderstanding of the logic of multiple causation and of statistical inference also reinforces free will misconceptions about crime causation.

Examples of such misunderstanding are common in everyday conversation and even in official reports on crime. Their basic form is as follows: many children who grow up in slums nevertheless do not end up committing delinquent acts; therefore it is silly to say that slum life is a cause of delinquency.

Such statements commit a number of fallacies. They assume that for a factor to be a cause of something it must *always* cause it—that is, it must be wholly sufficient. In this case all slum children must commit offenses, otherwise being raised in a slum is dismissed as a cause. They also often assume that a causative agent must be a necessary cause—that is, *only* slum children will commit offenses, and if this is found to be false, then again the effects of slum life are dismissed. But the real world is rarely like this. Single causes of social behavior are uncommon. Usually a great many factors may separately or in various combinations contribute to a given outcome. If slum children are more likely than nonslum children to commit delinquent acts, and if this difference cannot be explained away by some factor other than slum life, then we properly infer that slum life is at least one factor which contributes to the delinquency rate. These and similar fallacies about delinquency are dealt with in definitive fashion by Hirschi and Selvin.[2]

Crude free-will notions of human behavior predominate among the police and are widespread among the American public as well. But such notions are discredited in many important sectors of our society, particularly among governmental, judicial, religious, business, and academic leaders. Consequently, policies governing police action tend to favor social science rather than free-will assumptions. Indeed, social science views predominate in nonpolice agencies such as penal and probation departments with whom the police must coordinate their actions. Disagreement on such basic assumptions about the nature of man and the world inevitably causes conflict in such a system of relationships. Indeed, various programs based on social science theories and aimed at reducing crime and social disorder are commonly seen by the police as coddling criminals or, in the case of recent ghetto programs and campaigns to recruit minorities into police work, as selling out to lawlessness.

A radical free-will image of human nature is not the only source of dubious theories about criminality among the police. Free-will thought has always been serenely inconsistent (had it not been it would have been too implausible to survive). Thus, although claiming that nothing excuses human failings—since choices are personal and freely made—persons committed to free-will doctrines have consistently held that certain social and cultural factors are necessary for the maintenance of human morality, and that others are a source of moral decay. Thus, while rejecting poverty, political grievances, and the like as determining human actions, these same people have denounced welfare programs as not merely irrelevant—since poverty is the result of human free will—but also as harmful. Welfare programs are thought to destroy individual initiative. Similarly, firm religious training and religious participation are deemed vital to keeping men on the path of righteousness—even though falling from this path can be blamed on nothing.

Current police views share this traditional inconsistency. Thus police publications and spokesmen regularly denounce welfare and other "do-gooder" schemes as destructive of individual initiative, while rejecting poverty as capable of similar effects.

Similarly, law enforcement officials widely blame the current rise in crime on a turn away from traditional religiousness. Indeed, on these grounds judges sometimes sentence juvenile offenders to attend church. Yet, the best recent evidence shows that religiousness—whether belief, participation, or both—has no detectable effects on preventing juvenile criminality.[3] But because law enforcement people believe a loss of faith is producing rising criminality, and because most policemen are strongly committed to the importance of religion, they are encouraged to take an alarming view of modernist trends in religion as a sign of an impending moral breakdown.

Perhaps the main *bête noir* in current police thinking is permissive child-rearing. Many policemen interviewed by the Task Force echoed the views of Dr. Norman Vincent Peale that instant gratification and permissiveness in child-rearing (which he blames on the influence of Dr. Benjamin Spock) has led to a generation "that thinks it can get what it yells for." Indeed, one Oakland officer justified the use of physical force on offenders as a corrective for lack of childhood discipline. "If their folks had beat 'em when they were kids, they'd be straight now. As it is we have to shape 'em up." While much recent evidence has shown that students most concerned with social issues, with peace, and with active participation in protest movements have been reared in more permissive homes than those who are uninvolved in these matters, this is not to say permissiveness leads to criminality.[4] In fact, the evidence shows that persons reared in authoritarian homes and who received considerable corporal punishment while young are more likely to commit criminal acts than those from permissive backgrounds.[5] *Furthermore, the best available data show there has been no drift towards permissive child-rearing in America.*[6]

Like so much else, the furor over permissiveness partly rests on conflict over free will. Since, in the judgment of the police, criminality stems from individual volition, the proper response is punishment, both as deterrent and as just retribution. Repeated studies have failed to show that severe punishments, including capital punishment, do serve to deter crime. Nevertheless, efforts over the past several decades to find more efficacious methods for reducing crime outrage the police who retain their faith in deterrence, and even when they don't they still regard severe punishment as no less than simple justice. One officer with whom I discussed the fact that there was no evidence that severe punishment deterred crime put it this way: "Well, maybe it doesn't reduce crime, but people who break the law have to be made to suffer.... It's a moral debt they owe to society. They made their choice."

An equally important consequence of a radical free-will image of man for police thinking is the way it encourages the police to employ conspiracy theories. Because they reject social and cultural factors as causative agents and look instead to individual motivation, the police are unable to find most episodes of mass protest or civil disturbance explicable except in terms of conscious conspiracies. They do not ask *what* was responsible. They want to know *who* was responsible.

Dubious Theories of Conspiracy

Conspiracy is an elusive, almost mystical concept. In this section I attempt to isolate and assess the core meaning of conspiracy as it is used by the police and others to characterize certain kinds of group activities. I shall ignore the legal definition of criminal conspiracy. It is mainly irrelevant to most controversies over the presence or absence of conspiracies behind events. Criminal conspiracy statutes merely require that two or more persons discuss the commission of a criminal act. It doesn't matter whether or not they ever perpetrate the act or whether they succeed in carrying out their plans. For example, two persons are guilty of criminal conspiracy if they meet and discuss how to produce violence during an anti-draft rally. The fact that in the event no violence took place, or that while violence took place the two conspirators had nothing to do with bringing it about is legally beside the point (although it may matter in actual legal practice). Legally, their discussion of intentions is all that matters. But if our interest is in understanding larger events, not in the isolated behavior of a few individuals, then it matters very much indeed if intentions are turned into actions and whether or not such actions prove effective.

The real concern about conspiracies among Americans is not in the conversations held by several persons, whatever the criminality of the propoals they discuss, but with actions; more particularly we are concerned with actions of some appreciable seriousness such as assassinations, riots, or price-fixing. My concern with police adoption of conspiracy theories, however, is narrower still. The main abuse of conspiracy theories is their use as explanations of events involving the behavior of large numbers of people: demonstrations, political movements, protests, riots, rebellions, revolutions, and the like. It is *conspiracy explanations* imputed to incidents of mass behavior which I shall analyze. The question raised about such incidents is whether or not they were *produced* by a conspiracy.

As will be shown in detail later, the police are highly predisposed to explain such events as the product of a conspiracy. Many others, from sophisticated journalists to official commissions appointed to investigate some such events, typically challenge these views. In order to understand and assess these disagreements, it is necessary to discover the essential point of conflict: what is being asserted?

A useful starting point is to recognize that part of the disagreement is on whether or not some group activity grew *naturally* out of a particular social situation, or whether it was manufactured and thus unnatural and essentially alien to the situation in which it occurred. Consider the following examples. If students at some university become increasingly angered by administrative rules prohibiting political expression on campus, organize themselves to seek changes in these rules, and ultimately conduct demonstrations against the administration, I would call this a *natural* event. It is natural in the sense that the ingredients which produced it resided in the setting in which it occurred. But if, on the other hand, a group of outsiders, persons not members of this university community, come onto a campus with no previous significant student discontent, and, posing as students, raise false inflammatory charges against the administration and thus cause a demonstration, this is a *manufactured* event and should be called a conspiracy. The elements which produced it did not naturally reside in the situation in which the event occurred.

Of course, in reality things are not usually so simple as this. For one thing conspirators may be present in natural events. For example, off-campus radicals may well appear during a natural student protest and try to influence events. (More typically, in order to enhance their own prestige they try to convince others —especially the police and the press—that they are influencing events. Too often they find the police easy to convince). Thus we must recognize that a key issue in evaluating whether or not an event is a conspiracy is in judging who has how much power. The presence of conspirators is not enough to confirm an imputation of conspiracy. The conspirators must also be able to influence the course of events significantly.

But we still have not grasped the essence of the problem. If events are only conspiracies when they are significantly controlled by conspirators, we still do not understand what properly constitutes being a conspirator. I must admit that I spent more effort trying to provide a responsible and usable answer to this question than I did on any other in the book. My method of seeking a solution was to review a great many specific events over which there has been controversy as to whether they stemmed from the work of conspirators. In each instance I tried to decide on the evidence whether the conspiracy theory was sustainable. Then I tried to identify the common elements in my judgments— to find the critical assertion of conspiracy theories. My conclusion follows.

Given that we are discussing conspiracy only in terms of group or collective action and not simply criminal conspiracy, *the imputation of conspiracy explanations to such events rests entirely on the degree to which there is a lack of integrity in the relationships between the leaders and the followers.* I shall now try to make clear what I mean and to demonstrate that this is in fact the critical assertion in conspiracy theories.

When it is charged that a particular action by a group of persons stemmed from a conspiracy, the words most commonly used imply deceit, primarily deceit by the leadership: dupes, tools, mistaken, misled, sheep, and the like are applied to followers, while words such as plotter, demagogue, phoney, agitator, subverter, and the like are applied to leaders. The imputation is that the majority of rank-and-file participants were told lies about the aims of the activity, and the aims which enlisted their participation were not in fact the real reasons why the leadership enlisted them. For example, it is commonly charged of contemporary protests and demonstrations that the leaders do not want to achieve the goals which animate the rank and file, but instead want the rank-and-file efforts to fail in order to further the leaders' actual, but unstated, goals of frustrating and radicalizing participants so they will later be willing to adopt revolutionary tactics and goals.

When there is integrity in the relationship between leaders and followers it becomes irrelevant to speak of conspiracy, *regardless of the aims of the group*. For example, if all participants agree to launch the revolution now, their act may be characterized as rebellion, riot, vandalism, civil war, or damn foolishness, but it is not a conspiracy. Consequently, exhaustive legal efforts have been made to explain street events during the 1968 Democratic Convention as the work of conspirators—to show that the masses of demonstrators and even the press were duped by the likes of Jerry Rubin, Abbie Hoffman, and the rest of the Chicago Seven. But no such effort is being made to show that the violence of the Weathermen faction of SDS in the streets of Chicago a year later was a conspiracy. The Weathermen were not duped by their leaders. One may judge their efforts puny, foolish, or the first round in the revolution, but it is senseless to speak of conspiracy; even the *Chicago Tribune* has not done so. For the Weathermen are believed to be what they appear to be, while conspiracy entails the judgment that things are not what they appear to be, or more specifically that things are not as leaders say they are and the rank and file believes they are.

This hardly means that leaders may not have any secrets from their followers or they are to be labeled conspirators. Clearly leaders must have some secrets and these may even extend to some minor deceptions of followers on such matters as tactics. But faith must be kept over goals. The goals which sustain rank-and-file commitment must be the goals actually pursued or at least hoped for by the leadership. When the leadership in fact pursues or hopes for goals which are contrary to the aims of the membership, then this is a conspiracy and events stemming from such leader–follower arrangements sustain the imputation of conspiracy explanations.

This is the fundamental charge leveled by the police when they call certain events conspiracies. They almost universally preface their remarks with some statement of the probable good intentions of participants—"No doubt many of these students think they are acting from the highest sense of idealism," "Many demonstrators had a sincere concern for peace,"—but then they attack the leadership for base motives and for exploiting the good intentions of participants.

And this is the fundamental basis for refutations aimed at police conspiracy charges: there was no important breach of faith between leaders and followers.

A major qualification must be taken up at this point. Leaders must be able to exert power over the course of events—to impose their decisions on the rank and file—in order for conspiracy explanations to be sustained *regardless* of whether or not the leaders broke faith with the rank and file. This may seem tautological: by defintion, don't leaders have such power? But in fact in the kinds of events being discussed—mass protests, student demonstrations, ghetto riots, and the like—leaders often have very little power of any kind and no independent power at all. In a number of student demonstrations, for example, it has been clear that leaders were little more than discussion leaders and regardless of their private intentions could do nothing more than lead in precisely the directions the rank and file wanted to go. (See the subsequent discussion of the Free Speech Movement at Berkeley, for an example.) The same can be said of the general powerlessness of leaders of the Peace Movement as the Skolnick Report has so convincingly shown.[7] In such situations a group of conspirators may seize formal leadership only to find they are powerless to carry out their aims. Their private motives thus become irrelevant to an explanation of what occurred. That they *could not* break faith with their followers is adequate to disqualify the event as the product of a conspiracy.

Having clarified the prime feature of conspiracy interpretations, it is now possible to assess the grounds on which the police perceive many group actions as stemming from a deception of followers by their leaders.

In my judgment the fallacious use of three main "proofs" are responsible for police misjudgments of natural events as conspiracies:

1. The mere existence of resourceful leadership and effective organization frequently strikes the police as unnatural and a sure sign that outside—and thus conspiratorial—leaders are in control of events. The police have been especially prone to such judgments of campus disturbances and of political demonstrations and protests. But contrasting police perceptions and reports with those of highly competent commissions and special inquiries suggests that not only is this police judgment of conspiracy nearly always unfounded, but that it seems to stem from an ignorance of student and middle-class culture and an inability to comprehend the extent to which high intelligence can be a substitute for experience and instruction.

A classic instance of such police misperceptions appears in police discussions of the Free Speech Movement at Berkeley during 1964, especially in the lengthy analysis published in the influential *The Police Chief*.[8] In fact this article dwells on repeated signs of conspiracy in the practicality and efficiency of student activities, obviously the work of "well-coached leaders." "The initial phases of the student revolt were blueprinted with some finesse . . . ;[at a later stage] the FSM was ready to move with a smoothness and strategy that would do veteran politicians justice."[9] The authors quoted with approval a letter to a local newspaper which stated: "The handiwork of professionals is everywhere in evidence—information booths, buttons, machine-printed signs, bull horns, walkie-talkies. . . . Can this be the spontaneous rebellion of downtrodden students?"[10]

The article reported other ominous clues. During a sit-in: "From some unknown larder there came hundreds of loaves of bread with peanut butter, cheese, and salami from which sandwiches were made . . ."[11]

Rather than representing either a miracle equal to that of the loaves and fishes, or evidence of conspiracy, the unknown larder was simply the nearest supermarket. Students know how to find such places. The rest of the ominous signs turn out to be equally banal. The walkie-talkies were from a local toy store and were as much a put-on as they were a communications network. Buttons are a major Berkeley industry. The use of commercial printers is not unknown to students. To speak of student leaders acting with the finesse of veteran politicians overlooks the obvious fact that campus leaders *are* veteran politicians. They have served apprenticeships on countless committees and boards in countless organizations. In less turbulent times this was called training for democracy. As will be discussed later in this chapter, many investigations of the FSM at Berkeley failed to find any outside direction. In general the police were confounded by student (and faculty) competence because they failed to understand the extraordinary resources of a world-famous university. The student protest, which eventually mobilized the majority of undergraduate and graduate students and aroused considerable sympathy from the faculty, not only had easy access to the organizational and leadership abilities pointed out by the police, it also had on call persons versed in Sanscrit, matrix algebra, molecular biology, and the construction of nuclear weapons. Recruitment and training of intelligence is what universities are all about.

Furthermore, the police overlooked a very critical feature of leadership in the FSM and have continued to do so in subsequent student disturbances and in evaluating the peace movement—*the very limited amount of power leaders had over the rank and file.*

In the case of the FSM, the conflict extended over a number of months. Throughout, the leaders summoned student support. But their appeals were only heeded, and the FSM was only a viable protest movement, *intermittently.* Sometimes the students rallied by the thousands, at other times the leadership found its base shrunken to no more than several hundred. At these nadir points the leaders were unable to accomplish anything significant: on their own they were powerless. Several times the FSM was dead, despite calls from the leadership that important negotiations remained to be accomplished. Renewal of mass support for the FSM after each of these pauses was not the work of the leadership, but *only* occurred when the school administration took actions which rejuvenated mass student feelings of betrayal or inequity. The leadership remained constant in its calls for support, but the students gave, withdrew, and renewed their support independently, based on the issues. Clearly, then, the leaders could not foment student protest on their own. Whatever the intentions or political designs of many FSM leaders, they never had the power to manufacture the protest movement or even greatly influence its course. The FSM leaders were only permitted to lead when they accurately reflected the views of the mass of students. When they did not, their support evaporated. They were not free to conspire to any effect.

In an earlier study I found that such constraint on campus leaders is typical rather than occasional.[12] Students seem highly aware of issues and they support or desert the cause accordingly. Whether student positions on issues are "correct" is beside the point. They act on their positions, not on the appeals of agitators.

Similar findings on the role of leadership in the peace movement were reported in the Skolnick Report to the National Commission on the Causes and Prevention of Violence. The authors of this chapter of the Skolnick report concluded:

It is only a small exaggeration to say that the role of organizational leadership in the [peace] movement is restricted to applying for permits, holding press conferences, announcing the time and place of demonstrations, and mailing appeals for funds.[13]

Their data suggested that citizen turnout and response to the calls of leadership were almost entirely shaped by events in Vietnam and Washington which lay wholly beyond the influence of movement leaders. Response rose and fell independent of the actions of the leaders.

A major flaw in the police understanding of events seems to come down to an inability to imagine that collective behavior can occur without being planned and led. Somehow they conceive of people as sheep and that whatever people do is in response to some authority—someone *must be* telling them what to do, when, and how. Consequently, police analyses and evaluations of civil disturbances nearly always lay great stress on outside agitators who are responsible for starting and directing riots. Yet in riot after riot the police have not been able to catch any of these agitators or even determine who they are. If that were not frustrating enough, the police find that august groups such as the Kerner Commission and the Violence Commission deny that riots are the work of outside agitators. The police seem to find it incredible that riots can just happen without a "blueprint," or "the guiding hand of communists and extreme leftists,"[14] or some kind of conscious direction.

Los Angeles Police Chief Edward M. Davis provided a vivid example of such police thinking during a 1970 student demonstration at UCLA. While circling above the campus in a helicopter with right-wing newscaster George Putnam, the chief detected the plan behind the event.

Putnam asked: "Would you say that this is the second day of the planned revolution to take over the United States of America? Is it that serious?"

Davis replied: "I think it certainly is. I think the whole thing is in the Bible...."[15]

2. The second faulty proof the police rely on to demonstrate that certain events are conspiracies rests on detecting the presence of potential conspirators—radicals, leftists, agitators, or outsiders of various kinds—without inspecting the actual power of such persons to influence events and without showing that they in any way deceived the rank and file.

Often the police fall into the most uncritical and disreputable practices of guilt-by-association to establish the existence of a conspiracy behind events. In the case of the FSM, police lists of the "swarm of sympathizers" which help establish its "insidious nature" included such pillars of the civil rights movement as James Farmer, Bayard Rustin, and James Baldwin.

Others were characterized as persons who had once picketed the House Un-American Activities Committee, and a young man who had refused to sign the loyalty oath required of students enrolled in ROTC.[16] In subsequent student protests and peace demonstrations, finding leftists and subversives has been a major police activity.

Chief Davis of Los Angeles has for the past year waged a campaign to convince his city that all unrest in the black and chicano communities is a product of communist conspiracy. The chicanos, Davis claims, are being exploited by "sophisticated bolsheviks" as "prison fodder." During a chicano peace demonstration in 1970 Davis had his men photograph several old leftists who were in the crowd. He then mailed them to all the local papers with the statement that these were the communists who were causing all the trouble. When the pictures and his charges were mainly ignored, Davis complained "The goddam editors didn't want them printed." He believes the press is "inflaming the American people with yellow journalism."[17]

Sometimes the police are at least correct in identifying persons present during protests and demonstrations as leftists or Marxists. But they are typically incorrect when they infer from this that such radicals are in control of what occurs. Many policemen and newsmen are also drawn to such events. No one assumes that they are the conspirators. The police are encouraged to blame radicals for events because radicals often claim to be responsible for demonstrations in which they have played no significant role; it is much to their benefit to receive the credit. As will be discussed later, the police often perform as the primary "red dupes" by authenticating the fraudulent claims of radicals to power and foresight which they do not have.

A great many investigations of student protests have found the students bitter because radicals have been credited with the work others have done. In fact, at a New York press conference during the height of the Berkeley FSM, student leader Mario Savio expressed the bitterness he felt because "the Communist Party is getting so much credit for what [the students] have done themselves."[18]

Unwittingly, to what extent have the police enhanced the role of radicals in these events? Similarly, in countless recent protest demonstrations across the country when the police have violently treated moderate citizens as if they were bomb-throwing revolutionaries, how many bomb-throwing revolutionaries have they created? As recent events have tragically shown—quite a few.

3. The police are frequently misled into imputing an underlying conspiracy to events on the basis of similarities in tactics and expressed grievances in a number of scattered places and situations and when there has been communication among leaders of various events.

The fact that the FSM at Berkeley was the start of a rash of student protests across the country is used as retrospective proof by the police that a conspiracy is behind it all. How else, they argue, can we account for the fact that on so many different campuses remarkably similar tactics and grievances are manifested by students? Similarly, the police point to the similarities among ghetto riots and ask, if they aren't plotted by a nest of conspirators, why are they so similar? The same is said of peace demonstrations and other political protests.

There can be no question that there has been considerable

contact among student protesters from many campuses, if only because students frequently change schools. But there is little evidence that the spread of student protest has been essentially the work of some campus version of typhoid Marys carrying alien germs from place to place and manufacturing unnatural student protest movements, or at least not movements attracting significant mass support. (The several examples which most closely fit this police model, including the famous Tommy the Traveler, turned out to be paid police agents, which is carrying self-fulfilling prophesy to an absurd extreme.)

One could argue that the communication among student dissidents itself constitutes a conspiracy. But one still must show that such a conspiracy was effective and instrumental in producing subsequent "unnatural" episodes. Furthermore, the conspiracy theory seems needlessly unparsimonious. Students everywhere know the details of what happened at Berkeley—after all, the television devoted enormous news coverage to it—and at other campuses as well. Student newspapers and books popular among students have articulated general grievances against the modern college experience as well as other aspects of contemporary society. Similarly, tactical information has been widely disseminated. Students share not only these opinions and information, but similar circumstances: most schools suffer from similar defects and lack of relevance to which students object. For similar events to occur widely and to follow a recognizable pattern thus seems quite ordinary. Much less admirably motivated movements, such as panty raids, have spread through the student subculture in the past without producing conspiracy theories. People sharing similar circumstances and with a similar culture will often follow similar courses of action. That is not to say that the events at Berkeley did not inspire many students at many campuses to similar attempts to organize a protest movement. Many of these undoubtedly fizzled for lack of mass concern or through mismanagement. Others gained widespread student support. The important point seems to be that such events seem to require essentially natural sources to occur at all.

The same can be said of minority protest and civil disturbances. Issues and circumstances are not mainly idiosyncratic to particular communities. The grievances of blacks, chicanos, and other minorities are relatively constant from one community to the next. So are the available alternatives. Furthermore, the articulation of grievances and the demands for justice are widely shared. If nothing else, the mass media offer sufficient means for transmitting a common understanding of issues and tactics. It would be very odd if events differed significantly from one city to another.

Obviously if one followed the line of police reasoning one could as easily characterize the various police protests and strikes as the work of a conspiracy. The issues, tactics and rhetoric are pretty much the same in San Francisco and Los Angeles as in New York and Boston.

Finally, it is obvious that if communist conspirators were even 10 percent as powerful and clever as police literature claims them to be they would have taken over the nation years ago instead of skulking on the edges of protests and demonstrations carrying their banal picket signs.

The susceptibility of the police to inaccurate conspiracy explanations of natural events has a great number of unfortunate consequences. As has been discussed in earlier chapters, belief in conspiracies markedly affects police tactics in ways that often prove disasterous. For example, as pointed out in Chapter 1, the misconception by Los Angeles police officials that the peace movement represented only a few noisy radicals caused them to make preparations for a much smaller crowd than actually appeared in the Century Plaza march and this played a major role in subsequent police violence. Similarly, a number of investigators have concluded that police violence during the Columbia University crisis partly resulted from the police belief that there were many fewer students inside the administration building than there were. In surprise, the police resorted to violence. In similar fashion, police tactics to "get" the leaders of protests, demonstrations, or militant groups often result in greatly increasing the size of the original group rather than removing the active agents thought to be behind the events. Indeed, the ability of the rank and file to produce new leaders to replace the old seems *prima facie* evidence of the absence of a conspiracy.

Police belief in conspiracies also has had ideological consequences. Only among right-wingers can the police find political spokesmen who broadly support their views of conspiracy. In my judgment this makes the police especially susceptible to right-wing views in general, while exposure to right wing material further increases their belief in conspiracy and their sense of being an embattled group of true Americans isolated from the political and intellectual establishment.

The Police Mentality: A Profile

Many aspects of the police outlook or mentality have already been discussed. Evidence has been presented that the police are predominantly prejudiced against minority groups, especially blacks, and against political and campus protestors and nonconformists generally. Chapter 6 will show that they are also antagonistic towards the political and cultural establishment. Rather than merely being the tools of a repressive establishment as many radicals have charged, the police condemn and often defy efforts by the establishment to restrain them. Much police repression is done on their own behalf. Indeed, the majority of American policemen feel estranged from the general citizenry. They feel the public does not respect them, support them, or like them.[19] They believe the media are out to get them.[20]

Furthermore, the police believe that society stands on the brink of disaster which only tough police action can hold back. According to the *New York Times* some policemen in Cleveland recently were advocating a "takeover by the military" because civilian rule had failed.[21]

Based on their free-will conceptions of man, the police tend to be economic conservatives (except on police pay and benefits). On religion, it is clear that the police are predominantly conservative too, be they Roman Catholics or Protestants. This does not necessarily mean that the police are unusually active in religious institutions or ardent in their faith. It does mean that their religious preferences are orhodox and traditional regardless of the intensity of their commitment. There are no systematic survey data to support this generalization, but many signs point to it. Activities such as prayer breakfasts are more common among the police than among members of most similar occupations. Police textbooks, magazines, and journals contain a relatively large amount of religious inspirational material, which is not true of the publications for such professions as social work or teaching.

These generalizations add up to a portrait of the police as

right-wingers. In the remainder of this section I try to assess the validity of such a characterization.

There is no disagreement among observers of the police or even among police spokesmen that the American police are overwhelmingly to the right of center of the political spectrum. The question is how far right. Are the police predominantly conservatives, mainly falling within the Nixon-to-Goldwater portion of the political spectrum, or are they predominately right-wing extremists of the George Wallace, John Birch Society, Ku Klux Klan variety?

Without doubt there is a sizable number of right-wing extremists among the police. Spokesmen for the John Birch Society have often claimed large numbers of their members were law enforcement officers. Society spokesmen are reluctant to state actual figures, but several years ago estimates of 500 in New York City and several thousand in Southern California alone were claimed.[22] In 1964 a Newark patrolman was granted a three-month leave of absence to do coordinating work for the Birch Society.[23] In 1965 a New Jersey state patrolman resigned to take a job with the Society.[24] Subsequently, there have been short-lived furors in a number of cities, from Los Angeles to Philadelphia, over the activities of Birch police cells. John Harrington, President of the Fraternal Order of Police, has said he admires the anticommunism of the John Birch Society and would join it if he had time: "A lot of Catholic priests are members, and I figure they know what they're doing."[25]

The widespread membership of Southern lawmen in the Ku Klux Klan is well known. But Klan views have some general appeal for Northern policemen as well. In 1967 a Klan group was uncovered within the Chicago police department.[26]

The 1968 campaign by George Wallace and his American Independent Party brought momentary unity among feuding right-wing groups as well as bringing the Southern Klansmen into a common cause with the Northern ultraconservative. Estimates in the news media—by experts on the police and by policemen themselves—were that a majority of the nation's policemen were solidly behind George Wallace.

Task Force interviews with police commanders and police union officials in a number of cities revealed unanimous belief that "most of the guys in this department are with Wallace a hundred percent."[27] Policemen in Syracuse, New York, told a *New York Times* reporter that the great majority of officers in that department would vote for Wallace, because, as one officer put it, "Wallace is saying the things in public that we'd like to say and can't."[28] What they wanted said, judging by their reported remarks, was condemnation of civil rights and poverty programs. One officer said, "If we got back to nightsticks more often it would help. It was okay when we started to give the Negro an even break. Now they're taking advantage of it. . . . If it was up to me, I'd stop everything being done for them."

Despite the widespread belief of experts and of the police themselves that Wallace was the favorite of most policemen, I remained skeptical. Having long worked with survey research findings, I am accustomed to experts being quite wrong when they try to judge distributions of beliefs and attitudes among large numbers of persons. Indeed, if this were not frequently the case, no one would spend the substantial sums required to conduct large-scale surveys or public opinion polls. Furthermore, it has been found that when some portion of a population, even a minority, holds its views militantly enough, those opposed to them, because they remain silent, often substantially underestimate the numbers on their side. For example, it has been found that Southerners considerably overestimate the proportion of persons in their community who oppose integration. Having been told privately by several officers in the same department that each was the only liberal in the department I grew suspicious of images of the monolithic police support for Wallace, and consequently of their right wing extremism in general. No large-scale poll of police political and social beliefs has been conducted, although undoubtedly such a study would be of immense value and probably would shatter a number of widespread impressions about the police, including some I have used in this study. Nevertheless, the findings of a small survey of policemen in two midwestern communities do support my suspicions about Wallace support among the police and provide a better basis for characterization than unsystematic impressions.

Interviews with a randomly chosen sample of policemen in these two communities, conducted by James Leo Walsh,[29] yielded the following voting distributions for the 1968 election:

Richard M. Nixon	39%
George C. Wallace	35
Hubert H. Humphrey	26
	100%

(N = 78)

Far from carrying the majority of police votes in this sample, George Wallace did not even receive a plurality, but ran second to Richard Nixon. It is possible, of course, that policemen in these two communities are not as right-wing as policemen elsewhere. Nevertheless, it seems extremely important that these same policemen, the sum of whose own votes gave Wallace barely more than a third, *believed that the majority of officers in their departments were supporting Wallace!*

What seems obvious is that the prevailing climate of opinion in police circles is dominated by militant right-wing views. While on some measures, such as voting, this climate of opinion does not reflect majority sentiments, it is not entirely sustained merely by the clamor of the right-wing minority being mistaken for the majority view. It is further sustained because on some issues the overwhelming majority do accept the right-wing view. This is especially true on law and order issues. Policemen in this same sample were asked "Whose fault is it that certain ethnic and economic groups receive inadequate or second-rate treatment under the law?" Forty-two percent said it was because "these people are just too lazy" while an additional 23 percent rejected the premise of the question and claimed such people actually "get better treatment than they deserve." Clearly, this is Wallace talk. And thus the majority of policemen may have admired Wallace for his stand on law and order issues. This widespread approval seems to have been interpreted by many as full-fledged support. But when the time came, many of these policemen, and probably many policemen elsewhere, were unwilling to vote for Wallace.

Nevertheless, these data strongly support the impressions of many police observers that the majority of the police are at least conservative. If Nixon voters are added to those who backed Wallace, then 74 percent of the policemen in this sample could be classified as at least somewhat on the conservative side. Furthermore, simply that one-fourth of them voted for Humphrey does not necessarily mean that one-fourth of these policemen are liberals. Given the working-class origins of policemen, the traditional Democratic voting patterns of the working class and the fact that working-class Democrats are often very illiberal on non-economic issues, these Humphrey-voting policemen may be mainly conservative Democrats. In any event it is clear that the political climate among the police, as perceived by individual policemen, is strongly right-wing. Furthermore, although this climate may be sustained by a minority on some issues, on others a substantial majority accept right-wing positions. This climate is also supported because those policemen who are not sufficiently right-wing, for example, to vote for Wallace are predominantly quite conservative. Finally, even if these voting data suggest that right-wing extremists are in the minority among the police, one-third is still a very substantial minority. Judging from the reported instances of police political activism it seems likely that this right-wing minority is substantially more politically active and outspoken than the less extreme majority. On these grounds the American police, if not necessarily the American policeman, can be characterized as right-wing. I shall now try to explain why this is the case.

II. Sources of Police Ideology

Why do the police believe the things they do? Where do they get their ideas, and why do they find them convincing? The first of these questions has to do with who tells the police what, and on what authority. The second with what kinds of people policemen are, what kinds of education and training they have had, and the kinds of problems they must confront.

The Indoctrination of the Police

It is, of course, obvious that acceptance of many of the dubious theories concerning crime causation, of the false application of conspiracy explanations to naturalistic events, and conservative political, religious, and social values is not restricted to the police. A great many Americans share these views, and they are frequently enunciated from the pulpit, in the press, and from the political platform. The general prevalence of such beliefs is probably a major source of police acceptance of them because, as I shall discuss in the next section, the police are not recruited from among the more educated or enlightened members of society. However, although the police are predisposed to accept such views through the same cultural processes that lead many other Americans to accept them, the fact remains that the police have received special and prestigious indoctrination into the correctness of these dubious beliefs. Literature prepared solely for policemen stridently proclaims these notions as certainties. Widely respected police spokesmen reaffirm their faith in them. Perhaps most influential and most unfortunate is the role played by the FBI, especially by its famous and revered director, J. Edgar Hoover, in lending the full weight of his expertise, prestige, and nation-wide publicity facilities to dubious theories and right-wing points of view. Indeed, the FBI has often used the imposing credibility of its "secret" information to convince the police as well as the public of dubious theories of criminality and ill-founded assertions of communist conspiracies.

In his testimony before the National Violence Commission on September 18, 1968, J. Edgar Hoover flatly asserted:

> Communists are in the forefront of civil rights, anti-war, and student demonstrations, many of which become disorderly and erupt into violence. As an example, Bettina Aptheker Kurzweil, twenty-four-year-old member of the Communist National Committee, was a leading organizer of the "Free Speech" demonstrations on the campus of the University of California at Berkeley in the fall of 1964.
>
> These protests, culminating in the arrest of more than 800 demonstrators during a massive campus sit-in, on December 3, 1964, were the forerunner of the current campus upheaval.
>
> In a press conference on July 4, 1968, the opening day of the Communist Party's Special National Convention, Gus Hall, the Party's General Secretary, stated that there were communists on most of the major college campuses in the country, and that they had been involved in the student protests.[30]

Thus, according to Hoover, the whole spread of student protests, and specifically the FSM, was initiated and managed by the Communist Party (as are peace and civil rights protests).

Hoover thus puts the credibility of his glamorous organization behind a conspiracy explanation of the Berkeley Free Speech movement. On what grounds? The word of Gus Hall, the nation's number one communist! In so doing, Hoover rejects the results of careful investigations by some impeccably respectable and competent loyal Americans. Of the dozens of studies and reports written by responsible scholars, none ascribes the motivation or the management of the FSM to the Communist Party, or even to extreme radicals. Furthermore, a committee was appointed by the Regents of the University of California to fully investigate the FSM. Many members of the committee, made up of prominent citizens, were well known for their conservative views. Attorney Jerome C. Byrne was appointed special counsel to the committee. He conducted an intensive and careful investigation of the FSM (at the time students were very suspicious that his report would be badly biased against them). On the question of communist influence the Byrne report, issued by the blue-ribbon committee, stated:

We found no evidence that the FSM was organized by the Communist Party, the Progressive Labor Movement, or any other outside group. Despite a number of suggestive coincidences, the evidence which we accumulated left us with no doubt that the Free Speech Movement was a response to the September 14th change in rules regarding political activity at Bancroft and Telegraph, not a pre-planned effort to embarrass or destroy the University on whatever pretext arose.[31]

Despite the fact that the best and most complete investigation rejected the communist conspiracy theory, Hoover continues to advocate it on the basis of Hall's claims.

Similarly, Hoover has denounced subsequent student protests —especially the one led by the SDS at Columbia—as communist-inspired. He stated before the Violence Commission that:

The Students for a Democratic Society has been described by Gus Hall, General Secretary of the Communist Party of the United States of America, as part of the "responsible left" which the Communist Party has "going for us."[32]

Yet, the committee which investigated the Columbia disturbances, headed by Archibald Cox, former Solicitor General of the

United States, reported: "We reject the view that ascribes the April and May disturbances primarily to a conspiracy of student revolutionaries."[33]

But, again, Hoover rejects the judgment of Archibald Cox and his colleagues, and the fruits of their months-long investigation, to offer instead the "Truth" according to Gus Hall. No prominent or responsible spokesman in American life, aside from Hoover, puts so much blind faith in the pronouncements of Gus Hall. As mentioned earlier, to take credit for such events is extraordinarily to the advantage of the Communist Party. If all these moral causes are theirs, and theirs alone, then persons who support such causes may be led to reevaluate their negative judgments of the Communist Party and perhaps embrace it. Unless one has more faith in the word of Gus Hall than in that of sober, responsible, and informed citizens, one must conclude that J. Edgar Hoover may function as the number one "Red dupe" in America. Certainly he is the number one source of dubious conspiracy and communist infiltration notions in America.

Such a statement may seem outrageous. How can it be justified? The answer lies both in what Hoover says and what he does. Among his functions is that of being the number one spokesman for law enforcement in American society; his is the authoritative voice. And his voice is heard by all American policemen. Even if Hoover's words were not typically widely publicized by the news media, the relationship between the FBI and local law enforcement departments would be adequate to carry the message. The FBI conducts countless seminars and briefings and trains local policemen. Hoover gave the Violence Commission a summary of these activities in his testimony on September 18, 1968:

> To implement a program along this line [education of local police], the FBI has long furnished instructors and conducted police schools throughout the United States in cooperation with local police agencies. The Omnibus Crime Control and Safe Streets Act of 1968 authorized the FBI to assist in conducting local and regional training programs for state and local law enforcement personnel when requested to do so by a State or a unit of local government, and Congress has appropriated $3 million for this purpose. The FBI's training assistance will be materially increased with the construction of our new academy complex at Quantico, Virginia, a facility that will enable us to train approximately 3,000 police officers annually.[34]

It is not my intention to fault Hoover or the FBI for conducting training programs. Indeed, only through such means does it seem possible to raise the level of professionalization and general competence of the American police But whether such a program accomplishes these worthy ends depends very much on the *substance of what is taught*. And what is being taught is in many instances dubious at best and false and even incendiary at worst. Through the FBI program the American police have been convinced—if they ever doubted it—that student protest is communist-inspired, as are civil rights and peace demonstrations.

Consider Hoover's testimony to the Violence Commission in response to Chairman Eisenhower's question:

Dr. Eisenhower: There is one situation that has not been mentioned either by you or by the Attorney General; whether people are right or wrong, there is an enormous number of individuals in this country who feel strongly that the Vietnam War is not justified. This has led to vast protests and these protest movements have been infiltrated by the kind of people that you have discussed with us.

Would it be your judgment that when the Vietnam War is concluded, that the situation in the field of violence, violent crime, mob violence, would greatly diminish?

Mr. Hoover: No, it would not be, because they would find something else to agitate about and to pass propaganda upon.

The present activities against the war in Vietnam that has been carried on in this country has largely originated in Hanoi, to which some of these very people who participated in the agitation in Chicago had visited and had conferred in Hanoi, North Vietnam.

Also, Red China has been very active in advancing the criticism of this country in regard to Vietnam. So my feeling is that if the Vietnam War was ended, through peaceful negotiations or otherwise, that we would again find something that would be agitated about.

For instance, they will agitate in regard to housing. Now there is an area—housing should be improved. A great deal has been done, but not sufficient. But none of these things we talked about that are necessary can be done overnight. It takes a little time to do it. But I think—and I think that's the thought of the very informed Negro leaders—that it is something that you've got to be moderate in doing, but don't wait and drag your feet in doing it. I think that is the picture with regard to any issue that might be raised if the Vietnam issue was eliminated.[35]

The peace demonstrations are directed from Hanoi and from Red China, according to Hoover's testimony. And should the war end, the protestors will turn to something else, he presumes, probably the civil rights movement. In Hoover's eyes all protest is one: a symptom of communist-led agitation to destroy America.

When Judge A. Leon Higginbotham of the Commission asked Hoover if perhaps the present prominence of militant black leaders such as Stokely Carmichael and H. Rap Brown could not be partly explained by the fact that progress in such areas as housing, education, and justice has not been fast enough over the past eight years, Hoover gave the following answer:

Mr. Hoover: I think we have made great progress. We need to make a great deal more. I think it is imperative that the Negro, himself, be proud of the progress he has already made, of the position he has already been able to attain, of the opportunities that have already been afforded him.

But many more should be, of course, afforded him, the problem in regard to joining labor unions and things of that kind which ought to be corrected.

I think they ought to have the same opportunity that anyone of any color has.

But I think they also should show pride for what they have done. They have some great leaders.

In the history of the Negro movement, men who contributed tremendously.

George Washington Carver was one of the leaders, that I knew. Little is ever said about him, or I believe ever taught about, in our schools.

I think there should be more of that, the people of which the colored race could be very, very proud.

At the same time, improve the conditions which exist today, which are deplorable in many areas of the country, so they could not have just cause for criticism of that.[36]

Both Hoover's choice of words and his ideas are remarkably dated, clearly belonging to the era when attitudes towards "the colored" were expressed in such sentiments as: "Joe Louis is a real credit to his race." Perhaps this is not surprising for a man in his middle 70s, but it seems tragic for the director of the federal agency most responsible for civil rights investigations. Furthermore, it is this man who heavily influences police as well as public opinion on such questions as black militancy and political dissent. It is by now public knowledge that the FBI maintained a tap on the telephone of Dr. Martin Luther King for some years until his assassination. And it is an open secret that for months prior to the assassination FBI agents conducted briefings of local police officials across the nation during which they linked Martin Luther King with communism. When the media deplored the climate of hatred as a major contributor of King's death, they could well have indicted the FBI for contributing to that climate.

Finally, let us consider Hoover's worth as a prophet. The following quotations are taken from a report on black militance and radicalism prepared by J. Edgar Hoover for the United States Attorney General:

> [There can] no longer be any question of a well-concerted movement among a certain class of Negro leaders of thought and action to constitute themselves a determined and persistent source of radical opposition to the Government, and to the established rule of law and order.
> [He accused these Negro leaders of increasing] insubordination [and of] the utterance of inflammatory sentiment—utterances which in some cases have reached the limit of open defiance and a counsel of retaliation.
> [He charged that the key points in this defiance were] ill-governed reaction toward race rioting; [their] threat of retaliatory measures in connection with lynching; [and their] identification of the Negro with ... radical organizations ... and an outspoken advocacy of the Bolsheviki or Soviet doctrines.
> [Behind all this, Hoover reported, lay an] increasingly emphasized feeling of race consciousness ... openly, defiantly, assertive of its own equality....[37]

These were Hoover's warnings in 1919! His targets, the insubordinate radicals whom he condemned, were none other than the NAACP, the Urban League, and spokesmen such as A. Philip Randolph!

It would be unfair to put all the blame for dubious police theories and right-wing attitudes on J. Edgar Hoover or the FBI. Although it would be hard to underestimate the impact on the police of Hoover and FBI pronouncements, theirs are only the lead voices of the chorus. Police literature, as indicated in the earlier excerpts from *The Police Chief* and from Fraternal Order of Police publications, is, if anything, less enlightened and restrained in its embrace of moral decay, free will, crime crisis, and conspiracy assertions. This is true of the best and most responsible publications aimed at the police! In addition, there is a whole spate of lesser police periodicals which can only be described as shrilly right-wing extremist. One of these, a slick magazine named *Law and Order,* is under the editorial direction of W. Cleon Skousen, a regular lecturer for Fred C. Schwarz's right-wing Christian Anti-Communist Crusade and for the John Birch Society. Skousen can legitimately be called a veteran right-wing agitator, and the magazine reflects this. Consider the following excerpts from a Skousen editorial:

> Recently, I picked up an old magazine for January, 1960. It was filled with hopes and possibilities of the "fabulous 'sixties'." What went wrong?
> First, we heard about a "new" morality. It turned out to be a campaign against morality. We heard about a "new" religion. This religion turned out to be a campaign proclaiming God is dead. We heard of a new, militant but nonviolent program to achieve civil rights and equality. The next thing we knew the country was engulfed in a whirlwind of burning, bombing, looting, and violence greater than anything the United States had witnessed since the draft riots of the Civil War.
> ... We heard about a new Free Speech movement and soon found ourselves wading in the slop of hard-core obscenity and a flood of four-letter gutter words. We heard about a movement for the "free" university, then discovered that its advocates wanted a free rein to plunge youth into every conceivable form of human depravity, drug addiction, perversion and intellectual emasculation.
> We were told by certain people that the only threat from communism was "external," and then discovered these same people busily disarming the United States and wooing Communist bosses by selling them practically everything forbidden by the Strategic Material Embargo Act.
> A half-million American youth were shipped to Asia and commanded to fight Communist aggression in Vietnam while a hard core of five men on the Supreme Court proclaimed that it was all right for identified Communists to work in U. S. defense plants, teach in American schools and boss American labor unions.
> What has been happening in this country? Why are we floundering in this miasma of credibility gaps, protracted ideological confusion, institutionalized filth, judicially pampered crime, legalized subversion and politically touted violence?
> Somebody has been tampering with the soul of America. To go forward, we have to go back. We are off the track.
>
> W. Cleon Skousen[38]

Here is fully articulated the apocalyptic outlook which has been creating fear and militance among the American police. Society is in the last stages of a trip to hell and depravity. "Someone" has been "tampering" with religion and morality. The "hard core" in the Supreme Court have been selling us out to the communists. Youth is riddled with depravity, perversion, subversion, and immorality, and so on. All of the elements in this vision of impending social breakdown are spelled out monthly at length in *Law and Order* articles. The subversion and conspiracy behind black protest and anti-war demonstrations are revealed. The courts are continually lambasted.

But in addition to magazines such as *Law and Order,* which have a national circulation, the police are bombarded with conspiracy and moral decay charges by a number of locally-produced publications. A prominent example of these is *FI-PO NEWS,* published by the Fire and Police Research Association of Los Angeles. This periodical is a classic of right-wing extremist writing. It concentrates on finding communists everywhere and revealing all under the masthead doctrine: "What you believe depends largely upon what you believe in!" A major editorial preoccupation is to reveal that various legislators or congressmen have opposed bills favored by FI-PO and to list all the "subversive" groups that also oppose the bill. The attempt at guilt by association is not meant to be subtle. It is an article of faith among FI-PO writers that the American Civil Liberties Union is a communist organization and thus they have a field day identifying persons who attend ACLU meetings. In fact, as will be mentioned in the next chapter, this is a common police belief about the ACLU. Los Angeles Police Chief Davis spoke for many police leaders when he said recently about the ACLU, "I'm not saying they're communists, but I've noticed that when the Communist Party takes a deep breath, the ACLU's chest goes out."[39]

Similar examples could be extended almost indefinitely. But besides official or semiofficial police literature, the police have been for some years subject to considerable proselytizing from right-wing organizations. The John Birch Society's "Support Your Local Police" campaign has been designed to attract police membership. As mentioned earlier, there is considerable evidence that the John Birch Society has successfully recruited a number of policemen in most major cities. In addition, police have been courted by Fred C. Schwarz's anti-communism schools, which are the major activity of his touring crusade. Prearrival promotion advertises special rates for policemen who would like to attend the sessions and in many cities such as Oakland and Los Angeles, police have received considerable departmental encouragement to attend. This massive campaign to bring the right-wing message to the police has not been countered by any major effort by other sectors of the political spectrum. The right wing has been free to operate unopposed. Furthermore, the police find the line taken by right-wing groups fully compatible with the interpretations offered by their own periodicals and such leading police spokesmen as J. Edgar Hoover and the late William Parker of Los Angeles. In the light of the extent to which the police have been proselytized, it would be surprising if they had not embraced a fairly right-wing ideology in recent years. Much of the blame rests with the whole of American society for neglecting the police, for providing no educational or informational programs for the police other than those of the right.

Recruitment and Experience

The police are also inclined to accept right-wing views, including conspiracy and faculty theories of criminality, because of their social origins, and because of the nature of police work itself.

There are a number of extremely important characteristics to recognize about today's police recruits:

They are poorly educated.[40] For the nation as a whole, more than half of high school graduates enter college, and for Northern city-dwellers the proportion is much higher—80 percent of California high school graduates begin college, for example. In virtually all occupations the average educational attainment of new members is rising. Among the police it has been steadily declining. The overwhelming proportion of American policemen have no college credits. Indeed, many were high school drop-outs who qualified as high school graduates through armed services-administered equivalency examinations.

They come from blue-collar homes and are of non-WASP ethnic origins[41] (although in the Far West many policemen are from the South).

They are young; most departments will not accept candidates over the age of 29 and a large proportion of American policemen are under 30.

They became policemen because it was the best-paying job they could get. For most recruits in most cities their occupational alternatives to law enforcement were of considerably lower pay and prestige. Those who later can find better jobs typically resign, thus further exacerbating the fact of initial selection from the bottom of the labor pool.

In combination these characteristics of police recruits play a considerable role in sustaining the police mentality.

In the Introduction I dismissed theories blaming the police mentality on the psychopathology of police recruits. Clearly, the police are not disproportionately psychologically abnormal. Instead, I believe the evidence suggests it is the *normality* of the police—that they are quite typical of the social strata from which they come—that plays a significant role in sustaining the police mentality. To a considerable extent the outlook held by policemen is also held by nonpolicemen of similar backgrounds.

The police are from lower-middle and blue-collar origins. A number of studies have shown that these strata of Americans are relatively hostile to civil rights and civil liberties,[42] as are the police. A recent *Newsweek* poll of "middle Americans" found that two-thirds believed the "police should have more power"; 85 percent thought "Black militants have been treated too leniently," and a similar proportion thought this was also true for college demonstrators.[43] Police sentiments on such issues, then, are congruent with prevailing views among white Americans of similar backgrounds.

Similarly, views which are current among the police are characteristic of Americans with limited educations. A recent study by Gertrude Jaeger Selznick and Stephen Steinberg has shown that the very strong negative relationships between education and various kinds of prejudice and anti-democratic views seem to be accounted for by the fact that the education process exposes people to more enlightened and tolerant views.[44] Lacking this exposure, the less educated cling to traditional prejudices and fears. Furthermore, Selznick and Steinberg's findings suggest that little education is partly the reason the police are so prone to conspiracy explanations of events. Agreement with items such as "Much of our lives are controlled by plots hatched in secret places" was heavily concentrated among the less educated.

Thus the bigotry, anger, anti-libertarian, and pro-conspiracy views of the police are normal in the sense of being common among people of similarly limited backgrounds (perhaps what is abnormal is that we hire such important professionals from this sector of society, a practice we do not follow in selecting teachers, social workers, sanitation engineers, and other public-service professionals).

Furthermore, the police are young. In the din of talk about the generation gap, an enormously important fact has been overlooked. Among whites, the greatest "gap" is not between old and young, but between *the young who have been or are in college and the noncollege young.*[45] On such matters as peace, race, police power, and the like, educational differences among the young disclose much greater polarization than between young people as a whole and their elders. Where young people do not differ is in their dissent from present social arrangements and in their willingness to resort to militant tactics. But while the college-educated young people seek liberal and radical reforms, the young noncollege people have turned increasingly to right wing, traditional orientations. These facts make comprehensible the repeated observation that it is the young policemen who are the militant activists. In the words of a New York police lieutenant:

What we're seeing, I think, are dissident youth on the police force. They're exploding. They're fighting back against what they consider an intolerable situation. Just as there seems to be a new left on the campuses, there seems to be a new right among younger men in the police department.[46]

Thus the kinds of values and beliefs the police bring to their jobs are compatible with the police mentality. Nevertheless these tendencies are considerably reinforced once they have become policemen.

There are several aspects of policing as such which give rise to and reinforce the police mentality. First of all, policing is a difficult and unpleasant job. Police are perhaps inevitably somewhat isolated from the policed and thus suffer from estrangement (see Chapter 3). Furthermore, the police are necessarily exposed to a very unrepresentative slice of life. They mainly come in contact with law violators or the victims of law violation. Such an experience, continued for a few years, easily gives rise to the belief that the whole of society is riddled with crime. As one veteran police commander put it,

> It's hard not to go sour when you do this kind of work. After about five years most men ought to be retired on disability—simply doing the job that long makes them unfit to do it any longer. It's kinda like the way cons get hardened in stir. Sometimes the years of experience do make policemen wiser and more tolerant. But most often it makes them bull-headed and short-tempered.[47]

To some extent the present militance of the police is like that of other groups who handle the "garbage details" of modern society. School teachers, social workers, sanitation workers, and others similarly situated have all exhibited considerable militance recently demanding drastic changes in the organization of their tasks. The politicization of the police must be judged in this larger context as part of a pattern of rebellion by all public employees who have "dirty" jobs to do and whose jobs are becoming increasingly "dirtier" as the urban crisis worsens.

However, the police differ strikingly from these other rebellious groups of public employees in that all the others have turned to the liberal and trade unionist perspectives for programs and rhetoric while the police have turned to the right. Teachers direct their attacks and demands against social conditions which result in unruly or poorly prepared students. Social workers attack the economic and political arrangements which result in an unworkably confused welfare program which traps many persons permanently into welfare dependency and extreme poverty.

But neither teachers nor welfare workers are angry at their clients—students, and the poor. The police are angry at their clients—the public. And to the degree that the police are interested in social factors it is to restore society to an earlier simpler state (although a utopian version of those earlier days) and to free themselves from restraints on their dealings with individuals they regard as criminal.

Thus we confront once again a consequence of the police tendency to individualize; to regard men as free actors, unfettered by social structures or their past experiences. It is this that sets the police apart from other public employees who deal with social problems. And it is this which makes right-wing analysis so compatible with the police mentality.

In trying to explain why the police are so prone to free-will conceptions of human behavior it is instructive to look at church history. Similarities between police and religious institutions suggest that a strong pull towards free-will thought is inherent in policing.

Orthodox Christian theology has required a free-will premise primarily because of the doctrine of salvation. God judges men. Those whose faith and lives are deemed sufficient are granted eternal life in Heaven, and those who fail the judgment are consigned to Hell. Orthodox Christian conceptions of God reject the idea that he can be capricious, arbitrary, or malicious. God is good and just, and wants all men to be saved. But men must achieve their own salvations. *Thus men must possess free will.* Men are free, for only then can a God who judges be just.

In my judgment, whenever persons or institutions are set the task of evaluating individual "sinfulness" there is a powerful urge to regard individuals as free to refrain from sinning. Recognition of constraints on individual freedom threatens the legitimacy of sitting in judgment on individuals.

Religious institutions have had a great deal of trouble with this problem in recent times. Indeed, the ability to accommodate notions that men aren't wholly free and responsible for their actions has been mainly limited to those sectors of the clergy who have surrendered a judging conception of God.[48] Without judgment the problem evaporates.

Similarly the courts have struggled with individual accountability. Such issues as compulsion, diminished responsibility, insanity, and the like represent decreasing reliance on simple free-will legal philosophies.

Like priests and judges, the police are asked to judge individual sinfulness. But unlike priests and judges they must do so on a snap judgment basis without the time to reflect on questions of responsibility or the information to do so. Furthermore, while priests, judges, and social scientists can think about people in terms of broad classes and general tendencies, the policeman is required and trained to pick out individual members of such groups and concentrate on specific acts and situations. As we discussed in Chapter 4, policemen tend not to regard crowds as crowds, but to pick out specific faces and persons for individual scrutiny. The over-riding consideration in policing is to catch the guilty *party*—to find out and bring in the responsible *parties*.

Thus the police are led to individualize because a free-will conception of man is compatible with the task of selecting the guilty and because this same task leads them to presume that individuals are in fact specifically responsible for lawless events. It is in no way surprising, consequently, that the Los Angeles police refer to Marquette Frye as "the man who started the Watts riot," and have harassed him considerably since the riot. Frye's arrest on traffic charges is regarded as producing the precipitating confrontation of the riot. But the fact that similar arrests had not produced confrontations between officers and black bystanders, or the fact that similar confrontations had not previously led to riots, or the fact that Frye was in custody when the rioting itself began, or the fact that the riot jumped around among widely separated locations during its early period—none of these considerations led the police to think in terms of larger social causes, or of long-simmering grievances, to say nothing of police actions. Instead, they talk of the man who started the riot, and of the bad individuals who made it spread and grow.

Thus the act of policing has inherent strains toward free-will imagery and conspiracy thinking. It is surely the case that people, not poverty, *commit* crime. And it is the day-to-day police job to arrest people, not reduce poverty. But from this comes a tendency to reject poverty as in any way germaine to policing and to seek individual human faults as the complete explanation of events. Thus, when confronted by collective protest the police see "evil" people or "misled" and "misguided" people. When confronted with high black crime rates, the police see hordes of criminal blacks, each with individual faults of character (and they have a tendency to account for this on the basis of inherent flaws).

The police mentality is sustained both by the social sources of police recruits and by the experience, training, and indoctrination they receive as policemen.

Conclusions

This chapter has assessed the police view of man and society. I have tried to demonstrate that the police generally hold a narrow and unsophisticated outlook. They explain the world in terms of human intentionality. Individuals act solely out of evil motives, not because of social, psychological, or political factors. Collective behavior—demonstrations, civil disturbances, and the like—is also understood in individual terms: as produced by the evil designs of conspiratorial leaders. As a result of their beliefs about the world, the police are unreasonably alarmed and angered by what they see. This greatly shapes the kinds of tactical choices and responses they make and exacerbates their hostility when confronted by certain kinds of crowds. It is not simply that they hate political dissenters and militant blacks: they think such persons are bent on destroying the American Way of Life. These days the police often approach confrontations firmly believing that they are trying to head off the opening day of the revolution to take over America. Little wonder they then behave as they do.

6

Internal Control over the Police

. . . the police reject their historic role as the enforcers of established political and social policies. They now seek the power to determine these policies.

Previous chapters have been devoted mainly to the question: why do they do it; why do the police riot? The next two chapters raise the question: *how are they able to get away with it?* It seems clear enough that the police would be much less likely to erupt into rioting if they believed there was a high probability that such behavior would result in substantial penalties. Like the rest of us, the police generally conform to standards of behavior which affect their jobs and their promotions.

In principle there are a number of institutional restraints or control agencies which regulate police behavior. First of all, policemen are immediately answerable to their superiors for their conduct. Through a chain of command headed by the chief, observance of departmental regulations and standards is to be enforced. Furthermore, there are control agencies external to departments which also have authority and review power over police behavior. First among these is civil government—mayors, councils, and city managers who hold the power to hire and fire chiefs of police, to appropriate police budgets, and often, through civil service commissions, to review police hiring and firing decisions. A second external control over the police is the court and prosecutor system. Actions by policemen which are illegal are supposed to be subject to regular criminal proceedings. A third external watchdog of police behavior is the press and mass media. Police misconduct, corruption, and the like are presumably subject to press coverage and are thus to be brought to public attention. A final source of potential control over the police is the general public, whose attitudes, values, voting behavior, and the like are the final arbiters of how our society is to operate.

Given the fact that the police do riot and that rarely do they incur any punishment for such behavior, it is apparent that something is wrong with this set of presumed controls over the police. This chapter examines the failure of internal controls over police behavior. The next examines why each of the potential external sources of control over the police also fails to operate.

There are a number of reasons for the absence of authority *within* police departments. First I consider how police solidarity produces a cult of secrecy. I then take up a more serious and rapidly escalating challenge to internal police authority—the spread of political militancy among the police, which has reached such levels that many observers speak of a police revolt.

I. The Cult of Secrecy

It is a cliché in studies of the police that discretion is a paramount characteristic of the policeman's role.[1] Policemen typically work alone or in pairs and are usually out of sight of their superiors. In addition, the policeman is armed with considerable authority, not merely the authority to shoot people or arrest them, but also the authority to ignore particular violations and infractions. Moreover, the word of a policeman is considered exceptionally credible, particularly in court, as anyone who has contested a traffic ticket is likely to have learned. Thus, the police have a great deal of autonomy and discretion in their day-to-day work.

This line of analysis has been given so much attention by students of the police because it is seen as a major impediment to controlling police behavior. On these grounds, a central problem of police administration has been posed: how can commanders control what their policemen do when it is so hard to find out what they do?

But, the extent of individual police discretion has been exaggerated in these studies. The problem has not only been given undue emphasis, but has been somewhat misunderstood. For one thing, the analysis has been focused primarily on individual police discretion. The imagery is of policemen sneaking into back alleys to misbehave and the problem is defined as how to let the department know what took place in those alleys. But a careful and systematic study of the police has shown that most police violence does not occur out of sight.[2] It more typically occurs in the presence of other policemen and often within police buildings. *Thus, police violence is more often than not a group or collective activity which is inconsistent with the explanation that is sustained by its invisibility.* It is not that the department can't find out about it, because typically the department—at least in the sense of some other policemen—already knows. Indeed, in the case of police riots there can hardly be a plea of ignorance. They have all been public happenings in the presence of police commanders as well as newsmen and citizens. Thus, the nature of police discretion and the source of the policeman's sense of impunity to commit unlawful acts must be studied in terms of the internal operations of police organizations. How is it that such action is condoned, or at least unpunished, within police organizations? In addition, we must begin to investigate the basis for the collective discretion of police organizations. How do they manage to condone officer misconduct and remain immune from outside pressures for reform?

The collective discretion of the police is both a cause and a consequence of a lack of effective internal discipline. It is this lack of discipline and the resulting low risk run by the police when they engage in violence that are major factors in accounting for their propensity to riot.

In Chapter 3, much was made of the high degree of police solidarity. This solidarity is more than a preference for the company of fellow police officers, *esprit de corps,* or the bonds of fellow feeling and mutual responsibility ordinarily formed among persons who share danger and stress. The police may be regarded legitimately as a distinct minority subculture that feels itself profoundly isolated from the general public and is actively hostile towards certain other minority groups. Because the police see themselves as embattled, the sense of group solidarity usually found in any minority subculture group is greatly magnified: police solidarity in our society is obsessive. Its primary manifestation is a cult of secrecy and loyalty not unlike that attributed to the Mafia. The one overriding rule among the police seems to be: never squeal on a brother officer no matter what he does. As we shall see, this rule is also typically observed by police commanders, taking the form: protect an officer from outsiders, including the courts, no matter what he has done.

The examples below illustrate common police practices. No effort has been made to be exhaustive; the list could be extended almost indefinitely. Nor are these necessarily the most blatant instances; these are the only ones where the curtain of police secrecy was at least partially penetrated by outsiders. The episodes were selected to illustrate important variations in police solidarity and secrecy, to show how such events corrode police discipline, and to reflect how weak it is.

During investigations of the alleged execution of several young black men by Detroit policemen at the Algiers Motel during the 1967 riot, it was revealed that a State Police commander had withdrawn his officers from the motel because he could not condone what was going on. But he made no effective effort to interfere, nor did he report these actions of the Detroit police, to which he refused to be a party. Thus his disapproval did not serve as a deterrent, nor did his knowledge of events constitute detection. Following the indictment of several Detroit officers for murder in this episode, the Detroit policeman's organization officially came to their defense and financed their legal costs. The officers were freed on low bail and their trials were postponed for many months.[3] That they were eventually found not guilty does not alter the fact that the police treated serious charges against fellow officers in a way they do not when the suspects are civilians.

In San Francisco, during September 1968, police chief Thomas Cahill refused to suspend even temporarily an officer who fired his service revolver out a window of his home at howling cats, while allegedly "heavily intoxicated," and wounded a woman in a nearby home. Several weeks later after much pressure from the news media, the Police Commission found the officer guilty of misconduct and suspended him for 45 days. On the last night of his suspension, the officer rewarded Chief Cahill's faith in him by becoming involved in a hit-and-run traffic accident.[4]

On September 29, 1968, San Francisco patrolman Michael O'Brien shot and killed a 28-year-old black truck driver, George Baskett, following an argument over a minor traffic accident. O'Brien was off duty at the time. Chief Cahill told the press the following day that he was closing his personal investigation of the episode, and that the officer was exonerated of wrong-doing. This despite testimony from a number of eyewitnesses that the policeman had shot in anger—"[O'Brien] held out his revolver at George Baskett and said, 'I'm going to kill a nigger,' counted one, two, three—and then killed him in cold blood," was one witness's testimony. Another claimed O'Brien said, "I want to kill a nigger so bad I can taste it," before he fired. Only after the press revealed considerable damaging testimony, including that of a female companion of Officer O'Brien at the time of the shooting, did the police began to backtrack and continue the investigation. The *San Francisco Chronicle* spoke freely of a "switch from 'cover up' to investigation." The initial hard line taken by Chief Cahill began to collapse in the face of intense public indignation. However, simple suspension from duty only came a week after the shooting. Eleven days later murder charges were filed against Officer O'Brien. But the commitment of the police to the code of solidarity did not end here. The officer was immediately released on his own recognizance. Neither the press nor the District Attorney's office could remember a precedent for such a release. The next day the courts remanded Officer O'Brien back to jail. Officer O'Brien was accompanied into court by two officials of the Police Officer's Association and a lawyer hired by the POA to defend the case. On October 14, the POA filed a formal complaint with Chief Cahill calling for disciplinary action against Deputy Police Chief Al Nelder, three captains, a lieutenant, a sergeant, and an officer in the Community Relations Service for their part in the investigation of Officer O'Brien. In judgment of the POA, Officer O'Brien was being persecuted. Their fears proved somewhat unfounded when shortly thereafter the District Attorney took the unusual step of taking the case before the Grand Jury and, after failing to call certain witnesses who, in the judgment of some observers, were vital to the prosecution case, came out with an indictment for manslaughter. O'Brien was subsequently found not guilty and scores of policemen attended a testimonial dinner to honor his attorney, Jake Erlich, who had conducted a blatantly racist defense. At this dinner two reporters, one from *Ramparts* magazine and the other from KQED-9, the educational TV station, were beaten for no apparent reason other than that the magazine and the TV station are not considered pro-police. But more important, despite the fact that scores of policemen were present and despite the fact that a very clear photograph of one of the assailants was later available, police were unable to solve this case.[5]

Meanwhile, in Oakland, two on-duty officers strafed the headquarters of the Black Panther Party the night (September 10, 1968) following the conviction of Huey P. Newton, Black Panther leader, for voluntary manslaughter in a celebrated case involving a shoot-out with police during which one officer was killed and another wounded. Cruising by twice in their patrol car, the officers fired an estimated 30 shots into the building. The number of their squad car was reported by several eyewitnesses awakened by the fusillade. Acting on this information and an interrogation of the two officers, Police Chief Charles Gain dismissed both from the force within hours of the incident. But rank-and-file policemen were not pleased with his action. According to an officer of the Oakland Police Officer's Association, interviewed by the Task Force, Oakland police felt the two would not have been charged with a felony (firing into an occupied building) had they not been police officers and had it not happened in the wake of the Newton trial. Furthermore, Oakland police felt that while these officers had done wrong, their colleagues must not desert them. The legal fund of the POA provided their defense. They received probation.[6]

In New York City members of the militant right-wing police organization, the Law Enforcement Group (LEG), called a press conference (September 2, 1968) and charged that the suspension of a police officer awaiting trial on charges of severely beating a prisoner was "prejudicial and unconstitutional." In their judgment a policeman indicted for on-duty assault should remain armed and on duty until convicted.[7]

Earlier a mob of perhaps 150 off-duty policemen, alleged to

be members of this same group (LEG), attacked several members of the Black Panther Party in the hallway of the Brooklyn criminal courts building. The Panthers had come to attend the trial of several of their members. The off-duty policemen drove the Panthers from the building with blackjacks and then took over all seats in the courtroom. As of this writing, despite nationwide publicity, no charges (or other actions) have been filed against any participants. Police officials have indicated an inability to find out who they were. Officers on duty at the scene claim to have recognized no one.[8]

In Los Angeles bitter charges of police rioting, brutality, and unwarranted killing arose after police dispersed persons gathered in a park taking part in the 1968 Watts Festival. Three persons were killed and 38 more were wounded (as were six policemen) in the incident. Complete police silence in response to these charges continued so long the *Los Angeles Times*, a stout supporter of the Los Angeles Police Department, was prompted to publish an editorial under the headline:

Continuing Police Silence Unwise

Issue: What purpose is served by a prolonged official blackout of pertinent information relative to an incident in Watts?

Who shot whom—and with what?

That question remains unanswered by authorities despite the fact that the disturbance in Watts which gave rise to it occurred 11 days ago.

A concerned public should not be expected to wait that long.

The coroner's office and the County USC Medical Center refuse to reveal information which might provide clues as to the type of ammunition used.

Pertinent information which could clarify a confused situation should not be withheld simply to suit the convenience of some of the principals involved.[9]

In Detroit Mayor Jerome P. Cavanaugh complained during a press conference in early November 1968 that a "blue curtain" was preventing him from investigating an alleged police beating of three black youths. The charges stemmed from an outbreak of violence between off-duty police officers attending a dance sponsored by the Detroit Police Officers Wives' Association and black youngsters attending a church-sponsored dance in another part of the same building. The black youths charged that off-duty officers beat them without provocation during the course of the evening. Mayor Cavanaugh told newsmen after two days of investigation of the charges by high-ranking police officials that "We don't even have the names of those men who attended" the dance. Thirteen days after the event the mayor finally managed to get a report on what had taken place and nine policemen were suspended.[10]

In Berkeley, as reported in detail in Chapter 1, a great deal of evidence of police misconduct during the June–July 1968 confrontation was made available to the police and to the district attorney. There were dozens of victims of police hit-and-run attacks, and in many of these incidents there were a number of highly credible witnesses. Indeed, the city manager's report to the city council admitted a number of blatant police misdeeds, as did an internal police report on the affair. Yet, several years later no information could be obtained to indicate that any action had been taken against any police offenders. Since few policemen wore badges during the episode, citizen complaints were of the "Officer John Doe" variety. But researchers have been unable to locate any complainants who were shown photographs of officers in order to uncover the identities of their assailants. Indeed, during the ensuing year a number of even more serious acts of police misconduct occurred in Berkeley, and in many instances the officers' identities were known (it became standard practice for Berkeley demonstrators to carry cameras in order to make later identification of officers possible). Despite publication of many photographs which at least appear to support eyewitness testimony of police misconduct—including the shooting of demonstrators under conditions posing no threat to public or police safety—no departmental action is known to have been taken. Following newspaper publication of a picture of a Berkeley officer carrying an unauthorized, high-powered 30–40 Krag-Jorgensen rifle during the People's Park confrontation (May 15, 1969)—a flagrant violation of strict departmental gun regulations—Police Chief Bruce Baker declined to name the officer (Badge #101) and said the matter would be handled internally. Subsequently, Baker reported the matter had been dropped. "Keeping control of his department is probably one of the most difficult tasks any chief has," Chief Baker told the press. He said it is only maintained because "every officer knows that if he violates the rules he can be certain discipline will be administered."[11]

In Los Angeles a recent case in which the court found two police officers had planted a weapon on a person they had shot (an effort to establish a false self-defense justification) did not result in their criminal prosecution, nor, in the case of one of them, dismissal from the force.[12] Indeed, as reported in Chapter 2, the carrying and use of such throwaways—knives or guns to be used to establish a self-defense case—is neither uncommon nor especially secret among the American police. Obviously, many policemen and many commanders reject such practices. Yet, where are the complaints or the dismissals?

And then, of course, there is Chicago. No outbreak of police misbehavior was so widely witnessed and recorded on film. Yet, subsequent calls for action met hot denials from Mayor Richard J. Daley (backed by his police superintendent James Conlisk) that police had been guilty of wrongdoing. A few police commanders would anonymously admit to reporters such as D. J. R. Bruckner of the *Los Angeles Times* that things had gotten out of hand, but the public line was unwavering.[13] As press and public pressure built, Daley and Conlisk tried the "rotten apple" defense and suspended nine policemen for misconduct during the convention, primarily for not wearing their badges. Then came the *Walker Report*,[14] prepared under the auspices of the Violence Commission. Daniel Walker, General Counsel for Montgomery Ward & Co., and President of the Chicago Crime Commission, concluded in a report based on thousands of interviews and examination of hours of film, that the police had rioted. He demanded "prompt and severe" disciplinary action. "The blue curtain cannot be permitted to stay down," he told a news conference. Walker added that "the suspension of a handful of policemen will not be enough," because more than a handful were involved, *"and their lieutenants and sergeants know who they are."*[15] Indeed, according to his findings, during the Wednesday night battle in front of the Conrad Hilton Hotel, the deputy superintendent of the Chicago police rushed around pulling berserk officers off battered demonstrators shouting "Stop, damn it, stop! For Christ's sake, stop it!" But, predictably, nothing happened. Superintendent Conlisk took no action. According to an anonymous "police authority" quoted in the

Chicago Daily News, loyalty, not discipline, is Superintendent Conlisk's forte: "His men like him because he doesn't interfere, he doesn't cause anybody any trouble. He acts against them only if he is forced to."[16]

Most of the episodes reported above revealed the unwillingness or inability of police commanders to take action against officers charged with very serious offenses and the continued support given such officers by the police rank and file even when action is taken against them. It could be argued that this simply reflects the solidarity of the police and does not necessarily mean commanders have no power to discipline their men. Indeed, police commanders may simply share the views of their subordinates in these instances. The year after he had achieved international notoriety for his barbaric treatment of civil rights demonstrators, the nation's sheriffs elected Jim Clark of Selma, Alabama, to be president of their organization. However, the cult of secrecy and the consequent impotence of commanders cannot be denied given the findings of a recent *New York Times* study of "cooping"—the police euphemism for regular and premeditated sleeping on duty. Based on "scores of interviews" and a "number of late night inspection tours," the *New York Times* found cooping was a "widespread practice."

According to the *Times* account:

> Night after night, in obscure corners all over New York, policemen on foot and policemen in patrol cars disappear into their "coops."
> "It was often impossible to find more than one patrol car working in my precinct after 3 a.m.," said one sergeant, who was until recently a supervisor in a slum precinct. "You'd tell the guys to stay awake, to listen to the radio, but they'd just ignore you."
> Some patrolmen carry pillows and alarm clocks under their coats when they go on duty to make sure their rest is comfortable and that they do not oversleep. A popular practical joke is to distract a man then set his alarm clock for 11:55 so it will go off while the platoon is being inspected by the lieutenant just before it goes on duty.[17]

Clearly, that sergeants cannot keep men from cooping when they are aware of it—an "inspection" that does not prevent pillows and alarm clocks from being carried under uniforms or in which having an alarm clock go off under your uniform during inspection can be treated as a harmless prank, is hardly an inspection—

testifies to an extraordinary lack of intradepartmental discipline.

According to the *New York Times* this state of affairs is not limited to New York's "finest." It obtains in other major cities as well. New York's "cooping" is called "huddling" in Washington, D. C.; in some other cities it is called "going down"; and in San Francisco the police call it "kipping."

In sum, these instances support the assertion that the American policemen have considerable impunity. Their commanders are unable and/or unwilling to punish them for even flagrant misconduct.

It must be recognized that policemen must trust their superiors to back them up in the face of false accusations and to support them when professional police judgments of appropriate conduct differ from those held by laymen. It is also true that the police are often forced to make snap decisions about what they ought to do and that sometimes this will result in honest errors. Thus, the police must be able to count on legitimate backing by the department or they will be unable to make decisions under stress.

But, for all the anger among the police that the department and the courts do not properly back them up, the imbalance is much in the other direction. The exigencies of policing have been abused to produce impunity which encourages them to blatantly abuse the law and decency and makes them unresponsive to departmental authority. In their commitment to solidarity, the police have seriously impaired their organizational capacity. For the sake of morale, commanders rationalize their failure to discipline officers who break lines on riot duty, or who mount independent forays and beatings.

Police commanders seem afraid that if they should acknowledge charges of police misbehavior by disciplining or dismissing offenders that the public image of the police will be tarnished, that people will then know that the police indeed misbehave. But it seems likely that some such admissions would have the reverse effect, that they would convince the public that police commanders mean to run law-abiding forces; that undismissed officers can be presumed to be good cops and that police malpractices do not reflect departmental policy.

Most police commanders are hardly so naive or irresponsible that they do not want firm control of their officers. Why then do they permit these conditions to prevail? The answer may well lie in the fact that *to some significant extent police commanders have become the captives of a militant rank and file.*

II. The Police Revolt

The determination of the police to maintain secrecy and impunity at virtually any price and their transformation into a militant social movement stem at least in part from their reaction to the predicament in which they find themselves. In Chapter 3 the escalation of anger, fear, conflict, and violence between the police on one hand and the black community and protest movements on the other was outlined in detail. The deterioration of the police capacity to deal with the growing problems which confront them was also described. An examination of police responses to these developments shows that they facilitate police tendencies to rioting and mass violence.

Few policemen in America have responded to their present predicament apathetically. Some have reacted by refusing to perform their duties fully; many others have simply quit the force. But perhaps most have responded by taking part in building a militant, activist police movement in an effort to remove what they regard as the major sources of their grievances. The first kinds of response will be discussed briefly. Most of the remainder of this chapter will be devoted to the second, which is in many ways the most important feature of the modern police establishment.

The Cop-Out

Readers of the *San Francisco Chronicle* arose Tuesday, November 12, 1968, to learn that 195 officers of the San Francisco Police Department had put in for early retirement. This was approximately eleven percent of the force, which, like most urban departments, chronically operates at five to ten percent below authorized strength for lack of suitable applicants. The mass of retirement applications followed the June passage of a ballot proposition to improve police retirement benefits and permit retirement at an earlier age. The purpose of the new program was to aid the department in recruiting new officers. Ironically, its results thus far have been to increase retirement applications.

What reasons did these policemen give for quitting the force at the earliest possible moment? One veteran inspector said, "It's a dog's job. It's a job the average man wouldn't take. It doesn't have to be, but it is." Another inspector explained his decision this way: "... We're running scared ... If there are social injustices, that's society's bag. We can't cure them. All we can do is make arrests." In the judgment of Captain Charles Barca, the men leave because "It's just an ugly, difficult, uncomfortable way to make a living and will continue to be that way until the general public develops more appreciation for officers and more respect for them."[18]

Although the San Francisco episode was striking because a change in the law produced a sudden mass retirement, reports from urban departments across the nation indicate that the majority of officers retire as soon as they are eligible.

Those of us who grew up on Pat O'Brien movies have accepted the image of the aging cop who hides his infirmities to stay on the force as long as possible and then retires in a scene of tears and Irish sentimentality. Older police officers agree that things were once this way. But no longer. Many American cops can hardly wait to hang up their badges. A study prepared for the U. S. Crime Commission, based on a survey of policemen in four major cities, concluded that one of every four was wearing his uniform because he could "perceive no viable alternative."

Presumably, these officers would quit if they could find a better job. And in fact a substantial number of policemen do that each year. Many urban departments report massive resignation rates—as high as 15 percent per year—among officers short of retirement.

In an interview,[19] the then Berkeley Chief of Police William Beall said Berkeley officers quit the force at all stages of their career. "We lost many veteran officers with ten to fifteen years on the force, men who are at the peak of their efficiency." Almost none of these men take law enforcement jobs elsewhere—Berkeley is one of the highest paying and most admired departments in the nation—but take up other occupations. "The men who find these opportunities are among the best, as you would expect," Chief

Beall told me. Thus, for many policemen the way to cope with the predicament of modern policing is simply to get out.

A second way in which the police cop-out has even more serious implications: they simply stop doing their duty.

A New York policeman told a Task Force interviewer:

> ... things have changed a lot since I've been on the job. It used to be when you heard a call about a man with a gun you used to get two or three cars racing to get over there as fast as they could. Nowadays you hear that kind of call, you take your time, go slow. You get there, you don't look around too much. Don't worry too much about getting anybody, because you never know when you're going to walk into a shotgun blast.[20]

And a San Francisco police commander echoed this feeling.

> I've heard of men in radio cars who get a call—a 211, involving violence; it's in a trouble area, one where there are mobs who might try to interfere with the arrest.
>
> What do they do? They make a slow trip. Or they turn on the siren so as to warn the suspects to take a hike.
>
> Or they arrive in time to save the victim and stand a fair chance of getting involved in trouble and self-defeat. A little of this and they decide to turn in the badge and pump gas for a living.
>
> I don't blame them.[21]

These reports are confirmed by the findings of the Kerner Commission that police are very slow to respond to calls from minority group communities,[22] and by the reports of widespread "cooping" discussed earlier in this chapter.

But not all policemen can quit the force and many would not want to if they could. And for many, copping out on their duties is an unacceptable alternative. These policemen see the answer to their predicament and their grievances in militance. They have banded together to demand to be equipped and "unleashed" to get tough on crime and disorder. Furthermore, they seek fundamental changes in American society. This politicization of the police is a development that threatens to erode the rule of law, public confidence in the police, freedom of dissent, and the ability of police organizations to function responsibly in a free society.

The Politicization of the Police

In the days of the big-city political machines, the police were inevitably involved in politics in a small way (and to the extent that city political machines remain, such police politics continue). They often owed their jobs and promotions to local aldermen and were expected to cooperate with political ward bosses and other sachems of the machine. Sometimes they helped get out the vote or condoned election irregularities and even the harassment of opposition candidates (indeed, sometimes the police did the harassing, especially of radical candidates). They were also expected to permit or take part in various kinds of graft and corruption. Still, at most, they played minor roles in the political operation.

A more important way in which the police have been political is as the right arm of the political status quo. For decades the police were the main bulwark against the labor movement: picket lines were roughly dispersed, meetings were broken up, organizers and activists were shot, beaten, jailed, or run out of town.[23] Such anti-union police tactics are much less common these days when national labor leaders are firm figures of the establishment, but many of these same leaders survived nasty encounters with the police in their youth. Furthermore, unions with a majority of black or nonwhite members—for example, the garbage workers in Memphis and the farm workers in Texas and California—still find themselves confronted by the police and are the victims of police violence and harassment. Similarly, participants in the new protest movements of the 1960s and 1970s have harshly experienced the role of the police as enforcers of the status quo. Civil rights workers, first in the South and then in the North, suffered from the lack of police protection, and from police opposition, arrests, and beatings; some were even murdered by law enforcement officers. Subsequently, students and anti-war demonstrators have faced forceful police opposition. And minority communities, especially those of blacks and Mexican-Americans, regard the police as hostile, external agents of repression.

Still, the activities which will be characterized in this section as the police revolt are not these historic patterns of police political involvement. Instead, I am mainly concerned with a phenomenon new to American society: the emergence of the police as a self-conscious, organized, and militant political constituency, bidding for far-reaching political power in their own right. Indeed, in their new mood the police reject their historic role as the enforcers of established political and social policies. They now seek the power to determine these policies.

The militant new quest of the police for political power not only brings them into explosive opposition and conflict with minority groups and political and social dissenters, but also causes them to challenge radically the authority of their own commanders, the courts, civil authorities, and constitutionality.

The rapid politicization of the police seems to rest on four main factors:

1. Frustration As was shown in Chapter 3, the police feel embattled by forces beyond their comprehension, resources, or control. This has made them angry and fearful, and provided a powerful motive to do *something* to escape from, or at least improve, their circumstances.

2. A simplistic and apocalyptic ideology Chapter 5 examined what the police believe about what is wrong with society, who is to blame for police frustration and powerlessness, who is denying them the freedom to do what they believe must be done to save themselves and society. It must be recognized here that a fundamentalist, simplistic, right-wing point of view is an important element in police politicization for it brings them into conflict with the establishment.

3. Organization Police militance has been built upon a preexisting organizational framework through which their frustrations and ambitions could be readily expressed: their guild, union, and social organizations—in short, the police subculture. Police militants did not have to start from scratch to organize their fellow officers; they simply have been able to adapt old organizations to new goals and tactics.

4. Experience The lessons learned about their potential political power gained by the police through a series of successful battles to prevent the establishment of civilian review boards and to gain economic benefits have been a major factor in prompting the police to seek expanded power and more general goals. The overwhelming victories scored by the police in review board fights made them aware that they were a powerful political force. During these campaigns police leaders gained considerable political savvy and made contact with many potential political allies.

Perhaps the most revealing single case, both for what it reveals about the evolution of a militant police revolt, and for its importance as *an example for police elsewhere,* is New York City. Here the largest police force in America, led by the Patrolmen's Benevolent Association, successfully appealed to the public to vote out a civilian review board. Subsequently, the PBA leadership rebelled against orders from the police commissioner and the city government. Recently, the New York City police have produced a new organization of young right-wing extremists who are in revolt against the PBA as being too timid and who are devoted to direct action to challenge the courts, police commanders, and civil authorities. Because so many of the elements of the national problem are so fully developed in the New York City case, I shall briefly recount it here before considering evidence from across the nation bearing on the same points.

New York's Police Revolt

The battle broke out in summer 1966 when Mayor John Lindsay moved to fulfill a campaign promise to establish a civilian-dominated police review board. A preview skirmish had been fought a year earlier, when, on June 29, 1965, the police were given an opportunity to argue against the review board at hearings held by Councilman Theodore S. Weiss. The display of police militance on this occasion has been graphically described by former FBI agent William Turner:

The scene at City Hall that day was one that few New Yorkers who saw it will soon forget. Thousands of off-duty policemen in uniform, with service revolvers strapped on and wearing PBA buttons (the buttons were later removed at the request of the police commissioner) tightly ringed City Hall and packed its corridors. Many carried signs with such slogans as "What About Civil Rights For Cops," "Don't Let The Reds Frame The Police." Adding to the spectacle were dozens of American Nazis and John Birch Society members toting American flags and shouting encouragement to the police. Some of the police pickets yelled at a quiet group of CORE counterpickets, "Go home, finks," "Send 'em to Vietnam where they belong," "Wave a bar of soap at them and they'll all run," and other epithets and obscenities. Over the police radio crackled unauthorized messages urging as many police as possible to join the demonstration; one anonymous voice sang off-key the civil rights song "We Shall Overcome," at the conclusion of which another remarked sourly, "They already have."

Inside the City Council chambers, the PBA's rough-hewn president, John J. Cassese, in an echo of Senator McCarthy's celebrated bluff with a "list" of numerous communists in the State Department, was declaiming that a "black book" at police headquarters contained the names of many prominent proponents of civilian review—all Communists or communist sympathizers. Pressed for names, Cassese feebly named Roger Baldwin, the old warhorse of the ACLU.[24]

Despite this initial and continuing police opposition, a year later on July 7, 1966, Mayor Lindsay appointed a review board made up of three policemen and four civilians. Thus, the battle was joined. The PBA immediately tried to have a referendum placed on the November ballot to outlaw the board. This was turned down by the city clerk, but reversed by the courts. With the election set, the PBA conducted one of the most intensive and bitter campaigns in New York history. According to a number of accounts, policemen campaigned hard while on duty: patrol cars and wagons bore anti-review board signs, police passed out literature and even, it is widely charged, harassed persons campaigning on the other side. Many have claimed that at the height of the campaign cars with bumper stickers supporting civil review were flagrantly ticketed, while an anti-review sticker seemed to make autos almost ticket-proof. Billboards, posters, and ads were heavily exploited. One poster depicted damaged stores and a rubble-strewn street and read: "This is the aftermath of a riot in a city that *had* a civilian review board." Included in the text was a statement by J. Edgar Hoover that civilian review boards "virtually paralyzed" the police.[25]

Another poster showed a young girl fearfully leaving a subway exit onto a dark street; "The Civilian Review Board must be stopped! ... Her life ... your life ... may depend upon it."[26]

It was an alarmist campaign, heavily financed from PBA funds and by private sources. The New York Conservative Party made a maximum effort. According to a public statement issued by U. S. Senator Jacob Javits and the late Senator Robert F. Kennedy, the John Birch Society was also active in the campaign.[27]

On November 8, 1966, election night, the civilian review board was buried by a landslide of almost two to one.

Following their stunning victory at the polls the PBA officials began to see themselves, their power, and their goals in a new light. While the PBA (formed in 1894 while Theodore Roosevelt was a member of the Police Commission which ran the department) was originally conceived of as combining the functions of a trade union and a lobbying organization for police benefits, it now began a rapid transformation into a vehicle for the political sentiments and aspirations of the police rank and file. The growing political resentments of police towards minorities, demonstrators, the courts, and "leftist subversives" found a formidable channel for expression. The PBA now demanded the right to make police policy and political judgments. However, civilian political leadership—the mayor, the police commissioner, the city government—were unwilling to permit this development without a fight. Thus, the second round in the battle between the police and city hall soon began.

While the original battle had been over civilian review of police behavior, the second round was over the authority of police commanders. On August 12, 1968, PBA President John Cassese issued a directive to all members (about 99 percent of the force) to obey only lawful orders from superior officers, to wit: to disregard orders to refrain from arresting or shooting looters, vandals, unruly demonstrators, and other law violators.[28]

According to Cassese's explanations of this action, it stemmed from a resentment among policemen against directives to "cool it" during disturbances in the wake of Dr. Martin Luther King's assassination, and subsequent command restraint during demonstrations through the summer. Cassese charged that the police had been "handcuffed" and were ready for a "direct conflict" with city hall to end such interference.[29]

Police Commissioner Howard R. Leary countered with a directive of his own reasserting the authority of the departmental chain of command and promising disciplinary action against any officer who refused to obey orders.[30]

Here were the basic elements of what the *Christian Science Monitor* called a police "revolt." In the same editorial of August 15, 1968, *Monitor* warned:

It is intolerable that a police department anywhere disregard the orders of its civil superiors. That way lies self-assumed power, a breakdown of civil administration, and possible chaos.

The same day the *New York Times* expressed similar alarm:

> In clinging to his plan to issue his own orders to policemen on the handling of demonstrations and disorders, Patrolman John J. Cassese, president of the Patrolmen's Benevolent Association, arrogates to himself a policy-making role which, under law, belongs to Police Commissioner Leary and the chain of command he heads. For all its pretense of being a move in support of law and order, the Cassese decision represents a fundamental and intolerable challenge to orderly government.
>
> The patrolmen's delegate body, by its unanimous vote supporting the PBA president, put its members in exactly the same camp as those they profess to condemn—the overzealous black activists and other demonstrators who ignore rules protecting society and insist on obeying only those laws with which they personally happen to agree. Such an approach leads to anarchy. It chips away the foundation of law and order in an open society which provides ample legal avenues for securing change.
>
> New York's policemen confront infinite difficulties and dangers in protecting this largest of American communities. The challenges to them in a time of social change are especially demanding. In defending order under siege from chaos, they deserve society's fullest support.
>
> But a city cannot be ruled by its police force, any more than a free nation can be ruled by its military establishment. And, while flying banners proclaiming that the law ought to be enforced 100 percent, the union leaders of the police force now paradoxically undermine the whole system of law. Their defiance of the city's top elected official and the Police Commissioner becomes lawlessness in the name of law.

Thus far the dispute has remained rhetorical. No test incident has yet arisen during which a patrolman has been accused of following Cassese's instruction that "If a superior tells a man to ignore a violation of the law, the policeman will take action notwithstanding that order."[31]

However, Cassese's actions seem to have represented something deeper than an attempt to impose PBA authority over that of police commanders. According to anonymous sources quoted by Sylvan Fox in the *New York Times,* Cassese took these provocative steps in an effort to head off a grass roots, right-wing revolt within his own organization. "He responded just like the black militants to the guys coming up from below," Fox quotes one informant. "This was an attempt by a union leader to get out in front of his membership."[32]

This militant challenge from below was from the Law Enforcement Group (LEG), some of whose subsequent alleged actions in beating Black Panthers and taking over a courtroom were described earlier. And in fact, it would appear that Cassese was not able to appease these new young militants by his actions. The group has become more and more prominent, the first of the militant, young, right-wing police groups to receive national attention.

It must be recognized that "right wing," in this context, is relative. What is new with LEG, and with young right-wing cops generally, is tactical. Like their high school classmates who went on to college, the young police are activists—they believe in demonstration and protest. Some of them also accept the need for revolution rather than reform. Indeed, it is often hard to distinguish among the proposals of the young policemen and the young radicals. Both speak of regenerating a sense of intimate, participatory community. Some major spokesmen for both seem willing to dismiss civil liberties to achieve such goals. Both sides talk violently. Indeed, both are probably responding to the same set of injustices in American society (see Chapter 3).

The activism of the young police rump groups is probably an important factor in producing recent police militance. That John Cassese of the New York PBA was responding to pressure from young militants has already been suggested. More generally, I suspect that recent police use of such tactics as the slowdown, the strike, the riots, and the vigilante raid, all of which have appeared in New York and elsewhere (as will be reported subsequently), have been greatly stimulated by the militance of their younger members.

The Nationwide Battle against Review

Episodes of police revolt, based on PBA-type organizations, have followed in the wake of a nationwide campaign against review boards. In city after city the police have gathered sufficient political muscle to beat down citizen efforts to establish extradepartmental machinery for reviewing police behavior. In Philadelphia, the nation's first civilian review board was discontinued as a result of a lawsuit brought by the Fraternal Order of Police. The setback in court appears to be permanent since, as the *Washington Post* reported: "Mayor James H. Tate, whom the police helped to elect, has been reluctant to appeal the court decision."³³ In Boston, during November 1968, the Patrolmen's Association displayed sufficient influence with members of the city council to gut a proposed Model Cities Program. The program included such mild proposals as to allow citizens to receive, but not to judge, complaints against the police and an elected citizens' advisory panel to "provide guidance" for police in the model neighborhood. According to press accounts, council members bowed to heavy pressure brought to bear by an intense campaign conducted by the Patrolmen's Association.³⁴ John Harrington, national president of the Fraternal Order of Police, has inaugurated a nationwide campaign to oppose police review boards.³⁵

The intense hostility of the police to civilian review boards cannot be based on unhappy past experiences. In Philadelphia, under the civilian review board there was no appreciable increase in the proportion of complaints upheld against policemen as compared with previous departmentally conducted investigations.³⁶ Review boards must mainly rely on the police to establish the "facts" in any given case. Furthermore, members of civilian review boards are typically part of the city hall establishment and thus responsive to police pressures and preferences. Indeed, during fall 1968, a police review board in St. Louis rescinded extremely mild actions it had previously taken against officers accused of brutality towards black militants after police organized a massive protest.

Thus, from the point of view of strengthening control over police behavior it is difficult to see civilian review boards as very effective. Nevertheless, police everywhere regard them as a perilous threat. The widespread view among the police is that the force behind efforts to create civilian review boards is a Moscow-directed plot to destroy the police prior to an attempt to overthrow the government.

I realize that this statement seems extreme. Can many policemen really believe such a thing? I do not have systematic public opinion poll data to demonstrate what proportion of policemen do believe this. But I was able to review the printed material circulated among the police by the Fraternal Order of Police and other police organizations, articles in police magazines, speeches by prominent police spokesmen, and campaign material circulated by the police in efforts to block the creation of civilian review boards. It is virtually a universal theme in all these materials that the forces behind civilian review are left-wing subversives.

In a special compendium of articles from a variety of police publications on civilian review boards published by the Fraternal Order of Police this communist subversion theme is shrilly repeated throughout. An editor's note, inserted by the FOP, is in keeping with the other articles:

> No matter what names are used by sponsors of the so-called "Police Review Boards" they exude the obnoxious odor of communism. This scheme is a page right out of the communist handbook which says in part ". . . police are the enemies of communism; if we are to succeed we must do anything to weaken their work, to incapacitate them or make them a subject of ridicule."[37]

Also, the American Civil Liberties Union, the National Association for the Advancement of Colored People, and the Americans for Democratic Action are identified throughout as communist or communist-front organizations. Since these groups have been prominent in backing review boards the deduction repeatedly is made that it is all a "commie plot."

Indeed, "plot" is the central theme in police attacks on civilian review proposals. The editors of *FI-PO News,* published by the Fire and Police Protective League of Los Angeles, put it this way: "The American Civil Liberties Union's proposed Police Review Board still remains their number one local plot. . . ."[38] Similarly, Carl Parsell, president of the Detroit Police Officers' Association, wrote in a recent issue of his association's newspaper that charges of police brutality "are part of a nefarious plot by those who would like our form of government overthrown."[39]

But subversion is not the only apparent basis for police hysteria about civilian review. Racism plays an important role. To the police it is a simple case of "Blue Power" versus "Black Power." The demand for review boards has long been a major issue in the black community. Lately the issue has served as a lightning rod drawing to it much of the mutual fear and hatred between the police and the black community. Police opposition to review boards is seen by black Americans as simply an acknowledgement by the police that they do engage in widespread brutality and mean to remain free to continue to do so. As interpreted in police literature and statements, the black community's demands for review boards are seen partly as the work of extremists, subversives, and agitators who are bent on stirring up trouble, and partly as a reflection of black lawlessness and unreasonableness. In addition, anger and prejudice against black people is so widespread among the police that there is virtually automatic opposition to anything seen as "pro-black." Furthermore, it has been obvious that much police support at the polls, particularly in review board fights, has come from white backlash. The racist overtones to police review board opposition—that review boards will strengthen black militants in their struggle with the police—seem to have been mainly responsible for arousing public support. It has come to be widely understood by the public that "crime in the streets" and "law and order," like "neighborhood schools," is racist talk—referring to black crime, suppression of radical militancy, and unintegrated schools, respectively. Similarly, the public understands "police brutality" and "civilian control of the police" as radical militant talk, as the counter-charge to law and order. Public fear of and anger towards blacks is a major source of police political muscle. Thus, civilian review board battles have not only added to the cycle of greater and greater polarization between the police and the black community, but have shown the police that they have a substantial portion of the white community on their side.

The Battle for Benefits

A second major proving ground for "Blue Power" has been the successful use of militant tactics to secure increased wages and improved working conditions. The police have long been united in guilds to pursue the ordinary concerns of trade unionism: wages, pensions, hours, overtime, vacations, work rules, and various fringe benefits. Recently, however, these goals have been pursued with militant tactics unheard of since the Boston Police Strike of 1919. While the police review board battles have been largely restricted to intensive political campaigning (either directed at the general public or at city councilmen) or law suits, the battle for increased benefits has produced direct forms of protest, demonstration, and revolt.

An extreme example was the recent threat of a strike by the Patrolmen's Benevolent Association in New York. A strike, as such, did not occur, but a semi-strike in the form of a slowdown and a widespread attack of "blue flu" was called to put pressure on the city to meet PBA demands.[40] The "blue flu" epidemic seems to have begun in Detroit in 1967. According to newspaper accounts, an

aggressive police association steamrollered city hall into acceptance of one of the most generous salary scales in the nation by the classic trade-union device of "job action" and "blue flu," police vernacular for phony illnesses that keep police off the job as a display of power.[41]

Ray Girardin, the then Detroit police commissioner, recalls that city hall had no option but to concede. "I was practically helpless. I couldn't force them to work."[42] Since then "blue flu" has been spreading. An attack broke out in Newark, N. J., during November 1968,[43] and it has been discussed in other cities. Indeed, not even Chicago Mayor Richard J. Daley's immense popularity with the rank-and-file policemen has provided complete immunity to the dread disease.[44] During November 1968, the Chicago police organizations rejected a proposed pay increase of $1,008 for patrolmen and more for higher ranks which was contained in Mayor Daley's 1969 budget. They demanded more than twice this increase and broadly hinted that "blue flu" and other such ailments might break out in Chicago. The presence of New York PBA president John Cassesse, who came to confer with local police leaders, made the hints plausible. Indeed, Cassesse's activities prompted a *Chicago Daily News* writer to gently spoof the police about bringing in "outside agitators."[45] The *Chicago Tribune* editors did not find it nearly so amusing and referred to Cassesse as an "Unwelcome Adviser."[46] Eventual settlement was by negotiation. Since then police strikes and strike threats have spread to the west coast.

A second activist tactic used by police to win increased benefits involves varying enforcement of the law as a means of exerting pressure. In Detroit the police combined a slowdown in ticket-writing with their "blue flu" campaign.[47] Similar suspension of ticket-writing occurred in New York in fall 1968.[48] Overenforcement can also be used to apply pressure. During November 1968, Long Island policemen are reported to have given unprecedented numbers of traffic tickets and in unprecedented circumstances. Tickets were reportedly issued for such things as improper registration or for exceeding the speed limit by one mile an hour.[49]

Militant tactics by the police in pursuit of increased benefits raise many serious and sensitive issues, some of which will be discussed at the end of this chapter. However, if this were the extent of police militance one might speak of the *unionized* police, but hardly of the *politicized* police. Even the attack on civilian review proposals could be seen as a union concern with work rules and grievance machinery. But the police have not restricted themselves to such matters, nor to such tactics. Instead they see themselves as the last bulwark of the American way of life and are seeking political power to refashion society according to their own image. According to a five-city study by *Washington Post* reporters, the police are "reaching for political power in a fashion never dreamed of only a few years ago."[50] And their desire for power is based more upon "constitutional and moral" issues than on "monetary considerations," according to Michael Churns, one of the founders of the Law Enforcement Group in New York.[51] According to the *Washington Post* investigation, "Police are coming to see themselves as the political force with which radicalism, student demonstration, and black power can be blocked."[52] The police seek power in order to punish those they blame for causing our contemporary troubles.

The goals and tactics of the police revolt not only exacerbate and escalate conflict with blacks, radicals, students, and protesters, *they have also resulted in rising conflict with police commanders and in a further erosion of the power of commanders to command.*

Revolt against Police Commanders

Police antagonism is not as commonly directed against their commanders as it is against civil government and the courts. In part this is because often their commanders do not try to command. Some have adopted the style and policy of Chicago's police superintendent James Conlisk, who, it will be recalled, is said to act against his officers "only if he is forced to." For many commanders, the cult of secrecy serves to mute the possibilities of conflict with rank-and-file militants. Other police commanders are immune from rank-and-file antagonism because they are themselves militant activists in the police revolt. Philadelphia's police commissioner Frank L. Rizzo is a prominent example. But some commanders are neither sympathetic with the extremist conceptions of the police revolt, nor willing to abide abuses for the sake of peaceful relations with their officers. Such commanders have been quick to experience angry grass-roots opposition. Even some timid commanders have found themselves forced by events to take actions opposed by their subordinates. They have fared no better than their bolder colleagues (and sometimes worse).

The following brief summaries illustrate the diversity, character, and nationwide scope of the police challenge to command authority.

Cleveland, Ohio In the wake of an ambush of police (July 23, 1968) by black extremists, in which three policemen were killed and 14 wounded, growing police opposition to Mayor Carl Stokes and his administration moved towards open revolt. When police were withdrawn from ghetto duty for one night in order to allow black community leaders to cool down rioting and avoid further deaths, police reportedly refused to answer calls, and some poured out racist abuse and obscenities against the mayor over their radios. Officers in the 5th District flatly refused to travel in two-man squads, one white and one black, into the East Side. Subsequently, spokesmen for the police officers' wives organization have berated the mayor, the local Fraternal Order of Police has demanded the resignation of Safety Director Joseph F. McNanamon, and many policemen have reportedly been privately purchasing high-powered rifles for use in future riots, despite official opposition by police commanders. Plans for a two-day strike by the Fraternal Order of Police to arouse public sympathy were rejected by the group's national leadership. Instead, the FOP plans a nationwide campaign to secure "30 to 50 million" signatures on a petition asking the government to "take the handcuffs" off the police. On October 9, 1968, Mayor Stokes moved to quell the police revolt. He fired Police Chief Michael "Iron Mike" Blackwell and announced plans to restructure the department and personally lay down policy. At the same time he announced a $17 million program to modernize, reequip, and enlarge the force—changes which the police have been demanding. As reported by *Los Angeles Times*' roving police expert D. J. R. Bruckner, whether these moves "would satisfy the policemen in the force is unknown."[53] In fact they did not. Cleveland has had a succession of police chiefs, none of whom could gain rank-and-file support.

Portland, Oregon In August 1968, the Portland Police Association went to court in an effort to block plans of Police Chief Donald

I. McNamara to add six more Negroes to the city's 800-man force. The city had five Negroes on its police payroll at that time, *but none was assigned to uniformed patrol.* The chief proposed to recruit six Negroes subject to the usual rigid physical, psychological, and background tests but to defer their taking of Civil Service examinations (carrying them as temporary employees) until a special training program had prepared them for the tests. The lawyer for the Police Association charged this irregularity on scheduling the tests would hurt the morale and efficiency of the police. Feelings among the rank-and-file were reported to run high on the issue.[54]

St. Louis, Missouri[55] In mid-September 1968, acting only on the basis of information contained in the official police report, the five-man civilian police board suspended one policeman for 30 days, another for 10 days, and issued a letter of reprimand to four others for use of excessive force in the highly controversial arrest and detention of two black militant leaders. This action caused anger in the black community and among pro-civil rights whites who called it merely a "slap on the wrists" when blatant brutality and irregularity had occurred. Nonetheless, it produced an angry rebellion among the police rank and file. At an initial protest meeting against the board, more than 150 police officers attended. A second meeting produced a petition signed by more than 700 police, one-third of the total force, demanding the resignation of the police board and saying police on duty no longer had any confidence in the board. Subsequently, the city was rapidly polarized on the issue. Civil rights and student groups, the ACLU, and others came to the support of the board. Meanwhile the dissident police built a powerful coalition with unions, neighborhood clubs, political associations, the American Legion, civic groups, and various *ad hoc* committees. In the words of *Los Angeles Times* correspondent D. J. R. Bruckner, the polarization of the community was "a frightening situation."[56] Subsequently, the board backed down and rescinded its disciplinary actions, minor though they had been in the light of the charges on which they had been based. Still, the St. Louis police were not willing to settle. Despite opposition of the board, 1,300 officers formed a policeman's association to seek reforms which would restore the morale of policemen, which, the association charged, has been "seriously undermined" by the board.[57]

San Francisco What had been judged by all experts as the most effective police/community relations program in the nation, organized and led by Lt. Dante Andreotti in 1962, was stripped of most of its powers in 1967 after rank-and-file agitation against its goals, procedures, and personnel culminated in a virtual ultimatum from the nine district captains, backed by the 1966 grand jury police committee and the persistent efforts of the Police Officers Association. Andreotti resigned to join the staff of the U. S. Department of Justice. The short life of an active community relations unit was marred by constant harassment and abuse from other policemen who habitually referred to it as the "Commie Relations Unit." A community relations conference held in 1967 at which police attendance was mandatory was marred by such incidents as calls of "Nigger lover!" from the back of the room during a lecture by a representative of the NAACP, and "Christ killer!" while a Jewish community leader spoke. A captain of the California Highway Patrol, who sat in on a classroom session, was so shocked at the unruly and crude behavior he told Deputy Chief Al Nelder, "You have a bunch of hoodlums in uniform."[58] Following the death of a meaningful community relations unit, the San Francisco department has produced further evidence of a police revolt. Several members of the Tactical Squad have been indicted for an off-duty sweep through the Mission District during which they cleared at least a dozen pedestrians from the sidewalks with blackjacks. In the face of community indignation over a rash of such events the Police Officers Association has launched a campaign including large newspaper ads to denounce all complaints. Indeed, as mentioned earlier, the POA has demanded that disciplinary action be taken against Deputy Chief Al Nelder and six other commanders *because they conducted an investigation* of the conduct of an off-duty officer who shot and killed a black truckdriver following an argument over a minor traffic accident.[59] Subsequently, Nelder became chief and the POA was then taken over by a militant slate of "Bluecoats."

Santa Ana, California Chief Edward J. Allen suffered a long campaign of intense harassment and vilification carried on by right-wing officers on his force. He received constant abusive phone calls; unordered merchandise was sent C.O.D. to his home; false fire alarms were turned in for his house; unordered taxis were sent; ads were placed in newspapers that he had automobiles or dogs for sale. "Anonymous and libelous" pamphlets were distributed in the city, especially to city councilmen; some were openly handed out from patrol cars. Chief Allen attempted to dismiss two of the worst offenders, but ultimately had to settle for seven months' suspensions without pay of these officers. An uneasy truce was finally reached, but the embattled chief says that he assumes that his men still read all of his mail.[60]

Cincinnati On June 24, 1969, the local Fraternal Order of Police publicly expelled Safety Director Henry Sandman for "giving in too much to minority groups." Sandman, a 25-year police veteran, was chief of detectives prior to being appointed director of safety (equivalent to chief of police in most cities) three years before. FOP lodge vice-president, Police Specialist Elmer Dunaway, said the police rank-and-file organization revoked Sandman's honorary lifetime membership to indicate their opposition to several recent incidents when, they charged, Sandman "took the side" of the minority rather than that of policemen.[61]

These and many similar recent incidents across the country indicate the tenuous authority police commanders have over their rank-and-file. The solidarity of the police has gained political expression. The apparent complicity of commanders in justifying officer behavior in virtually any specific instance, with its obvious costs in discipline, can be at least partly blamed upon the fact that commanders have little freedom to do otherwise. The rank-and-file are in no mood to accept the official authority of commanders. Chiefs must rule mainly by moral suasion these days, which is a tenuous and limited basis for command.

Conclusions

It should now be clear that the police are unwilling and their commanders are in no position to set their affairs in order. The police cooperate to protect themselves against charges of wrongdoing and to seize the power to legitimate their use of violence and repression against protest and dissent. Restraint upon police behavior will have to be imposed from outside present police institutions.

7

External Control over the Police

The police worry about the press, and the majority of them are extremely hostile towards it, but they know it is a paper tiger.

We have examined the extensive freedom of the police from internal controls—neither their commanders nor their fellow officers often are willing or able to intervene to prevent or punish the physical mistreatment of citizens. But what about external authorities and institutions? The police do not function in a social or political vacuum.

This chapter assesses the inability of external forces to control the police at present. My thesis is that, for a variety of reasons, the police enjoy their own special version of the four freedoms: freedom from civil authorities, from the courts, from the press, and from public opinion.

I. Civil Authority

As was prominent in the New York City episodes recounted in the last chapter and in a number of other instances described, the current police revolt is heavily directed against civil authority, especially the power of mayors. A primary expression of this revolt has been through campaigns against civilian review boards and against police reorganization attempts proposed by city governments. But more recently they have broadened the scope of their concerns and have challenged civil authorities in a directly political way.

One prominent development has been activism on behalf of political candidates considered friendly to police aims and against those whose policies police reject or who have refused to cooperate.

During the 1964 Presidential campaign a number of departments had to issue special directives in an effort to curtail policemen from wearing Goldwater buttons on their uniforms and even from putting Goldwater stickers on their patrol cars. In 1968 there was abundant evidence that George Wallace enjoyed considerable support among American police (see Chapter 5), and there were a number of incidents of police campaigning on his behalf.

But perhaps the most effective direct political action found among police these days is activism on the part of or against local candidates. The next section will review evidence on police political action to defeat "liberal" judges, to elect judges committed to dealing "severely" with defendants, and with the implications of such police action. We will focus on police participation in local politics, especially with police campaigns on behalf of political candidates for local executive or legislative office.

The following excerpts from a story in the *San Francisco Chronicle*[1] reveal a practice that seems to be becoming more common across the nation:

Cops Are Peddling Favorite Candidate

Plans were announced yesterday to have policemen from all communities in Alameda County sell $10-a-person tickets for a testimonial dinner for Robert Hannon, Republican candidate for State Senate.

Detective Sergeant Jack Baugh of the Alameda County Sheriff's Department, cochairman of the dinner, said the record of Democratic State Senator Nicholas Petris is "repulsive to a police officer."

Baugh said tickets would be sold by police outside of their working hours and in civilian clothing.

Petris won reelection despite police opposition. Elsewhere, police political muscle has been more effective. On specifically police issues they have proved almost unbeatable. In New York City, Mayor John Lindsay has lost to the police lobby in the state legislature on his proposals to have police cadets take over traffic patrol duties, the use of one-man squad cars, and the consolidation of precincts.[2]

Similar police victories over city hall have been the rule in Boston. The PBA lobbied vigorously against Mayor Kevin White's decision to place civilians in most jobs occupied by traffic patrolmen, a move which would have freed men for crime work. The city council, which had to approve the change, sided with the police.[3] The mayor then went to the state legislature, but the police lobby again prevailed and White lost. In November 1968, the PBA again prevailed over the mayor when the city council substantially altered the police component of White's Model Cities Program. Changes included removal of a plan to allow citizens to receive (not judge) complaints against the police and removal of references to the need to recruit blacks to the police force.[4]

In a west coast city in which the Task Force conducted interviews, a graphic example of police lobbying was described. According to a policeman on the board of the local Police Officers Association, the practice has been to put "pressure" on city council members directly through phone calls, luncheons, and the like. So far the local POA leaders are uncertain how far this has gotten them. As one POA board member told a Task Force interviewer: "[We have gotten very little] although we have tried to wine and dine them and even blackmail the members of the city council. But they are too stupid to understand what the Association is trying to do."[5]

Militant tactics similar to those used by students, anti-war protesters, and blacks have also found their way into police activism. For example, New York and San Francisco police have marched on City Hall, and Detroit police have shown up in uniform at a city council hearing in what some councilmen are reported to have felt was a flagrant attempt at intimidation.[6] Moreover, because they are law enforcement officers, police can avail themselves of tactics beyond those available to most dissident groups—and of even more questionable legitimacy. The examples of slowdowns in ticket-writing and overenforcement of the criminal law have already been discussed. In addition, an extraordinary tactic has been reported in a confrontation between Philadelphia

Police Commissioner Frank L. Rizzo and the city's school board over the stationing of police in unruly, predominantly black schools. Rizzo is said to have told the school board that the police performed many duties of which the public was unaware—for example, keeping "dossiers" on a lot of people including "some of you school people."[7] The threat was left implicit. FI-PO, the Fire and Police Research Association, maintains dossiers on individuals and groups, compiled from "open sources." During the 1968 campaign FI-PO is reported to have passed the word that the son of a California senatorial candidate had once been arrested on a narcotics charge.[8]

The direct entry of the police into politics is so recent that it is difficult to assess. But one thing is clear—police political power in our large cities is both considerable and growing. The police are quite consciously building this power, and its impact is being felt throughout the political system. An example is given by an observer in New York:

> In fact, there's a growing danger of disagreeing with the cops. On precinct consolidation, for example, councilmen, rabbis, state senators privately would say, "It doesn't sound like a bad idea, but the police are getting everybody so hot, I don't see how we could go with it.
> See, these [issues] are not the exciting issues and a lot of people don't feel like taking on a political force like the cops.[9]

Some police spokesmen rate this power even higher:

> We could elect governors, or at least knock 'em off. I've told them, if you get out and organize, you could become one of the strongest political units in the commonwealth.[10]

Recently, there are signs that police political strategists are turning away from backing "acceptable" candidates in favor of running for office themselves. For some months there was considerable talk in New York of running PBA public relations director Norman Frank for Mayor—"talk which Frank encourages."[11] Ultimately Frank did not run. In Boston, political writers report Patrolman Richard MacEachern, activist police leader, has been considering running for Mayor or the city council.[12]

These aspirations, and those of police leaders elsewhere, have been greatly encouraged by the recent election of detective Charles Stenvig, business manager of the Minneapolis Police Officer's Federation, as Mayor of that city.[13] Stenvig ran a single issue—law and order—campaign, promising to end the influence of militants on city hall, but said little about any other actions he proposed to take. His victory was stunning. First he eliminated the Democratic Farmer Labor Party candidate—normally a certain winner in Minneapolis elections—and then in a run-off election overwhelmed Republican Dan Cohen, President of the City Council, by nearly two to one. Stenvig's first political announcement was the appointment of God as his "chief advisor, and don't you forget it!"[14]

With or without actually taking office, the police have become a potent political factor in civic government. Aides to New York Mayor John Lindsay are reported to feel that the mayor's office has lost the initiative to the police, who now dominate the public dialogue.[15] Political observers report that ultimate political power in Philadelphia resides in Police Commissioner Frank L. Rizzo, not Mayor James H. Tate.[16] Indeed, local officials of the Fraternal Order of Police believe they made Tate's election possible. As this is written, Rizzo is running for Mayor to succeed Tate and is considered the favorite. The implications are clear to Boston Mayor Kevin White (who is frequently called "Mayor Black" by the police): "Are the police governable? Yes. Do I control the police right now? No."[17]

II. The Courts

In principle, the court system could impose considerable control over police behavior. It could enforce the statutes violated by officers when they engage in unjustified use of force: assault, battery, unlawful use of deadly weapons, denial of civil rights, manslaughter, and murder carry considerable legal penalties. Presumably, the threat of prosecution and conviction under these statutes could inhibit the violent proclivities of many officers, as presumably citizens are deterred. Furthermore, the legal system provides the possibility for citizens to seek civil damages against officers and departments.

In practice, however, the legal system rarely operates to punish police violence. There are a number of reasons why it does not.

For one thing, the police are an integral part of the same system of justice. On a day-to-day basis prosecutors must work intimately with the police to prepare and try cases. Given the intimate character of this relationship it is not hard to imagine that prosecutors would be reluctant to bring charges against the police (except when such charges are initiated by the department itself). Furthermore, prosecutors are normally elected, as are most local judges. To gain and retain office, prosecutors and judges cannot afford an "anti-police" reputation.

Another impediment to the courts in controlling the police is the fact that neither prosecutors nor the courts have any substantial investigative resources of their own. In the ordinary course of things the police provide the investigative data on which cases are prosecuted and decided. Ordinarily this means that when allegations of police misconduct arise, it is the police themselves who conduct the investigation, and it is on this information that subsequent decisions by prosecutors and the courts are based. To a very considerable extent, control of the police by the judicial system actually is identical with control of the police by the police.

In addition, the police are "expert" witnesses in contrast with ordinary citizens who may have grievances against them. Quite simply, the police are accustomed to testifying in court and make very credible appearances. On the other hand, many of those who are victims of police violence are not upright middle-class citizens and do not make impressive witnesses in court.

A further constraint on court control over the police lies in the plea bargaining system. Chevigny has written a detailed account of how this process ordinarily prevents conscientious attorneys from pursuing actions against the police.[18] In situations when the police have used force on a citizen they ordinarily bring both misdemeanor charges such as resisting arrest, and felony charges such as assaulting an officer, against the arrestee. Subsequently, prosecutors are usually willing to drop the felony charges in return for a plea of guilty to the misdemeanor offense, especially when police actions seem to have been questionable. This puts a most difficult burden on the defense attorney. If he is to proceed to try to show in court that the police used illegal violence he must also advise his client to take the risk of a felony conviction. Typically, responsible lawyers cannot so advise their clients and contentions over police misconduct are dropped to protect the victim.

Finally, in the overwhelming proportion of recent cases when prosecutors have brought officers to trial for brutality, juries have refused to convict. Defenses based on the law and order crisis, the social or political deviance of victims, and the importance of backing up the "thin blue line" standing between society and anarchy have proven powerful. Thus the climate of public opinion, to be examined later in this chapter, operates to impede court control over the police.

At the present time a large number of civil suits against the police for physically mistreating citizens await trial in many major cities. This is a relatively new tactic in police–citizen relations, and it is not yet possible to judge its effectiveness. Experience with the failure of criminal proceedings, however, suggests that few such cases will be won by the plaintiffs.

But over and above these institutional and practical limits on the ability of the courts to regulate police behavior, is the extent to which police militancy is aimed at intimidating and changing the courts themselves. Increasingly, for the courts to crack down on the police entails arousing serious and powerful political retaliation.

Once again the most dramatic example occurred in New York City, although subsequently the New York tactics have been copied by police in a number of other departments.

The initial formation of the new militant right-wing group with the police (LEG) began with a petition calling for the removal of Criminal Court Judge John F. Furey from the bench because LEG alleged he permitted unruly conduct in his court during the arraignment of two members of the Black Panther Party.[19] Several weeks later LEG members moved from petitions and press conferences to direct confrontation during a hearing on charges of assaulting a policeman brought against three other Black Panthers. In the widely publicized incident mentioned in an earlier chapter, off-duty policemen, alleged to be members of LEG, took over the seats in a courtroom. The judge immediately scheduled the preliminary hearing in an adjoining courtroom. The crowd of policemen surged into the hallway—shouting "White Power" and "Win with Wallace," according to press accounts—and took over the seats in the new courtroom. Many policemen were unable to find seats, however, and it was these off-duty officers, plus an undetermined number of nonpolice white men, who attacked and drove from the building several Black Panthers who arrived to attend the hearing of their fellow Panthers. Meanwhile, in the courtroom—now packed with militant off-duty policemen—the defense lawyer objected that their presence was intimidating the court and asked that each be made to rise and identify himself. The judge refused.[20]

Subsequently, the LEG campaign against the courts has continued. They have demanded a grand jury investigation of what they charge is the "coddling" of criminals in the courts. They also conducted a campaign to support senators seeking to prevent "another Warren Court" by blocking the appointment of Abe Fortas as Chief Justice. But perhaps the most extraordinary tactic of LEG is its system of court watchers. LEG has arranged for off-duty officers to attend court sessions and note what they deem misbehavior by judges, prosecutors, probation officers, and others involved in the judicial process. Police Lieutenant Leon Laino, one of the founders of LEG, described this program as follows to a Task Force interviewer:

> The courts have a lot to do with the crime rate the way they handle people, let them out on bail or without bail so that they can commit the same crime two or three times before coming to trial. Nowadays the courts let people get away with anything, even disrespectful conduct while in court. But since we have instituted a policy of court watchers ... we have noticed a change in the behavior of these judges. What we want to do is to not just watch the court, but watch other agencies and make note of how they are handling law violators and the general public.... The way it stands now, policemen have a lot of feelings about things not being done right, but we can't document them. We feel that if we set up a system of watchers in the courts and in the other agencies, that then we know just what's wrong and we can figure out what to do to prevent it or change things.[21]

The announced purpose of this court-watching tactic is to challenge the competence and "toughness" of judges at election time or even to campaign for their impeachment. LEG has already singled out several judges as "coddlers" of criminals. Furthermore, the LEG court-watching tactic has been taken up elsewhere. The new militant group called the Blue-Coats, which recently took control of the Police Officers Association in San Francisco, has adopted this technique despite strong opposition by city officials and the press. In Oakland and several other western cities, the police have chosen to back court-watching programs ostensibly organized by concerned citizens groups, thus evading departmental opposition. Plans to publish ratings on judges and conduct election campaigns for and against particular judges have been announced in all these new instances.

As the intervention of policemen and police organizations in election campaigns of judges grows, there has been a tendency for candidates for the bench to announce they will be "tough" on criminals. The legal implications of electing judges who have promised to be tough seem profound. How can a judge fulfill this promise and at the same time impartially oversee due process and the rule of law? More important, if judges feel politically intimidated by police reactions to their judicial conduct a major balance of power in our system is threatened, and an important part of society's potential authority over the police is nullified.

Police pressure on the courts includes the District Attorney's office as well. DAs seem almost notoriously reluctant to bring charges against police officers. In two recent San Francisco incidents, one involving a cop who shot out the window at a cat and hit a neighbor and another involving an off-duty policeman who killed a black man following an argument over a minor traffic accident, no charges were filed by the DA until a local attorney brought victims and witnesses to the DA's office to sign complaints against the policemen. Similarly, in Detroit the DA's office proved extremely unaggressive in charging and prosecuting officers involved in the Algiers Motel incident, as did the courts who freed the officers on very low bail.

Recent police opposition to the courts has even extended to defense attorneys. In the celebrated Huey P. Newton case—the Black Panther leader charged with killing a policeman, and found guilty of voluntary manslaughter—Bay Area police dug into the past of his defense attorney Charles P. Gary. An official of the San Francisco Police Officers Association told a Task Force interviewer that the SFPD intelligence detail had passed along intelligence findings on the background of Gary which were alleged to document that Gary was a communist, or affiliated with the communists. The Task Force interviewer was told the same thing by a top official of the Oakland Police Officers Association.[22]

Attacks on the character and loyalty of attorneys who defend unpopular clients are hardly new in our society. But when the police assist in such tactics they are lent the aura of official credibility.

None of the officers mentioned above seemed aware of or concerned with the fact that the political past of a defendant's attorney, whatever the facts actually might be, has no bearing on the guilt or innocence of a defendant.

Thus, not only are there inherent flaws in the ability of the judicial system to regulate police behavior, police militance seems to be eroding even the limited power of the courts.

III. The Press

A third potential source of control over police behavior is newsmen—both press and television. In principle it would seem that to the extent that the news media make police misbehavior visible public concern would be aroused. Presumably, extended news coverage of particular instances might pressure police chiefs to take action or cause the district attorney to bring charges.

It seems certain that this is exactly what newspaper and television newsmen covering the 1968 Democratic Convention in Chicago thought when they gave so much indignant and detailed coverage to the misbehavior of Mayor Daley's officers. But that's not what happened.

Since Chicago, even the most staid and respected newspapers and magazines have attacked and exposed police violence. But on the whole their efforts so far have not had very great impact. Much of this ineffectiveness stems from structural features of the news media themselves.

It is a poignant reality of newspapering that today's last edition—a triumph of creative organization—will be fit only for wrapping fish tomorrow. Today's big story will not even be remembered by most readers by week's end. Because the news that sells is understood to be the newest and the latest of events, news media do not sustain coverage of a given story for very long. As a result, the media are ill-designed to deal with chronic problems—only the occasional crisis or strange event growing out of a chronic problem surfaces. Indeed, to keep a particular long-term story in the news requires good press agentry—the creation of newsworthy events (or nonevents, such as buying cocktails for the press) in order to get the story into the news again. The victims of police brutality lack press agents. If their story attracts attention in the first place, and most don't, it will not sustain coverage for very long. Soon it will all "blow over." And the police, who do employ press agentry, will help bury it with a newer story involving police heroism, martyrdom, or steadfastness.

In addition, the press looks for big stories. Most acts of police brutality, like most murders, don't really add up to a big enough story to attract press coverage. Of course, usually a police riot is sufficiently "big" to attract press attention. That's why police misconduct has received so much press attention over the past several years. Still, even when covering police riots, the press faces many limiting factors.

For one thing they are often not present at the scene of the event. When this is the case they must rely on after-the-fact accounts, of which the police will always offer the most comprehensive version. Even when reporters are on the scene they must rely on police accounts for a great deal of the material they need for an accurate story—who was arrested, on what charges, how many injuries, and so on. In fact all police reporting is greatly dependent on police information. In the huge majority of crime stories, neither victim nor suspect is ever spoken to by a reporter. The whole is taken from official police reports. Reporters must rely on the police most of the time, and they must be able to count on cooperation by the police in order to function effectively in their job. A police reporter who angers the department often finds his job made impossible. Furthermore, most police reporters are permanently assigned their jobs. They work out of police stations. Their editors become voices on the phone. Over time, they tend to become policemen rather than reporters.[23] They adopt police attitudes and accept police norms about covering up. When big police scandals—the police burglary rings in Chicago and Denver, for example—come to light they are not the result of digging by police reporters.

A further barrier to press coverage of police violence is the commitment to objectivity, which so often simply means recounting the opposing tales of two obvious liars.[24] The press is loath to point out when statements by public officials cannot possibly be true in light of other evidence. Rather, they hope to run a story quoting someone else pointing out the untruth. But often such spokesmen do not speak up, or fail to see the critical inconsistency.

All reporters know they are often being had by self-serving press releases and statements. But, when the police say officers acted with restraint, or claim special law enforcement expertise to "know" when officers are in fact in danger and had no choice but to use violence, the press often can do nothing but recount these statements. The other side is often a disorganized mass of angry citizens without an experienced press officer or the group discipline needed to permit a coherent rebuttal of the police version.

Finally, the public has learned to be somewhat suspicious of the press. The press loses credibility, necessarily, by treading upon private prejudices and fears. For example, while one-third of the American public thought Martin Luther King brought his assassination upon himself,[25] the press treated King's death as the tragedy it was. On the other hand, Americans are inclined to trust the police. Thus when it seems to be the word of the newspapers and some dissidents against that of the police, they believe the police. In all these ways the press has failed to serve as a restraint on police behavior. The police worry about the press, and the majority of them are extremely hostile towards it,[26] but they know it is a paper tiger.

IV. Public Opinion

Chapter 2 established that, at a conservative estimate, several million Americans have been beaten unlawfully by the police. Much of this activity has, of course, been relatively invisible. But as just mentioned, in most major cities in the past several years some very blatant instances have periodically been brought to light by the news media. Furthermore, in the past several years there have been a number of instances of mass misbehavior by the police—police riots. These are public events and often claim white, middle-class victims (instead of the less visible victims of much routine police violence). Still, hardly any punitive action against police offenders has resulted.

A number of reasons have already been outlined—the failure of political authorities, of the courts, and of the press to impose controls on the police. Each of these failures implicitly involves public opinion. It is the public that provides jurors. It is the public that supports "pro-police" candidates, and it is to the public that the news media have unsuccessfully appealed in efforts to arouse indignation over police actions.

These recent reactions by the American public suggest to most observers that Americans in fact condone the police use of force outside legal limits—that the average American has a taste for rough-and-ready "justice."

Those of us who are experienced with data on public opinion are always inclined to suspect simple generalizations about what the average American believes, knows, or feels about anything. Too often "expert" judgments in these matters prove incorrect when adequate data become available. Fortunately, I was able to obtain adequate data on this question, "Do Americans generally support police use of excessive force?"

The data are based on a representative national sample of the adult population of the United States interviewed by Louis Harris and Associates during October 1968. The study was done under the auspices of the National Commission on the Causes and Prevention of Violence.[27]

I will not explain the sources of support for police violence; that has been taken up in other works.[28] Here I am concerned about the general contours of public opinion on the use of extralegal force by the police.

The first item in Table 5 reveals that three out of four Americans accept the principle that there are some circumstances in which the police may need to strike an adult male, while 25 percent said they would not approve of this in *any* situation. It seems surprising that so many Americans reject outright the acceptability of policemen striking people (I certainly could not do so). It is much less surprising that the majority of blacks would reject this statement given the present outrage of the black community over police violence. Sex, regional, and age differences are relatively minor, while approval of the police striking persons increases modestly with income and education.

The results for item 2 are virtually identical. Overall, 7 out of 10 Americans could imagine a situation in which they would approve of a policeman shooting an adult male. Blacks were much less approving of police use of deadly force, while males, the better educated, and those with higher incomes were above the norm in approving.

Table 5 American Views on Police Violence

Police Violence	Race		Sex		Region				Income			Education				Age				National Average
	Black	White	Male	Female	East	Midwest	South	West	$5000 or less	$5,000–9,999	$10,000 or more	8th grade or less	Some high school	High school graduate	College	30 and under	31–50	51–65	65+	
1. "Are there any situations you can imagine in which you would approve of a policeman striking an adult male citizen?"																				
Percent answering "yes"	48	77	76	70	70	75	70	80	64	73	82	62	65	76	83	75	75	71	67	73
2. "Are there any situations you can imagine in which you would approve of a policeman shooting an adult male citizen?"																				
Percent answering "yes"	46	75	75	68	68	75	66	77	61	68	84	57	61	74	85	74	74	67	62	71
3. "Any man who insults a policeman has no complaint if he gets roughed-up in return."																				
Percent agreeing	41	60	57	57	50	57	66	53	66	54	54	71	65	56	45	41	53	67	81	57
4. "The police are wrong to beat up unarmed protesters, even when these people are rude and call them names."																				
Percent agreeing	76	44	48	50	52	40	49	57	47	47	52	39	55	46	53	55	54	50	38	49
5. "Would you approve of a policeman striking an adult male citizen if he had said vulgar and obscene things to the policeman?"																				
Percent answering "yes"	9	22	22	10	20	22	20	18	19	23	19	27	21	23	15	14	20	29	22	20
6. "Would you approve of a policeman striking an adult male citizen if he "was demonstrating against the war in Vietnam and carrying a Viet Cong flag?""																				
Percent answering "yes"	5	17	16	14	15	14	13	18	14	16	14	16	16	16	12	13	14	19	13	15
7. "The police frequently use more force than they need to when carrying out their duties."																				
Percent answering "yes"	66	21	21	28	29	23	33	26	35	28	21	33	34	21	28	34	27	25	27	28

Neither of these items reflects approval of brutality or misuse of force. Both striking and shooting people is legal under certain circumstances. The items are mainly interesting as they establish the rock bottom base of opposition to the use of violent methods by the police under *any* circumstances. The fact that nearly 3 out of 10 Americans would deny the police all use of violence seems a sizable proportion and at considerable variance with assumptions about public support for police actions.

Item 3 crosses the legal boundary: "Any man who insults a policeman has no complaint if he gets roughed-up in return." A majority of Americans agreed with this statement (57 percent), but opposition is considerably more substantial than on the first two items. Again race differences are large; only 41 percent of blacks in contrast with 60 percent of whites agreed. Southerners, lower-income persons, and the least educated exceed the norm on approval. There is also a very marked age effect—the older a person is, the more willing he is to approve. However, agreeing with this statement need not (and, as we shall see, does not) simply reflect approval of the police hitting citizens who insult them. The item also appeals to a realistic outlook—that a man who insults the police cannot complain if he gets into trouble, because he brought it on himself. Many, especially among blacks and workers, who agreed with this item perhaps mainly meant to indicate that they think it is stupid and asking for trouble to smart off to cops, and that a person who does so deserves little sympathy.

The fourth item in the table gives some indication that this is so. A smaller proportion of Americans condone the police beating up unarmed protesters "even when these people are rude and call them names"—49 percent think the police are wrong in such circumstances. Thus, one of the most frequently used defenses of police rioting would seem to divide public opinion about 50–50. Among blacks, however, three-fourths disapprove of such police action, while among persons over 65 only about one-third think the police are wrong in taking such action. As will be reconsidered below, the wording of this question tends to imply that the police are not only wrong to do such things, but that *they do them*. This creates a greater impression of support for such police action than may be the case. Indeed, on item 5 only 20 percent of Americans said they would approve of a policeman striking an adult male citizen who "had said vulgar and obscene things" to him. Thus, the overwhelming majority of Americans do not think policemen have the right to enforce deference with a nightstick—even though they tend to feel rude citizens should not complain if they do get worked over. Only 9 percent of blacks approve of policemen striking people for dirty backtalking, and the college educated and persons under 30 also fell below the norm.

Approval of police violence falls even further on the question of political dissent: 15 percent would approve of a policeman striking an adult male who "was demonstrating against the war in Vietnam and carrying a Viet Cong flag." Although the police in several cities have behaved in this way, and although hard hat demonstrators solidly approve, the overwhelming majority of Americans of any age, sex, race, region, and social class say they do not.

Thus far, we have seen a surprising disconfirmation of stereotypes about the support of the "silent majority" for police violence used to punish profanity and dissent. The survey data show they do not approve of it. This presents a puzzle. Why does this public disapproval of police violence not manifest itself during the many conflicts over police behavior? Why do police civilian review boards fail at the polls?

The answer seems to be that *the public is unwilling to believe that the police do misbehave.*

In the wake of the angry media condemnations of the Chicago police for the behavior during the 1968 convention, the Gallup Poll reported that 46 percent of Americans refused to believe what they had seen on television and supported the actions of the police (13 percent had no opinion, and 31 percent disapproved). Similarly, a Gallup Poll conducted shortly after four students were killed and others wounded at Kent State in the spring of 1970 found that only *11 percent* of Americans would attribute primary responsibility to the National Guard. The majority (58 percent) blamed the students, while 31 percent had no opinion.[29] This was the public response despite outspoken press criticism of the Guard.

Item 7 further confirms the unwillingness of the public to recognize or admit police misconduct. Only one-quarter (28 percent) would agree that "the police frequently use more force than they need to when carrying out their duties."

It seems perfectly clear that the police frequently do use unnecessary force. But most white Americans will not believe it.

However, two-thirds of black Americans believe it. Since we have seen in Chapter 2 that blacks are disproportionately the victims of police misconduct, this is not surprising.

The data show that a potentially powerful means for restraining the police to the limits of law and decency is nullified by incredulity. In this way most Americans are like most chiefs of police. They strongly disapprove of police brutality, but they will not admit, or cannot see, that in any concrete instance it has actually occurred. Some of this blindness seems related to self-interest. In the case of police chiefs this is obvious. Working with these same data, Gamson and McEvoy[30] have demonstrated that in the public at large support for police violence is most prevalent among those who see the police as representing their personal interests.

Whatever the reason, the police need not fear the high-minded principles of the public. An elaborate conception of evil is useless among those who see and hear no evil.

The conclusion of this chapter is simple. The police are free to behave as they want because the potential forces of social control over them are ineffectual. Since we have previously seen that the police would like to work over certain kinds of people and believe that the nightstick is an effective solution to dissent and social unrest, it is no surprise that they act as they do.

The important question posed by this chapter is: what is to be done? Is there any way to restore or establish control over police misbehavior? In the concluding chapter I offer what insights I have into what might be possible and effective.

8

Changing the Police

A corporation that recruited its executives from the stockroom and offered no more training to employees than police get would go bankrupt.

How can we create effective and responsible police departments? In this chapter I outline a series of proposals. They are hardly definitive. They are starting points, not stopping places. Successful change will depend upon trying a number of proposals and seeing how they work and then making alterations accordingly. Reform plans often create new problems as serious as those they were established to solve. Organizations can only be kept responsive and effective by constant tinkering and reshaping. This is how I would begin tinkering with police organizations.

Three main areas must be changed: (1) the kinds of police officers we have, which means changes in recruitment and training; (2) the way police departments are organized and run, which means changes in policy and administration; (3) the effectiveness of external control agencies, which means the creation of strong external regulation agencies and institutions.

I. A Different Kind of Policeman

All recent commission reports on the police have called for upgrading the quality of police officers. Recently police pay has been substantially raised in many cities in an effort to attract more qualified applicants. However, the main effect has simply been higher pay for the same quality of policeman as before—higher pay has made it easier to obtain the needed numbers of applicants, but qualifications of applicants have remained low. More pay is undoubtedly necessary, but it has proved insufficient. Significant change will require different strategies of recruitment and a reorganization and extension of training.

Dual-Level Recruitment and Training

At present all policemen are hired for the job of patrolman. Those who show merit (or simply wait for seniority) eventually are promoted to sergeant, detective, and even chief. It has been said with some justice that chiefs of police are simply patrolmen who have been on the force for 25 years. The general weakness of police administration is not very mysterious considering that it is performed by men who were not chosen for their administrative skill or training, but for physical aggressiveness and willingness to pound a beat. It seems inconceivable that this practice persists. For example, consider what kind of army we would have if we only recruited privates. We would have generals recruited from the pool of young men who found being an army private an attractive occupational choice, who knew how to field strip a rifle with their eyes closed, but who didn't know a double envelopment from an amphibious landing.

But the army doesn't operate this way. Even in the Revolutionary War we relied on a professional officer corps. Army officers are recruited and trained *as officers* (those who rise from the ranks are wholly retrained at officer candidate schools). Nor is initial training all that army officers receive. There is continual training as officers are promoted. For example, it is rare to become a general grade line officer without completing the Army Staff College. In contrast, police commanders receive very little training once they have completed their initial training to become rookie patrolmen.

I propose that the police adopt a two-level recruitment system like that of the army. The qualities that make a good beat cop are probably ill-suited to administrative work. Men should be recruited who will make good patrolmen and who see this as a worthwhile career. Different kinds of men ought to be recruited for training to be police commanders. While it probably will be important to give these men some period of experience of actual street policing—in much the same way as army officer candidates receive intensive infantry training—this should be part of an officer training program. With separate recruitment, a different quality of manpower would become available. For instance, young men with law degrees or degrees in business administration who find police work attractive would not have to enter as beat patrolmen and wait years for promotion. At present this is the prospect they face, so they do not join the police. Nor would they become privates in the army in hope of someday being commissioned. Only through a two-level strategy can we recruit men of appropriate quality to run our police organizations.

Actually, this suggestion is not really very novel. European nations have been following similar procedures for some time:

The top 300 police positions in Sweden are filled by lawyers recruited directly into these upper ranks. Most chiefs of police in larger cities are lawyers. The head of the Swedish police is a former judge, while the head of the main police academy is an ex-teacher of French.[1]

France recruits half of its lieutenant candidates from among civilians with a baccalaureate degree and half of its inspector candidates from among law school graduates. Half of the executive positions in the French police organization are held by civilians. The head of the French police was promoted from the upper ranks of the Ministry of Education.[2]

In Germany all police commissioners are civilians and so are most of the division heads, including the head of the criminal police, or detective force. German police commissioners, and most division heads as well, hold *doctorates* in law. German police forces recruit about 10 percent of their detectives directly from the legal profession. Applicants to the regular police who possess the *arbitur* (equivalent to two years of college in the United States) are allowed to apply for officer training three years earlier than those with less education.[3]

But it is not enough to recruit better patrolmen and better officers; we have done a woeful job training our police. The average American policeman receives 300 hours of initial training. (The average for barbers is 4,000 hours, for embalmers 5,000 hours.)[4] In contrast, police recruits in Italy receive 33 months of training; in Sweden rookie training lasts a year, in France six months.[5]

For the American police, their first training is pretty much their last. While some departments require additional training for those promoted to higher ranks (California requires those promoted to sergeant to receive 80 hours of additional training within 18 months after promotion), this training is brief and usually haphazard. In Europe, promotions require additional full-time training typically lasting from six months to a year!

In the next section I shall have some suggestions about how police training could be best organized. But, however organized, we simply have to face the fact that policing is at least as difficult as barbering or embalming and we are probably getting better service out of our police than the amount and quality of training we provide them gives us a right to expect. A corporation that recruited its executives from the stockroom and offered no more training to employees than police get would go bankrupt.

Lateral Entry

All recent commissions have suggested that the police would benefit from lateral entry—permitting policemen to move from one department to another without loss of rank. At present most departments require that a man moving in from another department begin at the bottom. In my judgment, lateral entry would produce many benefits, especially in combination with dual-level recruitment.

First of all, the better departments would be able to attract superior officers from elsewhere, which would provide a clear stimulus for upgrading departments which can't keep their better men.

Secondly, it would greatly speed the transmission of innovation. Men moving from department to department would bring new techniques and new knowledge.

Most important, it would speed the development of an administrative police profession. The aim of dual-level recruitment is to create a new breed of police commanders. With lateral entry these men would be encouraged to define their future in terms of competence and reputation among police professionals, rather than on advancement in a specific department. A talented man whose promotion is blocked by equally talented men ahead of him could move, taking his skill where it is needed. Policemen would acquire experience in many departments instead of just one, which would give them a much broader understanding of policing.

At present many of the best men attracted to policing leave without completing their careers. With lateral entry these same men could better be retained within policing. Not only could they achieve faster promotion and thus be retained, but they could move to a community which suited them better. For example, older officers who have gotten worn down by the rapid pace of a metropolitan department could move to less demanding jobs in suburbs and small towns. Officers bored by the quiet of the suburbs could move to metropolitan departments.

Years ago corporations looked unfavorably on men who changed jobs. The notion was that a good man had company loyalty. Promotion was mainly restricted to those who spent their working lives with the company. Recently, corporations seem almost to be playing a game of musical chairs at the upper-executive level. It takes considerable space on the business pages just to keep track of the comings and goings. All experts believe that this is good for American business. Peter F. Drucker has pointed out that the superiority of American companies over European competitors does not lie in superior research and development, as is widely believed, but in a very noticeably superior cadre of managers.[6] We have produced this management talent by hiring young men from business schools directly into the lower managerial ranks instead of sending them into the plant to work their way up, and by the fast process of training and locating the most talented, which inheres in the heavy traffic of managers from one corporation to another. I propose to give the same advantages to our police organizations.

A Police Draft

My final proposal for changing police recruitment is perhaps a bit visionary—it will hardly be adopted quickly. Yet, I think it potentially solves a great many of the most difficult problems of maintaining police institutions suitable for a democratic society.

In earlier chapters I have pointed out that policing the streets is a nasty job. Data suggest that policemen get more angry, more prejudiced, more unsuited to the job as they have been on it longer. It is possible that it is too bad a job for any but the most compassionate and stoic persons to do very long. Perhaps it should be a short-term occupation.

It is also the case that the police do not reflect the ethnic, religious, and racial makeup of the populations they police. In consequence there is considerable hostility between the police and some sectors of the public.

Being a policeman under present conditions is also stigmatizing. Many, especially young people, minority members, and students, look at the man behind the badge and hate or distrust him because he has chosen to be a policeman.

All these problems could be greatly reduced if rank-and-file policemen were obtained through a selective service draft and served a two-year tour of duty.

A draftee policeman would not be someone who *chose* to be a policeman, but someone's son and brother who got drafted. (Students at Berkeley treated National Guardsmen very differently from the way they treated the police—"They're just a bunch of guys like us, and they don't want to be here either," was a common remark.) A man serving a two-year tour as a patrolman would not suffer from the "battle fatigue" that seems to sour most men who are policemen for a long period. Finally, a draftee patrol force would immediately proportionately represent all social classes, all race and ethnic groups. It would be difficult for ethnic communities to regard the police as their enemies when their own young men were among the police. Furthermore, it would be much harder for the police *to be* the enemies of minority communities with such young men among them.

But could draftees do the job? I don't think there is much question that they could. For one thing, a draftee patrol force in time ought to face less difficult problems then do the present police. They would engender considerably greater public trust. Furthermore, as classes moved through their police service and back to civilian life, the country would be progressively filled with persons with police training and experience. This too ought to make policing less difficult.

But the success of drafted patrolmen does not depend on their facing an easier job. They could be made much more competent than our present police. Presumably, drafted police would earn minimal salaries (as do army privates). With such substantial wage savings we could easily afford:

1. To intensively train draftees for six months (about three times as long as policemen now are trained).
2. To recruit and intensively train a superior cadre of police supervisors—the equivalent of military noncoms—to direct police operations at the street level.
3. To recruit and intensively train (and retrain) an elite corps of professional police administrators—the equivalent of military officers.

In passing, I ought to make it clear that I think a police draft would most suitably be part of a national service act under which *all* young men and women are required to do two years of service for the country. In the growing crisis of social services, we face crushing needs for hospital staffing, care for the elderly, child daycare, teaching aides, and the like. I think the most effective solution would be for everyone to give a term of service in one of these positions. I am also inclined to think that some of the other dirty jobs besides soldiering and policing might properly be performed by draftees. For example, I doubt very much whether any man should have to spend his working life hauling everyone else's garbage.

II. A Different Kind of Police Organization

It will not be enough to put better men in the same old police organizations. Presumably, over the long run the impact of a highly competent corps of police administrators would greatly alter present organizations. But there are some important things that can be done now to improve the situation.

Streamlining the Police Role

At present we ask the police to perform a great many services which are inappropriate, either because the police are ill-suited to do them or because they could be done by less expensive, unsworn personnel. Some of the nation's most innovative police administrators have already taken some major steps to remove many needless and unsuitable tasks from the police role. I will only suggest a few of the most needed changes.

Sworn officers are not needed for traffic direction. As meter maids freed policemen from writing parking tickets, unsworn traffic directors ought to take over rush-hour traffic direction. Such steps have been taken in Los Angeles and are planned in San Francisco.

Policemen ought not to be used to provide many of the auxiliary support services the police require. Civilians, under the direction of one senior commander per shift, have now replaced the several scores of officers previously assigned to the Oakland Police Department radio room. Oakland also plans to turn over its research and planning activities to a private firm of systems analysts. In my experience the nation's police departments—which have staffed their research and planning divisions with sworn officers—have had some of the most incompetent work in this area imaginable. Until recently, in San Francisco the work of the research and planning staff was mainly directed to repairing chairs and typewriters. Similarly, when data processing has been delegated to sworn officers, the computer operation is typically a multi-million-dollar fiasco. These services can better be done by civilians who already have the required competence.

The police ought also to spend very little time writing reports—they should probably spend *no* time typing them. Quite simply, most policemen are lousy and expensive typists. Reports should be dictated onto tape on the spot and dropped off at a typing pool at the end of each shift.

The police also spend a great deal of their time dealing with family fights. While it is perhaps necessary that police answer the majority of such calls, in case weapons or physical danger is involved, the police ought not to have to act as family therapists. They aren't trained for it, and they don't like to do it. A new type of public agent—a family troubleshooter—ought to be developed to take over such cases from the police. Along the same lines, the police ought to be able to refer a variety of the "troubled citizen" calls they handle at present to psychiatric social workers and the like. In particular the police should not have to spend their nights wrestling with drunks. Alcoholism ought to be redefined as a medical and social problem. It should not carry jail sentences. Cases of public drunkenness ought to lead to a clinic rather than the drunk tank.

As suggested by the perceptive authors of *The Honest Politician's Guide to Crime Control*,[7] we should also cease using the police to suppress "vice." First of all, as Morris and Hawkins point out, by removing vice from the crime category the present crime rate would be cut in half (much of this would be from the demise of "secondary" crime, acts such as burglary and robbery committed to support drug habits). That would be quite a streamlining right off the bat.

But a second reason for doing this is because vice suppression activities corrupt and disillusion the police and undercut their public support. Police payoffs stem mainly from those engaged in prostitution, gambling, and drug trafficking. With these legalized or otherwise controlled without the use of police, this source of corruption would vanish. Vice suppression is also morally corruptive. After officers have spent enough time peeking through holes in lavatory walls to catch men in homosexual acts, or hanging around in cheap bars trying to pick up whores, they cannot help losing their idealism and their sense of propriety. The techniques used encourage officers to rely on entrapment, trickery, and even fraud. Furthermore, vice suppression is perhaps the sphere of policing where enforcement is least evenhanded. Many "blue laws" aren't enforced. Other vice laws are enforced only against a certain class or neighborhood. Overall, the police are encouraged to regard enforcement as an arbitrary, particularistic activity. Finally, vice flourishes because a great many citizens don't regard it as vice. When police bust bookie joints or break up a large-scale football pool operation, few citizens applaud it, and a great many feel abused.

But perhaps the most important reason to take the police out of the vice suppression business is because they do it badly and have worsened many of the problems they have undertaken to cure. After a decade of vigorous efforts to stamp out marijuana, many more people smoke marijuana than before. Only now they smoke grass of less predictable quality, pay outrageously high prices for it, and thus support dealers (and ultimately police corruption), and many otherwise law-abiding young people have ended up with long jail terms and records. Suppression of hard drugs has been even more disastrous. It has resulted in an extreme rise in the serious crime rate, thus endangering the life and property of everyone instead of merely endangering the health of a few.

Streamlining the police role is an urgent task if we are to produce policemen good at a few major tasks—primarily patrol and investigation—instead of policemen who aren't much good at any of the great many things they are asked to do.

But perhaps the most important streamlining of the police role has been touched on many times throughout this book: the police should not have to be stand-ins for needed social and political reforms. Repeatedly we turn problems of racial conflict, poverty, political dissent, and the like into police problems. So long as we meet the problems merely by sending in the cops the problems only worsen, the police become increasingly frustrated and fearful, and violence both by and against the police is the major consequence. There is nothing in the police repertoire appropriate for dealing with these problems. Nightsticks do not heal racism or feed children. Tear gas does not offer solutions to political conflict. Shotguns do not create patriots out of students outraged by the war in Southeast Asia. The solution to police repression in these instances cannot be found within police institutions. The solution is to avoid the simplistic tactic of consigning serious social and political problems to the category of police business.

Reduction in Force

It seems implausible to suppose we can disarm the police at least until we have effectively disarmed the citizenry.* But we can do much about how and when the police use guns. We can also ask that the whole aura of training for violence (see Chapter 2) be modified considerably.

In recent years a number of departments have adopted strict gun regulations. Typically these limit the use of firearms to situa-

---

* But we ought to disarm immediately many private police and security guards—the Pinkertons, Burns, and other rent-a-cops. After one of these shot a young man sneaking into an Oakland Raiders game in 1969, the Oakland Colosseum disarmed its guards with no apparent loss of efficiency in traffic direction. It is as unreasonable to arm most of these private police as it would be to arm meter maids; it is more than unreasonable—it is unsafe.

tions where necessary to protect the life of the officer or of a citizen. Most of these new regulations specifically exclude firing at fleeing persons and ban all firing of warning shots. Such regulations give a very different tone to the way in which deadly force is regarded in such departments, as opposed to departments whose firearms regulations merely limit officers to shoot only when necessary to enforce the law. It hardly seems necessary to urge that all departments adopt strict gun regulations and strictly supervise them.

Similarly, an effort must be made to remove from training manuals discussions of the use of nightsticks and batons such as the one reviewed in Chapter 2. The police must be trained to operate without needing force, and to regard force as a very serious step.

Recent experience in several communities with demilitarizing the police uniform indicates this seems to have the effect of gentling the police. In Covina, California, for example, the police have discarded the traditional heavy leather belts with the big buckles and large holsters. They have adopted smaller pistols which can be unobtrusively holstered. The Covina police have found they seem to provoke much less hostility and anxiety in persons they come in contact with; since the change, altercations with citizens have dropped very noticeably, and they find they feel less "badge-heavy."[8]

The lesson seems clear. If the police relied less on force they wouldn't abuse it so often.

Training in a Civilian Setting

To the extent possible, police training should integrate the police into civilian society rather than separate them from it. To this end as much of their training as possible ought to be conducted within the general college and university system. Furthermore, when possible, their training ought to be in classes with civilians, outside police science departments. The recent influx of civilian students into the John Jay School of Criminal Justice, until recently simply the New York police academy, seems to be having a considerable beneficial effect on *both* the police and civilians. The police culture is isolated and its outlook tends to the monolithic. Policemen need their beliefs questioned and to view themselves and their practices from outside. Obviously, such things as weapons training and arrest techniques will have to be conducted in a police setting. But advanced instruction in such areas as management science, race relations, or urban problems ought not to be conducted in-house.

In addition, many policemen would benefit greatly from short apprentice periods in other agencies such as welfare and hospital emergency wards, with whom they are expected to work. The police must discover that they are not alone—that it's not them against us.

Separating Patrol and Investigation

In the interests of better policing and greater control over police misbehavior, I propose to reorganize the police in such a way as to institutionalize internal checks on performance. I would restrict the police to uniformed forces, responsible for patrol and for preliminary investigation only. I would transfer all plainclothes officers, whose main responsibility is investigation (detecting), to the district attorney's office. I believe this would accomplish two important changes:

1. Investigation would be much more greatly influenced by, and made more suitable for, the needs of prosecution. Investigators would become much more proficient at assembling cases adequate for trial. At present, 25 to 50 percent of all felony arrests are dismissed by DAs as unprosecutable. Over time, investigation would take on many of the norms and the style of the law, instead of a police style. This is likely to result in better investigation, fewer unwarranted arrests, and fewer trumped-up charges.

2. It would also change the tone of the patrol forces. They would have direct contact with investigators who are not fellow policemen, but who work for a different firm—the prosecutor's office. If their reports or arrest procedures were faulty (leading to bad arrests and to unprosecutable cases) they would hear about it quickly. At present there is virtually no feedback to beat cops from the district attorney; many probably blame the courts for softness when they let off suspects; actually, their own failures in making the arrests or reports may have been responsible. Furthermore, the necessary close contact between the uniformed force and the investigators would mean that uniformed officers would be

under close observation of others who are not part of the same organization. It is obvious that the norm of secrecy about the misbehavior of fellow officers would be much less strong across agency boundaries.

In my opinion, patrol and investigative forces also ought to be recruited and trained separately. This would further weaken the bonds between the two and increase the likelihood that they will keep an eye on each other. It also seems clear that patrol and investigation require different kinds of men. Obviously, the FBI has not suffered from the fact that its investigators are recruited and trained directly from civilian life, rather than from patrol duties. Similarly, men who join the police because they want to become detectives may often hate patrolling and may not be very good at it.

III. External Control of the Police

Obviously no reforms *within* the police can insure a marked suppression of police misbehavior and violence. Someone must watch the watchers. The proposal to separate the uniformed and plainclothes forces is a step towards setting two groups to watch each other. But additional watchers are needed.

Each experience with civilian review boards has been very disappointing, for all the police abhor them. No greater proportion of complaints against the police have been upheld by review boards than had been upheld during a comparable previous period by the department. There seem to be several reasons for this. Appointees to police boards are typically part of city hall politics; such persons are not usually boat-rockers. But perhaps the major reason is that review boards lack significant independent investigative capacities. To get good investigations of citizen complaints against the police, they must be conducted by men dedicated to detecting police misbehavior and whose reputation and promotion depend upon it.

Whether review of the police is assigned to a civilian review board or to an ombudsman it must include an adequate investigative staff of its own.

To further strengthen external review boards, we should explore means to make them broadly representative of the communities they serve. It is not clear how this could best be accomplished. If they were elected, we might just get into the kind of election campaigns as those for review boards. Hard-line police supporters might well be elected to a majority of seats and thus prove much less effective than city hall appointees. Surely the police at present would take a very active role in any such election campaigns. It might be worthwhile to explore the possibility of random selection along the lines of jury selection. Nevertheless, virtually any review board if empowered to pierce the curtain of police secrecy and if served by competent and motivated investigators is likely to be a great improvement over present arrangements. Most citizens would support disciplinary action against policemen if they believed the officers had actually beaten prisoners or gone on a rampage against a crowd; with effective investigation, citizens would be more likely to believe cases of actual misconduct.

Major gains in regulation of the police would also follow from greater public access to police affairs. At present the police are able to deny the press, the public, defense counsel, and even review boards access to reports and records that are in principle public records. Public agencies are required to make public much of what they do. The police have claimed special privilege in the name of security to deny such access. Administrative and statutory changes must make police records and proceedings open to public inspection. In particular, the details of internal complaint investigations and disciplinary action need to be publicly accessible. At present we rarely learn details on which to judge the adequacy of investigations or the suitability of disciplinary action (if any). I suspect that merely by being made public, disciplinary actions would much less often be *pro forma*.

These are only a few suggestions for changing the police. In general, it seems to me that it is not difficult to find technical solutions to the problems of making the police effective and responsible. That isn't really the problem. The main problem is political, not technical. For no matter how good the technical solutions offered, they will not be adopted by present police institutions. Change will only occur from outside and thus depends upon mobilizing the necessary political power. In the long run, I don't think it cynical to believe that we get the policing we deserve. It simply implies that we must become more deserving. And that is why I wrote a book for the general public instead of a manual for police administrators. If reading this book has made you concerned about police behavior, it will have served some purpose. If your concern leads you to take part in the political process of bringing the police under control, perhaps the long litany of reports on violent and lawless police can finally end.

Footnotes

Introduction   [1] Dec. 6, 1968.   [2] Dec., 1968.   [3] See Chapter 6.
[4] The Walker Report, *Rights in Conflict* (Chicago, Nov. 18, 1968), p. vii; this report is also available in trade editions, for example, New York: Bantam, 1968.   [5] "Beat the Press," *Newsweek* (Sept. 9, 1968), p. 70, provides an excellent account. Also see *ibid.*   [6] Syndicated in the *Washington Post*, Sept. 9, 1968, p. 3.   [7] *Ibid.*   [8] *Ibid.*   [9] April 27 Investigating Committee, Dr. Edward J. Sparling, Chairman, *Dissent and Disorder: A Report of the Citizens of Chicago on the April 27 Peace Parade*, Chicago: August 1, 1968, pp. 30–31.   [10] The *New York Times*, March 23–25, 1968.   [11] *Ibid.*, April 28, 29, 1968.   [12] Archibald Cox, *Crisis at Columbia* (New York: Vintage, 1968).   [13] The *New York Times*, Sept. 5, 1968.   [14] The *New York Times*, Oct. 30, 1968.   [15] Rodney Stark, "Student Protest + Police = Riot: Berkeley and Beyond," in James McEvoy and Abraham Miller, eds., *Black Power and Student Rebellion* (Belmont, Calif.: Wadsworth, 1969), pp. 167–196.   [16] The *New York Times*, Oct. 30, 1968; italics added.   [17] Studies supporting this interpretation include: John H. McNamara, "Uncertainties in Police Work: The Relevance of Police Recruits' Backgrounds and Training," in David J. Bordua, ed., *The Police: Six Sociological Essays* (New York: Wiley, 1967), pp. 163–252; and Arthur Niederhoffer, *Behind the Shield: The Police in Urban Society* (New York: Doubleday, 1967).   [18] *Ibid.*   [19] Sam McCormick, "Patterns of Involvement in Altercations between the Police and Citizens," unpublished M.A. thesis, Department of Criminology, University of California, Berkeley, 1968.   [20] Neil J. Smelser, *Theory of Collective Behavior* (New York: The Free Press, 1963), p. 226.   [21] *Ibid.*

Chapter 1   [1] *Report of the National Advisory Commission on Civil Disorders* (New York: Bantam Books, 1968).   [2] "Violence Commission, *The Politics of Protest* (New York: Ballantine Books, 1969).   [3] A virtually definitive study was prepared by the Stanford Research Institute for the Kerner Commission: Arnold Katz, *Firearms, Violence and Civil Disorders* (Menlo Park, Calif.: Stanford Research Institute, 1968), no. MU–7105.   [4] My use of the term "collective outbursts" or "collective behavior" follows the work of Neil J. Smelser, *Theory of Collective Behavior* (New York: The Free Press, 1963).   [5] See William A. Westley, "Violence and the Police," *American Journal of Sociology*, 59 (July 1953), pp. 34–41.   [6] American Civil Liberties Union, *Day of Protest, Night of Violence* (Los Angeles: Sawyer Press, 1967). Unless otherwise noted, all quotations in this section are from this document.   [7] Confidential interview conducted by the author.   [8] I wish to thank team members Ruth White, Andrea Saltzman, Henry Schroerluke, Steve Hart, Nigel Young, and David Minkus.   [9] Quoted in James W. Smith, *The Park,* unpublished report prepared with the cooperation of the Berkeley Police Department for the Lemberg Center for the Study of Violence, 1970.

Chapter 2   [1] See Philip H. Ennis, "Criminal Victimization in the United States, a Report of a National Survey," National Opinion Research Center Report, University of Chicago, May 1967.   [2] Black and Reiss

submitted a number of papers to the U. S. Crime Commission based on their study and have also published parts of their findings in other works. Much of this material is cited at various points throughout this volume.
[3] Albert J. Reiss, Jr., "Police Brutality—Answers to Key Questions," *Trans-Action*, July-Aug. 1968, p. 12. [4] Quoted in George Edwards, *The Police on the Urban Frontier* (New York: Institute of Human Relations Press, 1968), p. 51. [5] Quoted in the *San Francisco Chronicle*, Sept. 10, 1968, p. 1. [6] *Ibid.*, Dec. 18, 1968, p. 10. [7] *Proceedings of the National Commission on the Causes and Prevention of Violence*, Sept. 18, 1968, p. 110. [8] See *Newsweek*, June 23, 1969, p. 92, and the *San Francisco Chronicle*, June 12, 1969, p. 10. [9] *Ibid.* [10] Orlando W. Wilson, *Police Administration* (New York: McGraw-Hill, 1963); quoted in: The President's Commission on Law Enforcement and Administration on Justice, *The Challenge of Crime in a Free Society* (Washington, D. C.: U. S. Government Printing Office, 1967), p. 102. [11] "Violence and the Police," *The American Journal of Sociology*, July 1953, pp. 34–41. [12] Reiss, *Police Brutality*. [13] *Ibid.*, p. 18. [14] Ed Cray, *The Big Blue Line* (New York: Coward–McCann, 1967); Paul Jacobs, *Prelude to Riot* (New York, Vintage Books, 1968); Robert Conot, *Rivers of Blood, Years of Darkness* (New York, Bantam Books, 1967); William W. Turner, *The Police Establishment* (New York: G. P. Putnam's Sons, 1968). [15] William A. Westley, "Violence and the Police," *American Journal of Sociology*, 59 (July 1953), p. 39. [16] *Ibid.*, p. 39. [17] Interviewed Aug. 2, 1968, by Nancy Leonard of The Violence Commission. [18] Reiss, *Police Brutality*, p. 15. [19] Turner, *The Police Establishment*, p. 46. [20] Conot, *Rivers of Blood*, p. 174. Also reported in Turner, *The Police Establishment*. [21] The *San Francisco Chronicle*, July 11, 1968. [22] The *San Francisco Chronicle*, Oct. 3, 1968. [23] Interviewed by Sam McCormick, Task Force interviewer. [24] *Ibid.* [25] *Newsweek*, August 4, 1969, p. 54. [26] George T. Payton, *Patrol Procedure*, 4th ed. (Los Angeles: Legal Book Corp., 1971), reprinted by permission. [27] *Ibid.*, pp. 333–337. [28] Ernest Jerome Hopkins, *Our Lawless Police* (New York: The Viking Press, 1931). [29] Jerome Skolnick, *Justice without Trial: Law Enforcement in Democratic Society* (New York: Wiley, 1966), pp. 3–4. [30] *The Negro in Harlem*, unpublished report, p. 65. [31] The President's Commission on Civil Rights, *To Secure These Rights* (New York: Simon & Schuster, 1947), p. 25. [32] U.S. Civil Rights Commission, *Report V: Justice* (Washington, D.C.: U.S. Government Printing Office, 1961), p. 8. [33] The Crime Commission, *Task Force Report: The Police* (Washington, D. C.: U. S. Government Printing Office, 1967), pp. 181–182. [34] Kerner Commission, *Report of the National Advisory Commission on Civil Disorders* (New York: Bantam, 1968), p. 29. [35] Quoted in *Life*, Aug. 27, 1965. [36] Walter J. Raine, "Los Angeles Riot Study: The Perception of Police Brutality in South Central Los Angeles" (Los Angeles: Institute of Government and Public Affairs, University of California, 1967), mimeographed, p. 8. [37] Personal communications. [38] Baltimore, Boston, Chicago, Cincinnati, Cleveland, Detroit, Gary, Milwaukee, Newark, New York (Brooklyn only), Philadelphia, Pittsburgh, San Francisco, St. Louis, and Washington, D. C. [39] *Racial Attitudes in Fifteen American Cities*, Survey Research Center and Institute for Social Research, University of Michigan, June 1968. [40] The study appeared in *Supplemental Studies for the National Advisory Commission on Civil Disorders* (Washington, D. C.: U. S. Government Printing Office, 1968), pp. 3–67. [41] *Ibid.*, p. 44. [42] *Ibid.*, p. 43. [43] Peter

H. Rossi, Richard A. Berk, David P. Boesel, Bettye K. Eidson, and W. Eugene Groves, "Between White and Black: The Faces of American Institutions in the Ghetto," in *Supplemental Studies for the National Advisory Commission on Civil Disorders* (Washington, D. C.: U. S. Government Printing Office, 1968), p. 106. [44] Reiss, *Police Brutality*, p. 15. [45] *Ibid.* [46] *Ibid.* [47] From the Black and Reiss data, quoted in *Task Force Report: Police* (Washington, D. C.: U. S. Government Printing Office, 1967), p. 182. [48] Reiss, *Police Brutality*, p. 14. [49] *Ibid.*, p. 13. [50] *Ibid.*, p. 15. [51] *Ibid.* [52] Kerner Commission, *Report on Civil Disorders*, p. 302. [53] Reiss, *Police Brutality*, p. 16. [54] *Ibid.*, p. 12. [55] *Ibid.*, p. 18. [56] Ed Cray, "Memo on Police Violence," submitted to the Task Force on Violent Aspects of Protest and Confrontation, Aug. 16, 1968, mimeographed. [57] Reiss, *op. cit.*, p. 16.

Chapter 3 [1] "Mob," *Encyclopedia of the Social Sciences*, Vol. 10, p. 553. [2] William Westley, *The Police: A Sociological Study of Law, Custom and Morality*, unpublished Ph.D. dissertation, University of Chicago, 1951, p. 294. [3] Jerome Skolnick, *Justice without Trial: Law Enforcement in Democratic Society* (New York: Wiley, 1966), p. 42. [4] James Q. Wilson, *Varieties of Police Behavior* (Cambridge: Harvard University Press, 1968), pp. 21–22. [5] Skolnick, *Justice without Trial*, p. 10. [6] *Ibid.*, p. 48. [7] Colin MacInnes, *Mr. Love and Justice* (London: New English Library, 1962), quoted in Skolnick, *Justice without Trial*, p. 48. [8] Skolnick, *Justice without Trial*, p. 11. [9] *Ibid.*, p. 44. [10] *Ibid.*, p. 57. [11] *Ibid.*, p. 57. [12] Horace Cayton, *Long Old Road* (New York: Trident Press, 1965), p. 154. [13] Erving Goffman, *The Presentation of Self in Everyday Life* (Garden City, N. Y.: Doubleday, 1959). [14] Paul Jacobs, *Prelude to Riot: A View of Urban America from the Bottom* (New York: Random House, 1967), p. 36. [15] Skolnick, *Justice without Trial*, p. 57. [16] See *ibid.*, p. 53, also Jacobs, *Prelude to Riot*, pp. 35–36. [17] Robert G. Kaiser of the Times–Post Service, *San Francisco Chronicle*, Dec. 18, 1968, p. 10. [18] Skolnick, *Justice without Trial*, pp. 58–59. [19] Morris Janowitz, *The Professional Soldier: A Social and Political Portrait* (New York: The Free Press, 1964), p. 175. [20] Skolnick, *Justice without Trial*, pp. 49–50. [21] Kerner Commission, *Report of the National Advisory Commission on Civil Disorders* (New York: Bantam, 1968), p. 305; italics added. [22] Jacobs, *Prelude to Riot*, p. 26. [23] Kerner Commission, *Report on Civil Disorders*, p. 305. [24] *Ibid.*, p. 307. [25] Skolnick, *Justice without Trial*, p. 62. [26] *Ibid.*, p. 48. [27] *Ibid.*, p. 45. [28] Irving Piliavin and Scott Briar, "Police Encounters with Juveniles," *American Journal of Sociology*, 70 (Sept. 1964); pp. 206–214. [29] Kerner Commission, *Report on Civil Disorders*, p. 300. [30] Muzafer Sherif and Carolyn W. Sherif, *Groups in Harmony and Tension* (New York: Harper & Sons, 1953). [31] Charles Y. Glock and Rodney Stark, *Christian Beliefs and Anti-Semitism* (New York: Harper & Row, Publishers, 1966); see Chapter 2 especially. [32] *Ibid.* [33] James Baldwin, *Nobody Knows My Name* (New York: Dell, 1962), pp. 65–67. [34] Robert Conot, *Rivers of Blood, Years of Darkness* (New York: Bantam, 1967). [35] *Ibid.* [36] *The Negro in Harlem* (New York: The Mayor's Commission on Conditions in Harlem, 1935), unpublished. Nearly 40 years later the problems recognized in this study have become so pressing that the volume is finally to be published, with a special introduction by Anthony Platt. [37] Westley, *The Police*, p. 168. [38] "Patterns of Behavior in Police and Citizen Transactions." A Report to the President's Commission on Law Enforcement and the Administration of Criminal Justice, mimeographed, 1966, p. 111.   [39] Conot, *Rivers of Blood*, p. 42.   [40] *Ibid.*, p. 41.   [41] Kerner Commission, *Report on Civil Disorders,* pp. 315, 321–322.   [42] *Ibid.*, pp. 316, 321–322.   [43] Conot, *Rivers of Blood,* pp. 159–161; see also the special series on the police in "Insight," a section of the *Washington Post,* Dec. 15, 1968.   [44] Conot, *Rivers of Blood,* p. 160.   [45] *Ibid.*   [46] Kerner Commission, Report on Civil Disorders, pp. 321–322.   [47] Burton Levy, "Cops in the Ghetto: A Problem of the Police System," *American Behavioral Scientist,* (March-April 1968), p. 33.   [48] Black and Reiss, "Patterns of Behavior in Police and Citizen Transactions," table 25.   [49] Levy, "Cops in the Ghetto," p. 33.   [50] Unpublished paper quoted in *ibid.*, p. 33.   [51] Skolnick, *Justice without Trial,* passim.   [52] Black and Reiss, "Patterns of Behavior in Police and Citizen Transactions."   [53] *Ibid.*   [54] *Ibid.*   [55] *Ibid.*, p. 115.   [56] *Ibid.*, p. 115.   [57] Conot, *Rivers of Blood,* p. 40.   [58] Kerner Commission, *Report on Civil Disorders,* especially Part I. A virtually definitive study was prepared by the Stanford Research Institute for the Kerner Commission: Arnold Katz, director, *Firearms, Violence, and Civil Disorders* (Menlo Park, Calif.: Stanford Research Institute, 1968), no. MU–7105.   [59] Kerner Commission, *Report on Civil Disorders,* pp. 144–149.   [60] See Albert J. Reiss, Jr., and David J. Bordua, "Environment and Organization: A Perspective on the Police," in Bordua, ed., *The Police* (New York: Wiley, 1967).   [61] Marvin E. Wolfgang, *Crime and Culture* (New York: Wiley, 1968).   [62] *Ibid.*   [63] Kerner Commission, *Report on Civil Disorders,* pp. 307–309.   [64] Robert Blauner, "Internal Colonialism and Ghetto Revolt," *Social Problems,* 16 (Spring 1969), pp. 404–405.   [65] Quoted in the *New York Post,* Nov. 12, 1968, p. 53.   [66] *Ibid.*   [67] The Walker Report, *Rights in Conflict* (Chicago, Nov. 18, 1968), p. 117.   [68] *San Francisco Chronicle,* Dec. 11, 1968, p. 41.   [69] A. James Reichley, "The Way To Cool the Police Rebellion," *Fortune* (Dec. 1968), p. 111.   [70] *Time,* Oct. 5, 1968, p. 26.   [71] *San Francisco Chronicle,* Dec. 18, 1968, p. 10.   [72] *Time* (Oct. 4, 1968), p. 26.   [73] *Newsweek* (Sept. 9, 1968), p. 70.   [74] "Newsroom," KQED–9, San Francisco.   [75] John Hersey, *The Algiers Motel Incident* (New York: Bantam Books, 1968).   [76] Reichley, "The Way to Cool the Police Rebellion."   [77] Conducted for the Task Force by Sam McCormick.   [78] Interviewed by Sam McCormick.   [79] See James McEvoy and Abraham Miller, "On Strike—Shut It Down: The Crisis at San Francisco State College," *Trans-action,* 6 (March 1969), pp. 18–23, 61–62.   [80] *San Francisco Chronicle,* Sept. 18, 1968, p. 8.   [81] January, 1969.   [82] "A Policeman Looks at Crime," *U. S. News and World Report* (Aug. 1, 1966), p. 52.   [83] *Saturday Evening Post* (November 16, 1968), p. 28.   [84] *Ibid.*   [85] Task Force Interview by Sam McCormick.   [86] *Fortune* (Dec. 1968), p. 113.   [87] Arthur Niederhoffer, *Behind the Shield: The Police in Urban Society* (New York: Doubleday, 1967).   [88] *Ibid.*, p. 16.   [89] *Fortune* (Dec. 1968), p. 113.   [90] *Newsweek* (Mar. 8, 1971), p. 17.   [91] William Fulton, "Report from New York," *Chicago Tribune,* Nov. 19, 1968.   [92] *Time* (Oct. 4, 1968), pp. 26–27; Sandy Smith, "The Mob: You Cannot Expect Police on the Take to Take Orders," *Life* (Dec. 6, 1968), pp. 40–43.   [93] Task Force interview by Sam McCormick.   [94] *Washington Post,* Dec. 15, 1968, p. B3.   [95] Interview by the author with the then police chief William Beall.   [96] *Washington Star,* Nov. 13, 1968, p. 14.   [97] Interviewed by Sam McCormick.   [98] The *New York Times,* August 30, 1968, p. 10.

Chapter 4 [1] G. Wills, *The Second Civil War* (New York: New American Library, 1968), p. 47. [2] Joseph F. Coates, *Nonlethal Weapons for Use by U.S. Law Enforcement Officers* (Washington: Institute for Defense Analyses, Science and Technology Division, Nov., 1967), study S-271. [3] Especially, Chapter 1, VIII. [4] Kerner Commission, *Report of the National Advisory Commission on Civil Disorders* (New York: Bantam, 1968) p. 100. [5] *Ibid.*, p. 330. [6] Rodney Stark, "Protest + Police = Riot" in James McEvoy and Abraham Miller, eds., *Black Power and Student Rebellion* (Belmont, Calif.: Wadsworth, 1969), pp. 167–196. [7] Coates, *Nonlethal Weapons.* [8] Interviewed by Sam McCormick. [9] Especially see the Kerner Commission, *Report on Civil Disorders.* [10] Harold K. Becker, "Do Police Helicopters Justify Their Cost"? *The American City* (November 1968), p. 71. [11] George T. Payton, *Patrol Procedure*, 4th ed. (Los Angeles: Legal Book Corporation, 1971), p. 264, reprinted by permission.

Chapter 5 [1] A. C. Germann, Frank D. Day, and Robert R. J. Gallati, *Introduction to Law Enforcement* (Springfield, Ill.: Charles C Thomas, 1962), pp. 13–15. [2] Travis Hirschi and Hanan Selvin, *Delinquency Research* (New York: The Free Press, 1967). [3] Travis Hirschi and Rodney Stark, "Hellfire and Delinquency," *Social Problems,* Vol. 17, No. 2 (Fall, 1969), pp. 202–213. [4] Kerner Commission, *The Politics of Protest* (New York: Ballantine Books, 1969), Chapter 3, fn. 5. [5] *Ibid.*, Chapter 7, fn. 59. [6] Rodney Stark and James McEvoy, Jr., "Middle-Class Violence," *Psychology Today* (Nov. 1970), pp. 52–54, 110–112. [7] Kerner Commission, *Politics of Protest*, Chapter 2. [8] *The Police Chief,* April 1965. [9] *Ibid.* [10] *Ibid.* [11] *Ibid.* [12] "Protest + Police = Riot," in James McEvoy and Abraham Miller, eds., *Black Power and Student Rebellion* (Belmont, Calif.: Wadsworth, 1969), pp. 167–196. [13] Kerner Commission, *Politics of Protest*, p. 34. [14] *The Police Chief.* [15] *Newsweek* (April 26, 1971), p. 32. [16] *The Police Chief.* [17] *Newsweek, op. cit.* [18] *The Police Chief.* [19] Jerome Skolnick, *Justice without Trial* (New York: Wiley, 1966), p. 62. [20] James Q. Wilson, "Police Morale, Reform, and Citizen Respect," in David Bordua, ed., *The Police: Six Sociological Essays* (New York: Wiley, 1967), pp. 137–162. [21] *The New York Times,* Sept. 3, 1968, p. 40. [22] *The Christian Science Monitor,* Nov. 13, 1968, p. 14. [23] *The New York Times,* Nov. 20, 1964. [24] *Los Angeles Times,* May 17, 1965. [25] William Turner, *The Police Establishment* (New York: Putnam's, 1968), p. 212. [26] *The Christian Science Monitor, op. cit.* [27] Interviewed by Sam McCormick. [28] *The New York Times,* Nov. 3, 1968, p. 78. [29] James Leo Walsh, "The Professional Cop," paper read at the meeting of the American Sociological Association, 1969. [30] *Proceedings of the National Violence Commission,* Sept. 18, 1968, p. 56. [31] *Ibid.* [32] *Ibid.*, p. 62. [33] Archibald Cox, *Crisis at Columbia* (New York: Vintage, 1968), p. 189. [34] *Proceedings of the National Violence Commission,* pp. 74–75. [35] *Ibid.*, pp. 99–100. [36] *Ibid.*, pp. 86–87. [37] Arthur I. Waskow, *From Race Riot to Sit-in: 1919 and the 1960s* (Garden City, N. Y.: Doubleday, 1966), pp. 188–196. [38] *Law and Order* (May, 1968), reprinted by permission. [39] *Newsweek* (April 26, 1971), p. 32. [40] Seymour Martin Lipset, "Why Cops Hate Liberals—and Vice Versa," *Atlantic* (Mar. 1969), pp. 76–83. [41] *Ibid.* [42] Seymour Martin Lipset, *Political Man* (Garden City, N.Y.: Doubleday, 1960), especially Chapter 4. [43] *Newsweek* (Oct. 6, 1969), p. 35. [44] Gertrude Jaeger Selznick and Stephen Steinberg, *The Tenacity of Prejudice* (New

York: Harper and Row, Publishers, 1969). [45]*Fortune,* January 1969. [46]*The Washington Post,* Nov. 10, 1968, p. 12. [47]Interviewed by the author. [48]Rodney Stark, Bruce D. Foster, Charles Y. Glock, and Harold E. Quinley, *Wayward Shepherds: Prejudice and the Protestant Clergy* (New York: Harper and Row, Publishers, 1971).

Chapter 6 [1] For a summary see Albert J. Reiss, Jr., and David J. Bordua, "Environment and Organization: A Perspective on the Police," in David J. Bordua, ed., *The Police: Six Sociological Essays* (New York, Wiley, 1967). [2] Albert J. Reiss, Jr., "Police Brutality: Answers to Key Questions," *Trans-action,* July-August 1968, pp. 10–19. [3] See John Hersey, *The Algiers Motel Incident* (New York: Bantam, 1968); see also newspaper accounts at the time. [4] See "This World" section of the *San Francisco Sunday Examiner and Chronicle,* Oct. 13, 1968, p. 5; see also the *San Francisco Chronicle,* Nov. 25, 1968, p. 3. [5] See coverage in the *San Francisco Chronicle* and *San Francisco Examiner* during this period. [6] Interviewed by Sam McCormick. [7] See the *New York Times,* Sept. 3, 1968, p. 28. [8] See the initial report in the *New York Times,* Sept. 5, 1968, p. 1, 50, and subsequent accounts. [9] *Los Angeles Times,* Aug. 22, 1968, p. 28. [10] See the stories in the *Detroit Free Press* and the *Detroit News* beginning Nov. 3, 1968 and continuing through the month. [11] *San Francisco Chronicle,* June 20, 1969, pp. 1, 30. [12] Paul Jacobs, *Prelude to Riot: A View of Urban America from the Bottom* (New York: Vintage, 1967), p. 32. [13] See D. J. R. Bruckner's long essay in the *Washington Post,* Sept. 9, 1968, p. 3. [14] *Rights in Conflict* (New York: Bantam Books, 1968). [15] *Washington Post,* Dec. 3, 1968, p. 14; italics added. [16] *Chicago Daily News,* Dec. 4, 1968, p. 1. [17] Carried in the *San Francisco Chronicle,* Dec. 16, 1968, p. 17. [18] *San Francisco Examiner,* Nov. 13, 1969, pp. 1, 16. [19] Personal interview by the author. [20] Interviewed by Sam McCormick. [21] *San Francisco Examiner,* Nov. 13, 1968, p. 16. [22] *Report of the National Advisory Commission on Civil Disorders* (New York: Bantam, 1968, pp. 307–309). [23] Hugh Davis Graham and Ted Robert Gurr, *Violence In America: Historical and Comparative Perspectives,* a report submitted to the National Commission on the Causes and Prevention of Violence (New York: Bantam, 1969). [24] *The Police Establishment* (New York, G. P. Putnam's, 1968), pp. 222–223. [25] See *Ibid.,* and the *New York Times* reports. [26] *Ibid.* [27] *Ibid.* [28] The *New York Times,* Aug. 16, 1968, pp. 1 and 38. [29] *Ibid.* [30] *Ibid.* [31] *Los Angeles Times,* Aug. 16, 1968, p. 4. [32] The *New York Times,* Aug. 16, 1968, p. 38. [33] *Washington Post,* Dec. 15, 1968, p. B-1. [34] *Ibid.,* p. B-2. [35] *Ibid.,* p. B-1. [36] Arthur Niederhoffer, *Behind the Shield* (Garden City, N. Y.: Doubleday, 1967). [37] National F.O.P. Committee on Human Rights and Law Enforcement, "Police Review Boards," Philadelphia, 1962, p. 8, mimeograph. [38] *FI-PO News,* Vol. 9, No. 5, June 1960, p. 1. [39] *San Francisco Chronicle,* Dec. 18, 1968, pp. 10–11. [40] See front page stories in the *New York Times,* Oct. 16, 26, 27, 1968. [41] *San Francisco Chronicle,* Dec. 16, 1968, p. 12. [42] *Washington Post,* Dec. 15, 1968, p. B-1. [43] The *New York Times,* Nov. 30, 1968, p. 1. [44] *Chicago Tribune* and *Chicago Daily News* from Nov. 19, 1968 through the end of the month. [45] Mike Royko, whose column was reprinted in the *Philadelphia Inquirer,* Nov. 28, 1968, p. 29. [46] The *Chicago Tribune,* editorial page, Nov. 21, 1968. [47] *Washington Post,* Dec. 15, 1968, p. B-1. [48] *Ibid.* [49] The *New York Times,* Nov. 18, 1968, p. 1. [50] *Washington Post,* Dec. 15, 1968, published as a special supplement. [51] *Ibid.,* p. B-1. [52] *Ibid.* [53] See: D. J. R. Bruckner in the *Los Angeles Times,* Oct. 10,

1968, p. 13, and again on Oct. 28, 1968, pp. 1, 8, 9. Also a report by Jim Hyatt in The *Wall Street Journal,* Aug. 20, 1968. The most complete single treatment is Louis H. Masotti and Jerome R. Corsi, *Report to the National Commission on the Causes and Prevention of Violence—Shoot-out in Cleveland* (New York: Bantam Books, 1969). [54] The *New York Times,* Aug. 18, 1968, p. 43. [55] For an excellent account see D. J. R. Bruckner in the *Los Angeles Times,* Oct. 2, 1968, pp. 26–27. [56] *Ibid.* [57] *San Francisco Chronicle,* Dec. 14, 1968, p. 5. [58] See the account in W. V. Turner, *The Police Establishment* (New York: Putnam, 1969). [60] *Ibid.* [61] *San Francisco Chronicle,* June 26, 1969, p. 10.

Chapter 7 [1] *San Francisco Chronicle,* Sept. 28, 1968, p. 9. [2] *Washington Post,* Dec. 15, 1968, B-1. [3] *Ibid.,* B-2. [4] *Ibid.* [5] Interviewed by Sam McCormick. [6] *San Francisco Chronicle,* Dec. 16, 1968, p. 12. [7] *Ibid.* [8] *San Francisco Chronicle,* Dec. 18, 1968, p. 11. [9] *Washington Post,* Dec. 15, 1968, p. B-1. [10] Harry Wise, the labor lawyer retained to help organize and bargain for the Patrolmen's Association, as quoted in *Ibid.,* p. B-2. [11] *Ibid.* [12] *Ibid.* [13] *Newsweek* (June 23, 1969), p. 32; also the *Minneapolis Star and Tribune* for the election period. [14] *Newsweek* (June 23, 1969), p. 32. [15] *Washington Post,* Dec. 15, 1968, p. B-1. [16] *Ibid.,* p. B-2. [17] *Ibid.* [18] Paul Chevigny, *Police Power: Police Abuses in New York City* (New York: Pantheon, 1969). [19] The *New York Times,* August 16, 1968, p. 38. [20] *San Francisco Chronicle,* Sept. 5, 1968, p. 1 and ff. [21] Interviewed by Sam McCormick. [22] *Ibid.* [23] Rodney Stark, "Policy and the Pros: An Organizational Analysis of a Metropolitan Newspaper," *Berkeley Journal of Sociology,* Vol. VIII, Spring 1962, pp. 11–31. [24] Douglass Cater, *The Fourth Branch of Government* (New York: Vintage, 1965). [25] Milton Rokeach, "Religious Values and Social Compassion," *Review of Religious Research,* Vol. 11, No. 2 (Winter 1970), pp. 23–39. [26] James Q. Wilson, "Police Morale, Reform, and Citizen Respect," in David J. Bordua, ed., *The Police: Six Sociological Essays* (New York: Wiley, 1967). [27] The interview schedule was designed by a number of social scientists under the direction of Sandra J. Ball Rokeach. [28] William A. Gamson and James McEvoy, "Police Violence and Its Public Support," *The Annals of the American Academy of Political and Social Science,* Vol. 391 (Sept. 1970), pp. 97–110. [29] *Newsweek* (May 25, 1970), p. 30. [30] Gamson and McEvoy, "Police Violence and Its Public Support."

Chapter 8 [1] George E. Berkley, *The Democratic Policeman* (Boston: Beacon Press, 1969), and also his article, "How the Police Work in Western Europe and the U.S.," *The New Republic,* Aug. 2, 1969, pp. 15–18. [2] *Ibid.* [3] *Ibid.* [4] Seymour Martin Lipset, "Why Cops Hate Liberals —and Vice Versa," *Atlantic* (Mar. 1969), pp. 76–83. [5] Berkley, *The Democratic Policeman,* and "How the Police Work." [6] Peter F. Drucker, *The Age of Discontinuity* (New York: Harper and Row, Publishers, 1969). [7] Norval Morris and Gordon Hawkins, *The Honest Politician's Guide to Crime Control* (Chicago: University of Chicago Press, 1970). [8] My interview with the chief of police.

Index

Activism among police, 197–198, (see also Police revolt)
Alibi guns or knives, 64–65
Allen, Chief Edward J., 206
American Civil Liberties Union (ACLU), 23, 26, 27, 29, 32, 33, 170, 200
Americans for Democratic Action, 200
Andreotti, Lt. Dante, 205–206
Atkinson, Atty. Judith, 28–29
"Attitudes test," 61–62
Authoritarianism, 10–11

Baker, Chief Bruce, 185–186
Baldwin, James, 98, 118
Baldwin, Roger, 195
Baskett, George, 182
Beall, Chief William, 36, 43, 49, 50–51, 52–53, 190–191
Beating up in custody, 73–74, 75, 76, 80–81
Berkeley, Calif.: covering up police misconduct, 185–186; People's Park, 6–7, 21; police violence, 6–7, 44–48; rally in support of French student strike, 6, 21, 32–54
Bernard, L. L., 85–86, 96
Biderman, A. D., 133n
Black, Donald J., 56–57, 64, 79–81, 82–83, 99–100, 103–104, 105–106
Black Panthers, 45, 106, 107, 128, 135, 183, 184, 214–215
Black policemen, 67–68, 103–104
Blacks: crime rate, 107–108; police prejudice against, 98–106; victims of brutality, 45–46; views of the police, 106–108
Blauner, Robert, 108
"Blue flu," 202
"Blue Power," 194–203
Briar, Scott, 95
Bruckner, D. J. R., 4–5, 204, 205
Byrne Report, 164

Camejo, Peter, 34, 36, 51
Campbell, Angus, 75, 76–77
Cassese, John J., 195, 196, 197, 198, 202
Cayton, Horace, 90
Changes, suggested, in police departments, 225–239
Chevigny, Paul, 213
Chicago: covering up police misconduct, 186–187; Democratic National Convention riots, 3–4, 9, 58–59, 114, 115, 223; Gallup Poll, on riots, 114, 223; 1968 peace march, 4–5
Churns, Michael, 203
Cincinnati, police revolt, 206–207
Citizens killed by police, 65, 65n
Civil authority over police, 178–179, 193, 194–199, 208–212
Civilian review boards (see Review boards)
Cleaver, Eldridge, 45, 128

Cleveland, police revolt, 204
Clubs, use of, 68–70, 235
Coates, Joseph F., 128, 136
Columbia University crisis, 157
Communist conspiracy, police belief in, 113, 154–155, 157, 163–167
Conlisk, James, 186–187, 203
Conot, Robert, 64, 102, 103
Conspiracies, 146–150; police belief in, 113, 150–158, 163–167
Control, external, over police, 13–14, 178–179: civil authority, 178–179, 208–212; the courts, 179, 212–217; failure of, 208–224; the press, 179, 217–219; public opinion, 179, 219–224
Control, internal, over police, 178–207; police revolt, 189–207; police solidarity and a cult of secrecy, 179–189
Convergence stage of riots, 18–19
"Cooping," 187–188
Courts, and control of police, 179, 212–217
Covering up police misconduct, 179–189
Cox, Archibald, 164–165
Criminality, theories of, 141–146
Crowd control: crowd dispersal, 20; massive police presence, 130–132; mechanical and technical means, 135–138; military-type tactical formations, 125–130; police fear and obsession with safety, 132–135; tactical errors in, 125–138

Daley, Mayor Richard J., 4, 9, 58, 113n, 186, 202
Danger, degree justifying use of force, 56–57
Davis, Chief Edward M., 154
Day, Frank D., 142
Democratic National Convention (Chicago), 3–4, 9, 58–59, 114, 115, 223
Demonstrations: after massive police presence, 19, 131–132; natural vs. manufactured events, 147–148; types of people involved, 24, 30–32
Demonstrators: attitudes toward police, 113–116; police attitudes toward, 109–113
Detroit: Algiers Motel incident, 181; covering up police misconduct, 184–185; failure of military-type tactics, 128–129
Dispersal of crowd, 20
Dissenters: attitudes toward police, 113–116; police attitudes toward, 109–113
Drucker, Peter F., 229
Dunaway, Elmer, 206–207

Educational level of police, 119, 120–122, 171
Eisenhower, Dr. Milton, 166
Extended riot, 6, 21, 32–54

247

Index

Fascist pig theory, 10–11
Fear: police fear and obsession with safety, 132–135; of subcultures, 94, 96–98
Federal Bureau of Investigation (FBI) (*see also* Hoover, J. Edgar): statistics on number of police, 121; training programs, 165
Fire and Police Research Association (FI-PO), 211
FI-PO News, 170, 200
Frank, Norman, 211
Fraternal Order of Police, 62, 199, 200, 212
Free Speech Movement, 116, 150, 151–153, 154, 155, 163–164
Free-will concept of behavior, 141–146, 174–176
Frisking and rousting, 71, 72, 75, 76

Gain, Chief Charles, 183
Gallati, Robert R. J., 142
Gamson, William A., 224
Gary, Charles P., 216
Germann, A. C., 142
Ghettos, 19, 107–108, 117–119
Gleason, Ralph J., 113n
Gordon, Margaret, 112
Gun regulations, 234–235
Guns: misuse by police, 135, 137; National Guard regulations, 137

Hall, Gus, 164, 165
Hannon, Robert, 209
Harlem Riot Commission Report, 98–99
Harrington, John, 62, 141, 159, 199
Helicopter patrols, 137
Hersey, John, 112
Higginbotham, Judge A. Leon, 167
Hippies, police hatred of, 49–50, 94–95, 111, 112–113
Hirschi, Travis, 144
Homicides by police, 65, 65n
Hoover, J. Edgar, 58, 121n, 171: belief in Communist conspiracies, 163–167; on black militance, 167–168

Indians, police conflict with, 109
Institute for Defense Analysis, 128, 136
Interracial sex, police attitudes toward, 112

Jackson State, 21, 135
Jacobs, Paul, 91–92, 92n, 93–94
Janowitz, Morris, 92
John Birch Society, police members of, 159
Johnson, President L. B., 6, 23, 114

Kennedy, Robert F., 195
Kent State, 132, 135, 223
Kerner Commission Report, 15, 70, 75, 81–82, 93, 94, 96, 101, 103, 107, 114–115, 117, 128–129, 130, 153, 191
King, Dr. Martin Luther, 167–168, 219
Kobler, Arthur L., 65n
Ku Klux Klan, police in, 159

Law Enforcement Group (LEG), 183–184, 197–198, 214–215
Law and Order, 169–170
Levy, Burton, 104

Limited riot, 6, 20–21, 22–32
Lindsay, Mayor John, 194–195, 210, 212
Los Angeles: covering up police misconduct, 184, 186; limited riot during peace march, 6, 22–32; police brutality in, 71–75, 82-83
Low-risk conception of order, 88–89

McCabe, Charles, 111
McCormick, Sam, 11, 113, 120, 122–123, 136–137, 159–160, 183, 191, 210, 215, 216
McEvoy, James, 224
MacInnes, Colin, 88–89
MacNamara, Donal E. J., 104
McNamara, Chief Donald I., 10n, 204–205
McNamara, John H., 10
Mensh, Dr. Maurice, 121
Mexican–Americans, and police, 109
Military tactics, 125–130
Military training vs. police training, 125–127
Mobs, conflict situations causing, 85–86
Morris, Norval, 233
Mutual assistance pacts, 35

NAACP, 200
National Commission on the Causes and Prevention of Violence, 8, 163, 165, 220
National Commission on Law Observance and Enforcement, 70
National Violence Commission, 153
National Guard: ban on heavy weapons, 137; in Detroit (1967), 127, 128–129
"New Morality," 112–113
New York City: covering up police misconduct, 183–184; Patrolmen's Benevolent Association vs. police review board, 194–198; police violence, 6
Newark police riot, 16, 21
Newton, Huey P., 107, 183
Niederhoffer, Arthur, 10n, 119
Nightsticks, 68–70, 235
Nonprovocative persons, 17–18

Oakland, Calif., covering up police misconduct, 183
O'Brien, Patrolman Michael, 182–183
Order, conceptions of: low risk, 88–89; high risk, 88

Parker, Chief William H., 71, 171
Paterson, N.J., police violence, 6, 9
Patrolmen's Benevolent Association, 194–198, 201–202, 210
Payton, George T., 68–69
Peace Action Council rally and march, Los Angeles (1967), 22–32
People's Park, Berkeley, 6–7, 21
Piliavin, Irving, 95
Plainclothesmen: recognition by criminals, 92n; transfer to DA's office, 236–237
Police: activism of, 197–198; demands on, 117–119; and dissenters, 30–32, 109–116; educational level, 119, 120–122, 171; external controls, 13–14, 178–179, 208–224; and the ghettos, 19, 107–108, 117–119; internal controls, 13, 178–207; low-risk conception of

Index

Police: (continued)
order, 88–89; paramilitary organization of, 89; and people on beat, 93–94; police solidarity, 64, 91–94, 179–189; political power, 209–212; racism, 67, 95, 97, 98–104; recognition of plainclothesmen, 92n; recruiting problems, 119–123; salaries, 119–120; social isolation, 89–94, 158; as a subculture, 86–96; suggested changes in departments, 225–239; suspiciousness of, 92–93; voting patterns and political stance, 159–162; working hours, 93
Police brutality (see also Police riots; Violence): "attitudes test," 61–62; avoiding detection, 63–67; in Berkeley (1968), 18, 37, 39, 40, 41–49; black police protest against, 67–68; toward blacks vs. whites, 75–77; citizens killed by police, 65, 65n; defined, 56–60; degree of danger justifying, 56–57; incidence, 70–83; in Los Angeles, 28–30, 71–75, 82–83; mistaken intradepartmental shootouts, 65–66; police club, 68–70, 235; police solidarity in condoning or covering up, 64; toward the press, 66–67; following provocation, 58–60; reasons for, 58–62; as result of training, 68–70; as routine behavior, 55–84; tear gas, 20, 21, 37, 39, 42–44; throwaways, 64–65
Police Chief, The, 151
Police club, 68–70, 235
Police ideology, 139–177: belief in conspiracies, 146–158; conservatism and right-wing extremism, 158–162; educational and social origin factors in, 171–173; effects of police work, 173–176; free-will conception of behavior, 141–146, 174–176; indoctrination in, 162–171; influence of J. Edgar Hoover, 163–168; police literature, 168–170; police mentality, 158–162, 171–173; sources, 162–171; theories of criminality, 141–146
Police misconduct: covering up, 179–189; fascist pig theory, 10–11; public disbelief in, 223–224; rotten apple theory, 9–10, 11
Police Officers Association, 210, 215, 216
Police revolt, 3, 189–207: "blue flu," 202; against civil authority, 193, 194–199, 208–212; against civilian review boards, 194–201; the cop-out, 189–191; against the courts, 214–217; for increased benefits, 201–203; against police commanders, 203–207; police lobbying, 210; political activism, 203, 219–212; politicization of police, 192–194; resignation or early retirement, 189–191
Police riots, 3, 15–54 (see also Police brutality; Violence; see also under specific cities): as collective violence, 16–18; confrontation stage, 19; convergence stage, 18–19; crowd dispersal, 20; definitions of, 11–12, 15–18; indicators, 18; limited vs. extended riots, 20–21; police deployment in, 130–132; stages in, 18–22; use of force, 20
Political activism, 209–212

Portland, Ore., police revolt, 204–205
Prejudice: against blacks, 95, 97, 98–106; educational and social origin factors in, 172–173; against police, 94–95; against racial minorities other than blacks, 109; against subcultures, 94–98
President's Commission on Civil Rights, 70
President's Commission on Law Enforcement and Administration of Justice, 70, 79
Press: and control of police, 179, 217–219; police brutality toward, 66–67
Protestors: attitudes toward police, 113–116; police attitudes toward, 109–113
Public opinion and control of police, 179, 219–224
Public order, low-risk and high-risk conceptions, 88–89
Puerto Ricans, police conflict with, 109

Racism among police, 67, 95, 97, 98–106
Radicals: attitudes toward police, 113–116; police hatred of, 50–51, 94–95, 109–113
Raine, Walter J., 72, 73
Recruitment, 10, 119–123, 226–227
Reiss, Albert J., Jr., 56–57, 61–64 passim, 79–83 passim, 99–100, 103–106 passim
Report of the National Advisory Commission on Civil Disorders (see Kerner Commission Report)
Review boards: nationwide battle against, 63, 198–201; New York City police battle against, 194–198; racist overtones to opposition to, 200–201; seen as Communist-dominated, 200; strengthening, 237–238
Rights in Conflict (see Walker Report)
Riots (see also Police riots; see also under individual cities): 6, 20–21, 22–32, 32–54
Riot control, tactical errors in, 125–138
Rizzo, Police Commissioner Frank L., 204, 211, 212
Robin, Gerald D., 65n
Rotten apple theory, 9–10, 11
Rousting and frisking, 71, 72, 75, 76

St. Louis, Mo., police revolt, 205
Salaries of police, 119–120
Sandman, Henry, 206–207
San Francisco: covering up police misconduct, 181–183; police revolt, 205–206; police violence, 5–6
San Francisco State College, 6, 67
Santa Ana, Calif., police revolt, 206
Saunders, Charles, Jr., 122n
Schuman, Howard, 75, 76–77
Schwarz, Fred C., 169, 170–171
Searching of homes, 71–72
Selvin, Hanan, 144
Selznick, Gertrude Jaeger, 172–173
Shaw, George Bernard, 63
Shootouts, mistaken, between police, 65–66
Skolnick, Jerome, 87, 88, 89, 90, 91, 93, 95, 104
Skolnick Report, 15, 133–134, 150, 153
Skousen, W. Cleon, 169

Smelser, Neil J., 11–12
Smith, James W., 53–54
Social isolation of police, 89–94, 158
Sparling, Dr. Edward J., 5
Spiegel, John P., 110
Spock, Dr. Benjamin, 24, 145
Steinberg, Stephen, 172–173
Stenvig, Mayor Charles, 212
Stokes, Mayor Carl, 204
Stop and search, 71, 72
Students: attitudes toward police, 113–116; police hatred of, 112–113, 116
Students for a Democratic Society, 164–165
Subculture(s), 87: conflicts with police, 94–96; police as, 86–96
Suspiciousness of police, 92–93

Tactical formations in riot control, 125–130
Tactics, 13: crowd control, 135–138; military type, 125–130; police deployment, 130–132; police obsession with safety, 132–135
Task Force on Violent Aspects of Protest and Confrontation, National Commission on the Causes and Prevention of Violence, 8: interviews, 122, 123, 159–160, 183, 191, 210, 215
Tate, Mayor James H., 198–199, 212
Tear gas, 20, 21, 37, 39, 42–44
Throckmorton, Lt. Gen. John L., 129
Tijerina, Reies, 109
Training, 228: in civilian setting, 235–236; dual-level, 227; encouragement in

Training, (*continued*)
brutality, 68–70; vs. military training, 125–127; personal vs. impersonal conception of patrol, 127–128; in use of police club, 68–70
Turner, William W., 64, 194–195

U.S. Civil Rights Commission, 70
U.S. Crime Commission, 101, 190

Vice suppression, 233–234
Violence, 1–14 (*see also* Police brutality; Police riots; *see also* under specific cities): causes, 8; collective, 15–54; examples of, 3–7; police homicides, 65, 65n; in presence of Crime Commission observers, 79–83; as routine police behavior, 12, 55–84

Walker, Daniel, 186
Walker Report, 3–4, 110–111, 186–187
Wallace, George, police support for, 159–162, 209
Walsh, James Leo, 160–161
Watson, Nelson A., 57
Watts area, Los Angeles, 73–74, 75, 106, 107
Weathermen, 149
Westley, William A., 60, 87, 99
White, Mayor Kevin, 210, 212
Wilson, James Q., 87–88
Wilson, Orlando W., 59–60, 117

Yippies, 110
Young Socialist Alliance rally, Berkeley, 34–41, 43, 51–54